THE WORD

THE WORD

MYSTICAL REVELATIONS OF JESUS CHRIST
THROUGH HIS TWO WITNESSES

VOLUME 4 | (1977–1980)

ELIZABETH CLARE PROPHET

SUMMIT UNIVERSITY ❖ PRESS®
Gardiner, Montana

THE WORD
Mystical Revelations of Jesus Christ through His Two Witnesses
Volume 4 (1977–1980)
by Elizabeth Clare Prophet
Copyright © 2023 The Summit Lighthouse, Inc. All rights reserved.

Except for a single copy for your personal, noncommercial use, no part of this work may be used, reproduced, stored, posted or transmitted in any manner or medium whatsoever without written permission, except by a reviewer who may quote brief passages in a review.

For information, contact
The Summit Lighthouse, 63 Summit Way, Gardiner, MT 59030 USA
Tel: 1-800-245-5445 or 1 406-848-9500
info@SummitUniversityPress.com
SummitLighthouse.org

Library of Congress Control Number: 2023937478
ISBN: 978-1-60988-440-6 (softbound)
ISBN: 978-1-60988-441-3 (eBook)

Summit University ❧ Press®

The Summit Lighthouse, Summit University, Summit University Press, ❧, Church Universal and Triumphant, Keepers of the Flame, and *Pearls of Wisdom* are trademarks registered in the U.S. Patent and Trademark Office and in other countries. All rights reserved.

26 25 24 23   1 2 3 4

CONTENTS

FOREWORD vii

CHAPTER 1 . . . . (January 2, 1977)   1
  "Except Ye Eat the Flesh of the Son of Man . . ."

CHAPTER 2 . . . . (April 10, 1977) 11
  Be the Saviour of One Life

CHAPTER 3 . . . . (July 3, 1977) 19
  Our Sacred Labor of Love in the New Jerusalem

CHAPTER 4 . . . . (October 23, 1977) 27
  The Messenger and the Living Church

CHAPTER 5 . . . . (December 25, 1977) 39
  The Sacred Fire Judgment of the Holy Spirit

CHAPTER 6 . . . . (January 1, 1978) 47
  My Mission with Saint Germain

CHAPTER 7 . . . . (In Pisces 1978) 61
  Come to the Marriage Feast

CHAPTER 8 . . . . (March 26, 1978) 69
  As My Father Hath Sent Me, Even So Send I You

CHAPTER 9 . . . . (August 6, 1978) 85
  They Shall Not Pass!

CHAPTER 10 . . . . (November 23, 1978) 99
  The Communication of the Word

CHAPTER 11 . . . . (December 25, 1978) 127
   **Dedicate Yourself to the Issue of Abortion,
for upon This Issue Hang All Others**

CHAPTER 12 . . . . (April 15, 1979) 139
   The Symphony of the Resurrection Flame

CHAPTER 13 . . . . (May 6, 1979) 155
   Take My Cup, and Drink Ye All of It

CHAPTER 14 . . . . (May 24, 1979) 161
   The Words of My Father

CHAPTER 15 . . . . (December 25, 1979) 177
   Willingness to Confront the Adversary

CHAPTER 16 . . . . (April 6, 1980) 189
   Rekindling the Essential Identity of Every Living Soul

CHAPTER 17 . . . . (November 9, 1980) 201
   "Almost Free!"
      The New Era of the Rising Son of Righteousness

CHAPTER 18 . . . . (November 27, 1980) 219
   The Sacred Walk to the Immaculate Heart of Mary

CHAPTER 19 . . . . (December 25, 1980) 237
   The Hour of the Sword Is Come

NOTES 255

FOREWORD

Two thousand years ago, Jesus Christ appeared in the Middle East—an event of such import that we divide history into the epochs before and after his coming. He walked the Holy Land performing miracles, preaching to the multitudes, and imparting an inner teaching to the Apostles and the Holy Women.

After three short years, he ascended from Bethany's Hill. Yet that was not the end of Jesus' mission—nor the end of his teaching.

Paul proclaimed that he received his knowledge of Jesus' teaching *not* from the Apostles, but directly "by the revelation of Jesus Christ."[1]

John received "the Revelation of Jesus Christ"[2] while in a cave on the island of Patmos fifty years after Bethany's Hill.

In fact, Jesus has *never* ceased teaching. Through all the centuries since his departure from that scene, Jesus has spoken directly to the heart of his disciples.

Some, like Francis of Assisi and Catherine of Siena, were empowered by the Master for a very public mission. They were true spiritual revolutionaries.

Others found their lives transformed by his very personal impartation of the keys to their spiritual path. They have kept the flame by their profound inner communion with the Master.

Today, once more Jesus brings a new public revelation of his Truth. For more than forty years, he released his teachings through Mark L. Prophet and Elizabeth Clare Prophet, messengers for the ascended masters. And along with this new revelation, he also brings a torch of responsibility that he would pass to those who are ready to receive it.

Two thousand years ago, he told us that "the kingdom of God is within you."[3] Today he brings a more profound understanding of what this really means.

He told us then of the time of judgment that must come at the end of the age.[4] He tells us now that we are living through the fulfillment of that prophecy. He tells us that we have a key role to play in that judgment, and he tells us how to pass through it unscathed.

He demonstrated miracles then as proof of the promises he made. Today he explains the spiritual science behind those miracles. And he shows us how we can also work the "greater works"[5] that he promised those who follow in his footsteps.

The image in many churches is of Jesus on the cross—as if that were the defining moment of his mission. Jesus himself has reminded us that he was on the cross only a few brief hours. In fact, his life was not one of suffering but of great joy and a profound communion with God.

He bids us experience that communion.

He bids us experience the resurrection—a gift intended for the many, not the few.

He bids us embrace our sacred labor and become on earth, as he was, an agent of the Cosmic Christ.

And he offers the full cup of joy that he experienced, the abundant life promised to all who follow in his footsteps.

THE EDITORS

CHAPTER 1

*Understand the mystery of the absorption
of the Body and Blood of Christ.
Understand that all that I AM you must become.
You will become this as you open the door and sup with me,
partaking of that substance that God has given to me,
which is my very identity.*

CHAPTER 1

"EXCEPT YE EAT THE FLESH OF THE SON OF MAN…"

Bearers of light, sons and daughters of flame, I stand in your midst to perform the ceremony of the transfer of light. From out the Great Central Sun, the Elohim of God send forth a ray. The ray of light is a ray of hope. It is God's energy and his love. It is a ray of light that must be transferred from point to point and consciousness to consciousness throughout the body of God in heaven and on earth. And therefore the cycles roll and the energies flow, and I AM for the implementation of the God flame within you.

I come to transfer to you the light that is my own, which is the Father's light that he has made my own and that I have made my own by the opening of the valve of the heart and the allowing of the life that is God to flow. This day I stand before you and I ask you to do the same, to understand the alchemy: "I and my Father are one."[1]

It is the Father's work that is accomplished in and through you as you open the valve of the heart. It is the sacred heart of the eternal Christos of which I speak. It is the spiritual heart, and the valve of that heart is the open door which when once opened by the Christ and confirmed by your free will no man can shut.[2] I AM the open door and the opening of the door within you this day for the light, the light that is in the inner worlds, to manifest in the outer worlds in order that outer worlds might come into alignment and be according to that will that is the very formula of the creation.

The will of God, O children of the Sun, is not superimposed upon the creation. It is integral to the creation, inherent within it. It is the very fiber and the fabric, the warp and the woof of life. Whoso therefore is out of harmony with that will is out of life, out of the creation. Therefore let not the body of God be separated from that holy will.

ENERGIES THAT MUST BE ANCHORED IN TERRA

I come for the assimilation that you might assimilate energy that is necessary for the redemption of God's people and that we might assimilate the energy that is God's that is locked within you —locked within matrices of imperfection. We come to assimilate that which belongs to God, which men have thought to be their own, which they may make their own only when they ratify and confirm the will to which it was sent. I am sent this day also as the arrow that is shot from the bow of the Eternal Archer. I am come as the Son of God. And I transfer through this open door to your open door energies that must be anchored in Terra, posited in the very chalice of the hearts of a people for the turning of the cycles of the age and of the ages.

I come with the mystery—the eating of the flesh of the Son of man, the drinking of his blood. Unless this be accomplished in you, you have no life that is God's; for this flesh is meat indeed, and this blood is drink indeed. It comes from the Father. As I am of the Father, so as you are in me and partake of my consciousness, you are one with the Father and you have that flow of consciousness that is eternal life, and therefore you are sustained only by the energy that is God's.[3] The flesh and the blood of the Son of man is the energy consecrated as the fulfillment on earth of the light of the eternal Christos in Father, in Mother, in Spirit, in Matter, in the principle of adhesion, cohesion, and the polarity of every form of energy.

I AM the light of the transfer of the Elohim. Understand the mystery of the absorption of the Body and Blood of Christ. Understand that all that I AM you must become. You will become this as you open the door and sup with me, partaking of that substance that God has given to me, which is my very identity. Therefore the assimilation, therefore the integration, therefore this day heaven becomes earth, earth becomes heaven. And as you receive, you may give. But only if you are willing to receive will you have the wherewithal to give to life that portion necessary for the resurrection.

My life is lived for the sole purpose that you might become life, and I witness among all nations and peoples in this hour, and I give to the souls of earth the vision of their becoming the Christ. Behold, see the image of the Son of man! Behold, see the image of that Son being fashioned within you by the great kindling light of the Spirit! Behold, see the angelic hosts who come to minister to the newborn child!

THE CLEARING OF THE SACRED CENTERS OF LIFE BY THE SIGN OF THE CROSS

I AM the same yesterday and today and forever.[4] I come to bring to you the nearness of your own Christ Self and the understanding of the Law of the One. I AM the opening of the way of the Great Central Sun within you. I raise my hands for the clearing of the sacred centers of life by the sign of the cross, which is the God-control of that energy of the Great Central Sun that is released daily and hourly through each one of the sun centers within you—those spheres of light, the golden chakras. So let the flow of Alpha be the delivery unto the world of that energy garnered within the flame.

As the wise virgins have trimmed their lamps,[5] so let these lamps trimmed now with oil be the energy that is sent forth for the balancing of this earth and for the planes of consciousness and for the clearing of the air and the sea and the land by the action of the sacred fire. Let it be the purging of worlds within and worlds without. And let the return of that energy, which is sent forth through you in my name, be for the sustainment of that current within your being whereby the energy that flows also forms the ascending spiral that is the path to your eternal reunion with God.

I AM come that you might have life and that more abundantly manifest in the here and now![6] I AM come to remove the moneychangers from the temple of our God and from the temple of the people![7] I AM come for the thrusting of the energy of the Great Central Sun whereby all must give accounting this day in the Law of the One! Let them stand, then, before the judgment hall as I stood and as you stand, for none are spared in the hour of the judgment! And unto the souls of light is the judgment—the manifestation of that love whereby they are sealed in the Eye of God.

Let the judgment, then, be for the separation to the right and to the left of mankind's uses and misuses of the sacred energies of life. And let those who have been sown as the tares among the good wheat,[8] let the seed of the wicked also know that the hour of redemption is come and the hour of choosing to bend the knee and bow to the inner light of the Christ is also come. He that receiveth you receiveth me, and he that receiveth me receiveth the Christ of his own Self[9]—the Supreme One, the Mediator, the very God from the heart of the Great Central Sun.

I AM come for the transfer of that energy that is for the salvation of the soul of a planet and a people. Where is the source of salvation but in God? Why do mankind seek other sources? Why do they not give unto him the glory? Well, I will answer that question. It is because they have gone out of the way and not understood who I AM. If they would understand their very real identity in Christ, then they would know that the confirmation of that being, I AM THAT I AM, is the key to the solution of every problem of the age.

Understand, then, that the question may well be asked: If they do not seek answers in the Godhead and in the white-fire core of being that is the God within, then perchance may it not be that they are not in actuality desirous of finding solutions but of only giving the impression that they are seeking solutions? And in the meantime they are garnering unto themselves the precious energies of God that ought to be in the very hand of those who are committed to love and to life and to the great cosmic flow whereby all parts of the one whole receive proportionately that energy that is meted out according to the path of initiation, according to the inner attainment of the soul.

THE INNER ALCHEMY OF THE SOUL'S REUNION WITH THE MAKER

We do not ask for equality that distributes to mankind without regard for the inner development of the soul light those resources of the Spirit. We seek for that equality whereby each man must bear his own burden and each man is rewarded according to his works. And that grace that confirms the works is that grace that is the result of the soul's inner meditation on the Law of the One. This is true equality. It is equal opportunity to be the son of God and the daughter of God where you are, measure for measure. Therefore according to the measure of energy that is the input, so is the net gain of energy by the exponent of the Christ-potential. See how the multiplication factor of a holy science will teach to you a holy religion. See how each one abiding in the planes of Mater can find the principle of life whereby the increase and the law of the increase can be known as the inner alchemy of the soul's reunion with the Maker.

I AM come that all might have life. I AM come with the teaching of the law of abundance. And I send forth the light of the judgment upon those among mankind who have taken the abundance of the Almighty One to hoard it, then, for their selfish interest and for private gain, who have kept from the people the true energy of life and have given unto them only the husks.

I tell you, precious ones, God is a very real and integral part of life that is lived on earth. If mankind do not know this, it is because they have not invoked the flame of the very God of gods. It is because they have failed to commune, they have failed to flow upstream to the Source of life. But they have gone instead downstream—down, down the way of the misuses of that life energy, never knowing that that energy which they have in their hands each day is from the eternal fount of the living Spirit.

So let those who have ears to hear understand that the message unto the seven churches, the seven lights, the seven temples of being[10] is the message of the conservation of energy. As you guard the energies of life entrusted into your care, so you will have the energy that is for the dissemination of the Word, and you will find that by the Holy Spirit, by the infusion of the flame and of the Word and of the sacred fire breath, you will never want for that supreme resource to deliver the Word of God that is the Logos unto this age.

THE CRYSTALLIZATION OF THE GOD FLAME

Understand that the Word that goes forth from the altar of God and through his emissaries, the ascended hosts, is always for the alchemicalization of truth on earth. This is the crystallization of the God flame—that the Word is power, that the Word is wisdom, that the Word is love, and that the Word of God goes forth unto you and through you for that alchemy that is known as the judgment.

Fear not, for the justice of the Law is ever active. But then it is the patience of the saints that is the trying of the saints. "In patience possess ye your souls."[11] Wait and see the salvation of our God. And in the waiting and in the watching, apply the law of the energy of the rod and see how the sun center, the flaming yod, will send forth a light and a mighty action of the whirlwind fire that will be the transforming of energies on earth—that those who are called into the consciousness of the One may have that forcefield, that spiral, that movement that is the transfer of identity from the point of limitation to the point of the sense of the limitless abundance of a cosmos.

Stand fast, then, and see the salvation of our God.[12] See how he will implement his work through those who will to work his work on earth. See, then, that the testimony of the senses will not always tell you what is the reality of the moment. See how the points of time and space move in relativity and how you, coordinating time and space, move along the spectrum. See, then, that how the past, the present, and the future are nothing but the moving stream of the energy that is time. And your sense of awareness, of presence, here and there and everywhere in the being of God, is but the coordinate called space. See, then, that if these are moving, never the same, ever changing, that that which transpires in the veil—this veil that is the temporal plane—is also not worthy of permanent testimony or permanent witness or of the sense of an absolute science or an absolute religion.

A MOMENT FOR THE TURNING OF WORLDS AND THE TURNING OF CYCLES

What I am saying, precious hearts, is that all that seems to be is not, and all that is does not always seem to be. Therefore be not confounded by the burdens that are coming upon this earth or by the saturation of the elements by mankind's misqualified energies, for all of this can change, all of this can move as God moves. Therefore it is a moment of hope when the sons and daughters of God commune together to study the mysteries and the laws governing all energy, spiritual and material. It is a moment for the turning of worlds and the turning of cycles when sons and daughters of God on earth raise high the chalice to receive the light, the flesh, and the blood of the ascended sons and daughters of God.

In this cosmic interchange and in this interval, this cosmic pause, there is released a nucleus of energy containing the inner key for the resolution of all that is out of balance in Terra. Take this key, take this nucleus to your heart, and let it be the unwinding of an energy coil and let it be the unfoldment of the Word. Let God unwind through you the answer to the call and the solution to every need. Let it flow through you and let it be the flow of a holy science, a sacred truth, and a mission unfurled.

Study, then, all that must be studied in this octave for the solution of every problem. Then place the fruit of study upon the altar and meditate upon the living God. Then let the LORD God return to you, through the flame that burns upon that altar, the distillation of his mind, even as you have placed the distillation of your mind in that sacred fire. Let God be the one who draws together all areas of learning, all areas of discovery and experiment, and let him fashion within you holy purpose.

See how you can work a work, and when you have done your all in working that work, how you can give that work to God and God will infuse it with life, with fire, with dimension, and then fire it in the kiln of cosmic awareness and return to you the answer —the answer that is always life becoming life, life eternal becoming life eternal. This is the Law of the One! This is the law of transcendence and of the cycles of worlds within and worlds without.

I come. I AM in your midst always, the transformer of worlds below and worlds above. I come, I knock. You open, I enter. And I AM forevermore within you the great transforming energy of the Almighty One. I AM Jesus the Christ alive within you forevermore.

January 2, 1977
Pasadena, California
Elizabeth Clare Prophet (ECP)

CHAPTER 2

*This coming together, then, is for the opening of consciousness.
For we would set the seal of our being upon a way fully taught,
open, waiting—waiting for the soul's conversion from
the finite line and linear thinking to the infinite sphere
and spherical consciousness.*

CHAPTER 2

BE THE SAVIOUR OF ONE LIFE

Peace, my beloved. Peace in the flame of my heart. I have won for you that peace which passeth all understanding.[1] I have won for you that peace wherein you can always know that greater is he that is in you than he that is in the world.[2] Be of good cheer, for I have overcome the world.[3]

This is the rejoicing of our resurrection. That which I have done, you can—yea, *you must*—do also. This is the meaning of original Christianity. Let that meaning, then, be the regeneration of a religion that I have founded and yet that I have not yet sealed. For I cannot place the seal of my flame upon a doctrine that is erroneous or is an interpretation of my life that is unfounded.

And therefore the sealing of the dispensation of the Christed One in us all cannot come until the final writing of all that was conveyed by me unto the disciples, unto John and Mary the Mother and the holy women so that those lifewaves of the sixth root race —whose destiny it is to find grace through the Christ and through my personal flame—might have in hand that portion of the book of life, which it is decreed by God should be unto them the open book and the gospel of salvation unto that soul and every soul who has come under the aegis of the God and Goddess Meru, manus of our dispensation.

You will remember that Mary the Mother took her initiations in the retreat at Lake Titicaca[4] so that she might have within her soul the archetypal pattern of the type of the sixth root race.

These precious children of God, then, require the opening of the scriptures, which was given by God through my heart to the disciples who were with me all the way—from the original call of alchemy, the transformation of the water into wine, through the transfiguration, the persecution of the light, the Sermon on the Mount, the challenge of the entrenched order of the day, and then the crucifixion, the resurrection, and the ascension.

THE TEACHING PASSED BY THE TRANSFER OF THE INITIATION OF THE SACRED CENTERS

You see, that which we sought to accomplish while the Brotherhood worked with me for the quickening of souls was that these few disciples, and the other seventy whom I sent forth,[5] might have the acceleration of their God centers so that in the hour of the ascension their energies might also fulfill in the Matter plane that which I was fulfilling in both the Matter and the Spirit planes of consciousness. For those, then, who had proved themselves able to carry the light of Christ in each succeeding level of consciousness—which our demonstration proved and liberated—there was then given the sacred bowl, the chalice of the teaching.

And therefore the opening of the understanding of the close disciples was the opening of the crown chakra, the very same initiation that Lord Buddha gave to his disciples so that the teaching might be passed by the few—not hand to hand or word to word but that it might be passed by the transfer of this initiation of the sacred centers.

Each time, then, that you come together in celebration of those events of masters of the East and West who have overcome the law of sin and death, it is so that you might experience an increment of this acceleration of your centers in preparation for the moment when the Holy Spirit will reveal to you the full dispensation of the mission—the spherical awareness of the life of the master and not merely a recounting of a timeline or the episodes of space, but the spherical dimension of the coming into these octaves of the consciousness of God and the interpretation of that consciousness for lifestreams who must have that interpretation in order to fulfill their divine plan.

THE NAME OF THE MASTER OPENS THE WAY OF SALVATION FOR A PARTICULAR DISPENSATION

This coming together, then, is for the opening of consciousness. For we would set the seal of our being upon a way fully taught, open, waiting—waiting for the soul's conversion from the finite line and linear thinking to the infinite sphere and spherical consciousness.

This is the only way that the soul can enter into salvation. And therefore the believing upon the name Jesus the Christ or Saint Germain or Gautama Buddha is the acceptance *in that name* of the inner key, the very nucleus of energy and life that is released by that name and therefore conveyed to the heart and the soul of the devotee as the means of salvation. For in the name of the master, the one representing a certain consciousness of God, there is the opening into the way of salvation for a particular dispensation. And this is why it was written that there is no other name whereby mankind should be saved except the name of Jesus the Christ.[6]

This name, then, becomes the symbol for that which every son and daughter may become. More than this, it is the name that opens the causal body of God and his grace that is upon me and that is mine to give to all who are in the earth who are mine because God has given them to me.

You who walk in the teachings of all of the ascended masters have moved through the dispensations of the personal Christ (which I have brought) and into the spherical awareness of that Christ, until in that consciousness (whether fulfilled in this life or many previous incarnations) you have come to be aware of the fact that every son and daughter of God throughout all aeons who has ever won the ascension has passed through that same awareness—from the personal Christ to the universal Christ to the oneness of every part of life that is come forth from God.

And so, precious ones—you who now understand that the open door of every ascended master consciousness leads to new dimensions and paths back to the Great Source of Being—you can well afford to be patient with the children of God who require in this age one master and one flame in order to understand, through the mastery of that one flame, the multiplication of that flame in the many ascended and unascended avatars. For you see, we who are your elder brothers and sisters have been patient with you until your understanding of the One has become the understanding of the many and the return of the many to the One.

Salvation, then, is in the name of God and in his name alone! Salvation is in the name that God has given as the key to the light of the avatars of the ages! Salvation can be found and won through Krishna, through Brahma, Vishnu, and Shiva, through Mary the Mother and John the Beloved, through Saint Germain and Sanat Kumara, Omri-Tas, Maitreya, and Gautama!

YOUR INNER NAME IS THE INNER KEY TO A NUMBER OF SOULS

Understand these names as you would understand the combination to a safe—each turn, each number decoding, deciphering an energy field that is precisely for the opening of that door, the very special door that is the requirement of the hour for that individual soul whom God himself adores because that soul is the potential, the living potential of the flame, which he has made. And this is why it was written, "In my Father's house are many mansions."[7] These mansions are the great spheres of light that have been lowered into the Matter forcefield by the incarnation of the Word century after century.

Have you ever thought that your name, your inner name, is the inner key to a number of souls who, because you have given the teaching and become the teaching, have found the way back to their own God Presence, I AM?

You somehow think of the masters as being so far removed from yourselves. You wonder how your poor expression of the Godhead could possibly be the key to spherical consciousness for the few and the many.

Well, I tell you it is so. For you are not very far removed from us and from our Self-awareness in God. The only separation you experience is your own inaccurate assessment of your Divine Self, your *Christed* Self, and the Presence of God in you. Change your concept, change your perception, and you will find yourself *opening, opening, opening* for the vastness of a cosmos to flow through you to the children and to all.

Would it matter, then, if your life were lived for the saving of but one soul for the ascension? This would be the great glory of many idle and vain existences, which you have also known. And therefore to be the salvation of one soul is truly to be the salvation of all, for there is but one great Self, one God, and one Life.

If therefore your heart's love be the key to the rolling away of the stone and the coming forth of the Lord out of the tomb, is this not worth a million years of evolution?

For in that one soul who has become God is the liberation of the full *potential* of God for a cosmos. For every ascended master—free in God, whom God has freed and who has freed God—is then the opening of the way for all energy of God to flow from Spirit unto Matter.

I bid you consider *your* role as the saviour of mankind. I bid you consider *your* coming forth from the tomb this day as the risen Christ. And if you be the saviour of many, then this, *this* is the wondrous confirmation of your life. And if you be the saviour of one, then this too is the magnification of the flame.

But this is my question to you this day, and I leave you with this question: If you determine to be the saviour of one life, then why not let it be your own?

April 10, 1977
Pasadena, California
ECP

CHAPTER 3

*What do you think, that God shall work a work of love
in this age only for man to undo that work?
Nay! But it is God who comes, in the person of myself
and yourself as one, to undo the works of man
that would undo the works of God.*

CHAPTER 3

OUR SACRED LABOR OF LOVE IN THE NEW JERUSALEM

Peace, beloved. Peace, beloved. I AM come. I AM come in the flame of deliverance. I come to deliver your soul from perdition and from perfidy.

I AM come. For the hour is late, and we must be about our Father's business. Our sacred labor of love in the New Jerusalem awaits us. This is the calling to which we are called.

And I stand before you, the Prince of Peace, the King of kings, the Lord of lords. By your decree that is God's decree, I AM the authority and I AM the ruler of all that is below and all that is above. All who would rule in the footstool kingdom must come this day under the authority of my flame of love!

What do you think, that God shall work a work of love in this age only for man to undo that work? Nay! But it is God who comes, in the person of myself and yourself as one, to undo the works of man that would undo the works of God.

For the fulfillment of prophecy is come, and the prophecy of love must be confirmed and affirmed daily by your invocation of that love. As you manifest and align the energy of love within your being, so you compel my being within yourself. As I speak a word of love to your soul and you repeat the word of love, I AM made whole.

So I AM one in thee and thou art in me,[1] and we are one in the authority of the command of the All-Father. And therefore the All-Father stands within you when you receive the Son of Righteousness that I AM.

Therefore let God the Father be magnified! Let God the Son be magnified! Let God the Holy Spirit be magnified within you!

THE SECOND COMING OF CHRIST IS NOW

This is the Second Coming of Christ. For the first coming is the personification of the Christ within the master, within the teacher, within the Guru. And the Second Coming of Christ is the entering in of that Christ into the temple of the disciple, of the student, of the Guru's chela.

So let the chelas now proclaim the Second Coming of the Lord Christ this day. For this is the proclamation that I bring: Only love could bring forth the only begotten Son of God, and only love brings forth that son day by day by day. Let not the fallen ones allow you to continually postpone the day of the Second Coming. For there is no time and space, and the Second Coming is now.

The Second Coming is the transfer of the fire and light of the eternal Christos into your own chalice. And in that Second Coming, the Prince of Peace becomes the ruler of this world as well as the inner world of light. And with a manifestation of myself —the anointed one in you whom I anoint to be myself, my heart, my hands, my head, my temple—so is come the judgment. So is come the restoration of the will of God. So let it be the turning back of the fallen ones, as they have seized the energies of the children of God in government and in science, in education and in religion.

Let them be judged! For I sit at the right hand of Almighty God to judge the tribes of Israel this day. And I call forth the sons and daughters of God for the judgment of the holy ones of light and for the judgment of the fallen ones. For the judgment is as the Sun of living love that shines upon the just and the unjust.

THE RAIN OF THE JUDGMENT OF LOVE

Let it rain! Let it rain! Oh, let it rain the judgment of love! And let it come down as the intense fire of love upon the earth. And let there be the turning around of the energy. And let there be the baptism by fire.

I AM the shepherd of the sheepfold. I stand in the center of America. I stand to strip the sheep's clothing from the wolves who have seized their positions of authority. I stand to expose the lie, and I command all lightbearers to call for the exposure of the lie —by the flame of Jesus Christ, by the flame of Mary and Saint Germain, by the flame of every living ascended master, by the flame of the Lord of the World, before whose light I bow.

I AM a servant of the Most High God, who lives within you. Therefore I bow before the flame of God, and I say, now let all false doctrine and dogma and every demon thereof be bound! I AM the binding of the fallen ones, and they are stripped of their power! And therefore let the babbling of the voices of darkness cease, and let the truth be proclaimed. And let every Keeper of the Flame be kindled now in the Word of truth!

LET ALL MISUSES OF THE THROAT CHAKRA CEASE

Let the quickening of the throat center come forth from the very heart and throat center of El Morya, of beloved Hercules and Archangel Michael. Let the Word of God, which shall not pass away,[2] be transferred now to the centers of the will of God. And let the quivering of the flame of Alpha and Omega, which I send forth out of the mouth of the messenger, be unto you the opening.

Ephratha! Ephratha! Ephratha![3]

Be open now! And let the opening be for the coming of the light! And out of the mouths of those who are clear, let there come forth now all of the darkness and the dark and evil spirits who have been allowed to congregate in the mouth. Let the mouth be purified. Let it be purified of all misuses and all abuses of the sacred fire. And let the mouth be for the living witness of the I AM THAT I AM. Let all misuses of the mouth of God be consumed now!

I send forth the ray of the will of love. I call for the purification of the love of man and woman as the devotion unto the Word of God. Let all misuses of the throat chakra now cease! For I send forth a fire unto you, O beloved ones of God. It must not be misused by any manifestation whatsoever of misuse of the sacred life force.

Let the chakras which are above the heart be consecrated as the temple of the Most High God into which I may enter at will twenty-four hours a day. For the sacredness of the coming of the Prince of Peace is that this earth might receive the salvation of the Saviour, the eternal Christ within you.

O LORD, PREPARE THESE TEMPLES

O LORD, O LORD Almighty One, O LORD, descend, I pray! I stand before thy throne. I implore thy light—the impelling light that will draw these souls into a greater reverence for life and consecration of thy energy.

O LORD God Almighty, be the I AM THAT I AM, and prepare these temples. Make room for my coming. For I, the Son of God, would enter the temple of the devotee on earth. I would enter the temple. And I demand the temple be clean and white and blazing in the glory of the devotion of the God within to the God within.

I HAVE EMPOWERED THEE TO BE MYSELF

I consecrate now the bread and the wine. For I will pass to you a portion of myself, that you may know that through the hand of the Mother there will be released to you the sacred energy of Alpha and Omega—for the transformation of your very vibration and the quickening of your being, for the ritual of the return to love in the Victory of the ascension.

I stand before you. I AM *here!* I AM *here* in the victory of love. And I take the Body and the Blood of my Lord, my God, my Father, through myself, through my vicar that you might know that the open fount of Terra is the flame of my messenger.

And this day I send to you, through the opening of the heart, the immense light that is for our victory in the sacred labor of the New Jerusalem. First we begin with the securing of freedom to America and to every land, and we secure the freedom of the soul in the heart. And then we build the temple. Therefore let the fallen ones be contained by the lightbearers, by the Word and the science of the Word.

This day have I begotten thee.[4] This day have I empowered thee to be myself. Keep thyself holy in the purity of God, and know thyself as myself.

I AM with you alway, even unto the end of the age of the cycles of love, even unto the end of the cycle of your sojourn on earth. I AM with you alway, even unto the hour of your ascension in the light!

I AM in the heart of America, the Prince of Peace.

I AM come for the reign of love!

July 3, 1977
Pasadena, California
ECP

CHAPTER 4

*Blessed ones, it is a mystical union.
It is a oneness of the one person. Let it be, then,
that this is our triumph, this is our joy, this is our conquest
of all darkness, as love, true love for Christ is the universal
solvent of all evil, all error, all darkness, all intrigue,
all murder, and the lie of the Serpent.*

CHAPTER 4

THE MESSENGER AND THE LIVING CHURCH

Most beloved of my heart, I AM come in answer to your call. I AM Jesus, your Lord.

I come in the Word, and I come out of the Word incarnate. For God has placed the Logos within the heart of the messenger and as the seed of light, as potential in every living soul.

Because he lives within thy vessel, I AM come. Because you have prepared your tabernacle as a witness of the living God, I AM come. I enter the temple of the children of Israel. I proclaim my kingdom come and I repeat, "My kingdom is not of this world."[1] It is not of this cycle of materialism. Nay, it is of the Spirit. And so you have chosen to embody that Spirit.

Therefore, the LORD's Spirit be upon you this day in the infinite power of love that will give you the power and the authority of God to challenge the oppressor in the midst.

I have heard your prayers unto the Son of Righteousness. I have heard your desire to be the instruments of God. Truly, it is a difficult question of how to translate the vision of the kingdom to those who have neither the vision nor the imagination to behold our Father's kingdom.

BE EMPTIED THAT I MIGHT FILL YOU WITH MY BEING

You have accepted the challenge of an age. I come to remind you that there is no solution in Matter for the conquest of worlds, and therefore let your instrument be the sacred fire. Let it be your soul refined, containing the veritable droppings of that fire from the Great Central Sun. Let it be the virgin consciousness of the blessed saints who have gone before. Let it be even that consciousness of purity that brings the diamond of God's will to the point of action.

Look, then, to those who have gone before you who have influenced civilization, who have gone before the leaders and rulers of this world. And because they have contained myself, because they have cleared the temple to become exalted in the Spirit, men [and women] have listened, have been converted, have been infired by the light.

It is not that the saint brings a new word but that the saint brings the cup of my being, charged with the purity of his soul's conversion and conversation with me daily.

Dip into the fount of eternal life and know that you can use the pen and the sword and the sacred Word and that you can go forth. And a simple rebuke to error charged with love will cause the most callous heart to submit to the life universal. Put on, therefore, the whole armour of God[2] and recognize that the core of the armour is the purity of the saints robed in white.

Let the things of this world and its honors and its preoccupations become to you as loathsome, as filthy rags. Be uncomfortable in the ways of the world and then God will use you as the knife that descends to cut free the children of God.

You live for but one purpose, and that purpose is to bring my souls, the souls of our Father, Home to me. Let all else resume its lawful place before this goal of your life. And if you have more than you can accomplish in the day and more preoccupations that do not glorify the name of our God, then cast them aside. Be emptied that I might fill you with my being. Learn, then, the message that I gave to my beloved Catherine of Siena[3]—that you are unreal, that I AM Real, that I AM your Real Self, that you represent the not-self.

The realization that to you the reality of your life is God, is Christ, enables you to see the nothingness of all temporal consciousness and manifestation. And in that nothingness, in that awareness of the impoverished self, you will be emptied, swept clean, as though the winds of the Holy Spirit had blown through and swept away all but the very bare walls. And into this cell of your cloister, of your soul's utter devotion, I will come and be thyself.

This is the key to the kingdom and to the consciousness of the saints: "It is not I, but God in me!" Let your Christ Self reign as your Real Self, and do not allow room for the assertions and the subsequent desertions of the synthetic image.

As long as you are preoccupied with that lesser self, you will bar me from entering. As long as you attempt to be mighty in the human sense, you will fail and the plan of the age will fail. As long as you seek a separate identity from the flame—as your nation, as your culture, as your race, or as your private self—you will see that you will remain hungering and longing to be one, but you will find that I cannot come into the temple of your being.

THE EXAMPLE OF CATHERINE OF SIENA

Understand that this doctrine, proclaimed by one who became a Doctor of the Church, is for you, veritably, the key to your acceleration in the world scene.

Do you know that Catherine of Siena was able to move men, mighty men—kings and bishops, princes, lords, and even the pope —by the power of the pen, by the power of the written word? And therefore her correspondence with individuals of her time delivered the Holy Spirit and my Presence.

She had not excellence of speech or learning and perhaps even had a cumbersome way of expressing that light, and purposely so. For the mystery of God is revealed unto the simple of heart so that God might prove over and again that it is not the excellence of outer learning but it is this one gift—the soul's devotion to Christ, the Mediator, the soul's devotion to love, the soul's self-effacement, the realization that the soul is a nonpermanent facet of identity and only Christ can give it life.

Thus, beloved ones, as you give forth the sacred Word, the rebuke to error, the vision of truth, when you are filled with my being, you will have the power to deliver that Word and to confound the fallen ones, to rally the people of God. Let us make haste, for the Coming Revolution is based upon every living soul who will walk the earth as myself. Anything less will end in failure.

I send you forth, then. According to your purity, your desire for innocence, so will the power of God come unto you. I speak not of the "purity" of the Pharisees and Sadducees, their doctrine and their dogma. Nay, this is not the purity that I long to see upon you but it is the joy of the free Spirit born again in God—free to move, free to break the shackles of the former self, free to be one with me and to know the intimacy of our love forevermore.

You will find, then, that I have bestowed upon that blessed Catherine the light of the revolutionaries of God, that she has gone before you so that you might read of her life and be the imitators of her life and understand that this revolution is based on the same white cube. Indeed, her love of the Holy Church enabled her to become that Church, and she defended the Church unto the end. And by her intercession, even the pope[*] returned to Rome from his exile and thus was found keeping the flame, as he ought to be.

Blessed ones, this champion of the Holy Church comes again to bear my flame and stands before you in the person of your messenger, having the momentum of her life as blessed Catherine.[4]

---
[*]Pope Gregory XI

Understand, then, that this is why I have placed upon her the burden to be my vicar[5]—because she has bowed before the Vicar [of Christ] and championed his cause, because she has taught the children of the One the message of obedience to my representative.

And thus I have taken the Mother and placed her once again to defend the Holy Church, which is not a building but is a commission of my heart flame for every child of God and every soul of the twelve tribes to come again into that unity of Spirit whereby the very temple itself, the temple that is made without hands,[6] is the fortress, the veritable citadel of freedom. Within this citadel—which you comprise by your very life—the saints, the ascended hosts do enter. Thus the living Church is our cause, and we build unto eternity.

Come close, then, to the robes of the one to whom I gave my heart and the gifts and graces as the single flame that held the balance in those dark, dark years of chaos and the turning away from God. See, then, what a pillar of fire each one of you can be if you will follow in the footsteps of the many who have gone before. It takes but one soul filled with my being to command life and to set it free. But millions of souls who have not bid me enter the temple cannot effect that change that is required in this hour.

THE WEIGHT OF DARKNESS WITHIN THE CHURCH

Therefore, in this moment you see the blessed land of the Church, of the popes, and of the saints falling beneath the hordes of darkness, falling beneath that conspiracy of the dragon and the beast and the serpents, falling beneath the weight of that selfishness and indulgence.

O blessed ones, the pain upon my Blessed Mother is almost more than she can bear—to see the holy shrines, to see the places where you yourselves have walked within the monasteries, within the convents, consecrating your life lifetime after lifetime so that you might be found together as one in this age.

And therefore I stand with the Blessed Virgin to uphold and support her this day. And I ask that you shall give your promise to the Blessed Mother to receive into your heart the blessed momentum of the light of the saints, of the holy shrines, the flames that have burned upon these altars for centuries upon centuries, where miracle upon miracle upon miracle has taken place.

And yet in this hour there is not one who has been found able to be infilled with the fullness of that joy of the living Spouse, to stand and to unite the people in that nation of Italy. And therefore the fallen ones are marching, marching. And they are, blessed ones, as beasts and demons of the night. If you could but see them in the astral plane as they prepare for the great meal, as they plan their plans to dine upon the blood of the saints, O blessed ones, methinks you would faint to know the horror as I see that horror contemplated upon these souls who, for want of a rallying point, for want of leadership, for want of truth, integrity, and righteousness, are not able to pull themselves from their cups, from their pleasures, from all of that indulgence.

THIS IS OUR HOPE, OUR ONLY HOPE—THAT HIS FLAME WILL BE CONSECRATED UPON THE ALTAR OF YOUR TEMPLE

And so the hour is passed and we come for the gathering of the remnant. And when our remnant is gathered and when we may walk a thousand times a thousand across the fields, the hills, the deserts, through the towns and the cities, ourselves embodied within our disciples, then you will see how we will roll back—with the momentum of the archangels, by the flame of freedom from the base of Camelot—all of this darkness.

And we will not stop with America. We will go from the West to the East. We will cover the plains and the cities of Canada. We will move our legions and our troops through South America. We will leap to the continents of Europe, Africa, Asia. We will cover the earth and we will roll back the darkness in that notable day of the Lord[7] already proclaimed by angels and legions of Victory in the Great Central Sun, who can project themselves in the time-space frame and therefore live in the past, the present, or the future. They hold the balance with dynamic decrees, proclaiming the day of that victory even while you summon the light to fulfill the cycles of the past in the present.

Thus the movement of energy in the legions of light is foretold. Thus the inner blueprint is given. And the votive flame that is passed to the Blessed Mother, to the blessed children, to your very hearts, is our hope.

This flame is our hope because this flame is Almighty God. Almighty God will save the earth *because* he lives in you, *because* you prepare him room, *because* you make the decision this day to be wed to God, to call no man friend but God. Hear my call! This is our hope, our only hope—that his flame will be consecrated upon the altar of your temple.

Blessed ones, it is said that history repeats itself. It is our prayer that the history of the golden ages will be the history that repeats itself. And in order for this to come about, much light must pass through your hearts, your heads, and your hands for the dissolution of those records that serve as a magnet in the astral plane to bring forth into the physical plane those remembrances upon akasha that are the sordid manifestations of perversions of Mu and Atlantis and all that has caused the fall of civilizations and continents.

Let these records be swallowed up in the light of victory, in the fullness of the flame of freedom, which Saint Germain brings as the absolute dedication of his life. Let us, then, move forward, knowing that with God all things are possible, knowing that each of you—as you become the Lord's body and the multiplication of the blood and of the flesh of the Son of God—will be the catalyst. And it requires but one of you in each of the cities and nations of the earth.

Beloved ones, you may wonder at my speech. But think of yourself as the Word incarnate. Think of yourself as myself as I enter your temple, as your Christ Self is wholly and fully integrated with your four lower bodies. If you could accept this day that my presence in America could save America, then I say, accept that *your* presence can and will save America. And then, you see, you will gain the full perspective of your mantle of responsibility and the power of this mantle to divide the waters of Jordan[8] and to be the healing robe and the garment of the Mother.

I AM THE SON OF GOD IN YOUR BROTHER, IN YOUR SISTER, IN YOUR NEIGHBOR

O beloved ones, stay very, very close to your Mother, for in her has come the presence of the Blessed Mother. And therefore you need not fear, for to be disciples of the Blessed Mary is indeed to find yourself the Mother of God, the one who nourishes the life of the Christ incarnate.

Above all, let the writing be upon your wall and upon your heart: "Inasmuch as ye have done it unto one of the least of these my brethren, ye have done it unto me."[9]

I ask that you nourish me now. I ask that you take me down from the cross. I ask that you hold me in your arms, as the Blessed Mother did. I ask that you shall now minister to my wounds. I ask that you will go forth and know, no matter who it is, that you may look into the eyes of the sick, the ignorant, those yearning to be free, and you may see my own eyes in the pain, in the anguish of the terrible, terrible darkness that has come upon the earth.

Beloved ones, if you will but remember this, the code and the ethic of our Christian brotherhood, then, *then* you will not fail one test on the path of your becoming myself.

Can you not remember? Will you not remember? Look now to your right. Look to your left. And know that I AM the Son of God in your brother, in your sister, in your neighbor, that you cannot err when you minister unto me in joy. And think of this joy midst the darkness of these times, the joy of knowing that in this holy company, one by one you are with me as the body of God.

Blessed ones, it is a mystical union. It is a oneness of the one person. Let it be, then, that this is our triumph, this is our joy, this is our conquest of all darkness, as love, true love for Christ is the universal solvent of all evil, all error, all darkness, all intrigue, all murder, and the lie of the Serpent.

LET YOUR CANDLES BE LIT, AND LET THE CANDLE BE YOUR OWN HEART FLAME

I give you, then, according to your purity, the power to tread upon serpents.[10] Blessed ones, you need this power. Therefore, tie yourselves firmly to the umbilical cord of my Blessed Mother as she interpenetrates my blessed messenger. Understand that this tie, this blessed tie, binds you to the throne of grace, to Alpha and Omega, and that I AM your intercessor twenty-four hours a day.

Let it be, then, that the chosen ones of light are infused with the living spirit of liberty, and let this liberty be a *shout* for joy, a *release* of light, a *thunder*, an *acclamation*, a *descent* of the judgment of Almighty God, the *protection* of my little ones, and the *deliverance* of the captives of the astral plane.

I am grateful for your prayers. Let them continue. Let your candles be lit for those souls who are walking through absolute Darkness to find the way to my heart, walking through the astral night of horror to which they have been subjected. Let your candles be lit, and let the candle be your own heart flame.

I adjure you in this month to submit all selfishness and self-concern, all psychic variance into the flame, that you might receive the full power of the All-Seeing Eye of God and the full power of Cyclopea to release the energy for the penetration of evil. This is the true meaning of the scorpion's sting. It is the penetration, when translated by the divine alchemy, of the All-Seeing Eye of God.

I AM with you. I bless you. I charge you with light. I live in you. Blessed ones, know that when you accept me within your temple with that light and that Presence, you will be initiated. You will be required to subject your human will. And above all, you will begin to be uncomfortable with your old self and you will desire more and more to be the fullness of your own Christ Presence.

I have come for the deliverance of the nations. I have come for the salvation of the earth. Let the children of God be called to my heart. I walk among you. I AM with you. And we *shall* overcome!

October 23, 1977
Pasadena, California
ECP

CHAPTER 5

*We have drawn a hallowed circle around this forcefield
and around the earth, and within that circle
we have magnetized the souls whose inner commitment
to the flame will allow them to become candidates
for the ascension in this life.*

CHAPTER 5

THE SACRED FIRE JUDGMENT OF THE HOLY SPIRIT

H*ail*, sons and daughters of light! *Hail*, souls of infinite fire! I come into your midst, and I demand attention! I demand your obedience to cosmic law! I come for the quickening of your lifestreams to the higher discipline of the sacred fire, and I *rebuke* you for being out of alignment with that holy will of God!

Let the violet flame descend! And let your judgment be your incapacity to be receiving a greater light of freedom this day *because* of your indulgence and *because* of the indulgence of the nations of the earth!

While all of the earth wallows in self-pity, you dare not indulge in one speck of dust! And yet you have! And yet you have perpetuated those energies and that nonsense, which has become a burden to our endeavor, to our messenger, and to your own soul's evolution. Therefore let the selfishness and self-indulgence not be found in my house! For this is the Father's house, and within this house there will not dwell those individuals who cannot respond with alacrity when the command from the Son of God is given!

Therefore let the chelas of the light not take for granted the opportunity to accelerate on the path of becoming an ascended master. You must realize that the greatest gift of my incarnation is not the Bethlehem babe but the promise of that babe that all might become the ascended master. To trifle with that opportunity is unthinkable! It is unthinkable in our octaves of light and therefore we will not permit the trifling within our midst!

We have drawn a hallowed circle around this forcefield and around the earth, and within that circle we have magnetized the souls whose inner commitment to the flame will allow them to become candidates for the ascension in this life. Beloved hearts of fire, release, then, your resistance to the love of that path, and only that love.

DO NOT COMPROMISE

I come before you, and this is my Christmas message to every Keeper of the Flame, to every student in the teaching centers, and to those who stand offish from the organization, knowing well that here lies the fount, the victory, and the flame of the teaching.

And I say to you that your trifling with the teaching and with the directives that we send forth through our messenger will cost a great price to you individually, to you collectively, and to the world at large. Therefore understand that while you have the Word for the discipline, it is no time to be going after other forcefields because of this or that teaching or this or that dispensation that you think is manifesting.

Beloved hearts, how many have there been who have come as the Bethlehem babe? Were there twenty-five who came having the mission of Jesus Christ? Or was there one?

Do not consider, then, that we have messengers in every nation or here or there or that simply because someone applies great words and is able to portray before you a romantic telling of the story of the Law, that at last you have found "by your deep perception" another who can represent our consciousness and our flame to you.

Beloved hearts, this *is* our dispensation, and we demand electrodes who will appreciate that when the Lord God sends forth the dispensation, if it is to be carried over the thousands of years, then those who receive the initial impetus cannot compromise.

You will see in Christianity today the effects of the compromises of the apostles. Beloved ones, each compromise, each impetuous work, each act of stubbornness has been reflected untold times over and again within the Church until we have had to break the very vessel of that Church and form again that which would be acceptable in keeping the flame on Terra.

BE A PILLAR OF FIRE BY NIGHT

I tell you that cataclysm does threaten this coast and this area, and therefore we count upon the disciplined ones to be that fiery light day and night.

When you indulge, then, in your selfishness, when you look glum, when you are wondering who is going to do something for you next, and when you are concerned that you are not happy where you are, then I say, you are not the pillar of fire by night[1] and you are out of alignment.

Take this rod of light and see how it is connected to the heart of the earth and the heart of the Great Central Sun. When you are in harmony with love and joyous where I AM, then you will not consider the extension of time and space necessary for the fulfillment of your divine plan, but you will make the leap into the heart of God by love and you will see that that love itself can transcend the time and space that must evolve unto the fullness of your expression of joy in this octave.

See, then, how [when you are out of alignment] you are the electrode that moves aside from its connection to the heart of the earth and the heart of the Sun, and it is therefore useless. It has no polarity. It has no energy and no quickening because it is not attached to the filaments of God's being.

Blessed ones of light, I come, then, with the sacred fire judgment of the Holy Spirit. I come that you might be "burned" now rather than later. I come with sacred fire so that you might understand the mastery of detail in the Virgo action of the incarnation of the Mother. This is the hour, then, for fastidiousness, for *order* in the household of the Mother, for *order* in the organization, and for all to understand that unless there be order in your consciousness, there cannot be an orderly progression of the Law and the expansion of the teachings.

Let the obedience of my flame be upon you! Let my message be upon you! And let all those who have withheld a part of the price know that this day I have read your hearts and I, the Lord Christ, look beyond appearances to the very core of your being. And by the Eye of God I therefore can read in the projected future the judgment upon your life if you continue to withhold the best part of your love for the Almighty on earth.

In reading, then, of the judgment, I come to forewarn you of the judgment and to give you the action of the judgment this day so that you might receive it, correct that manifestation, and live.

BECOME DOERS OF THE WORD

Saint Germain stands with me. We are ready for the conversion of souls. We are ready to have an example in our midst whereby when souls come into our midst they see and know that this is indeed the place where those who have heard the Word have become doers of the Word.[2]

I speak directly to *you!* I speak directly to everyone who has had contact with the ascended masters! If every lifestream on earth this day who knew of me and knows of Saint Germain would come forward and submit even an additional 5 percent of their consciousness in the service of God, I tell you that the influx of light would be so great as to cause light of a cataclysmic nature (but a benign cataclysm) to occur within the very forcefield of the earth. And mind you, I have spoken only of those who know of the ascended masters and are familiar with their teachings.

Think, then, what a difference would come to earth if all of those who profess to walk in the way of the Lord in the world's major religions would also provide that additional 5 percent for the balancing of darkness on earth.

Blessed ones, I demand a sacrifice. As the LORD God demanded of me a sacrifice, so I stand the instrument of the judgment and I demand your sacrifice. And I will continue to demand it until all is consumed and you stand before the altar, ready to take your final vows for the ascension.

I have come. I have released the sacred fire into the midst, and I have released the energy necessary for the judgment of the individuals who are a part of this darkness that is abroad in the Holy City. Watch and see how the cycles of Almighty God are fulfilled. For every jot and tittle of the Law shall be fulfilled[3] ere this case is resolved. Therefore be not dismayed but be alert and vigilant. For there are many matters in America and in this organization that require your diligence.

BE UNTO ALL THE FULFILLMENT OF LOVE

Let this message be sealed in your heart and go forth in the joy of the incarnation and the joy of solstice. Go forth in the joy of the Holy Child and be unto all the fulfillment of love.

I AM your Lord. And while I have an instrument, I will speak as I will, and I will speak as God wills, and you will hear the wind of judgment.

Elohim, come! Press! Press down now upon these souls and let them feel the pressure of light that demands cosmic compensation —compensation for all gifts and graces, the compensation of an identity forged in God.

Be *sealed* in my ray! For I have directed it to your heart, and none shall escape—no, not one! Not one soul on Terra who has the teaching of the ascended masters will escape the ray of my flame! And let that flame of white fire be for the forcing of that hardness of heart, that human selfishness and willfulness, the forcing of that energy into a spiraling energy of light, driving it now into the white-fire core of sacred fire for transmutation, that you might be an angel among angels, an angle among angles of God's consciousness.

So I AM before you, the Faithful and True and the joy of the new cycle.

December 25, 1977
Pasadena, California
ECP

CHAPTER 6

I would that your heart would become a replica of the purple fiery heart of Saint Germain, . . . see the dazzling brilliance of amethyst crystal now in your heart, and above the crystal, eight points of diamond light—the eight points of the Eightfold Path of the Buddha, reminding you that it is how you live that determines how you will win.

CHAPTER 6

MY MISSION WITH SAINT GERMAIN

O Son of Righteousness blazing in all hearts, I stand before thee. I expand God consciousness. I AM the Lord Jesus Christ, the servant of the Son of Righteousness in each flaming one, and I come to address you on this New Year's Day, January 1, 1978.

I stand to release the spiral of my consciousness into the City of the Angels. And as that golden-white coil of energy proceeds from my heart, legions of angels now stand upon this coil, which forms a golden-white pyramid of energy that includes the entire county of Los Angeles, one indivisible unit of hierarchy. Thus the angels, the seraphim, the cherubim stand upon the spiral of the consciousness of the Son of God to ensoul, to personify, to embody, and to become the desiring of the Son of God for the resurrection and the life of every child of God within the City Foursquare.

The City Foursquare is a cube within your heart for the mastery of the Matter plane. As God intended you to be the alchemist of the sacred fire, so that God has placed that cube inaccessible to you until you bow before the Son of Righteousness within, confess the Lord Christ to be your Real Self, and confess the Lord Christ within the avatars of the ages, including my own humble incarnation of the Word but not excluding any other incarnation from the beginning of time and space unto the fulfillment of the cycles of eternity.

The City Foursquare, beginning with the cube within your heart, is, then, a continual extension of self. It is the cosmos. It is the solar system. It is the Matter sphere. It is your planetary home, the abode of evolution. It is your laboratory of fire, air, water, and earth. It is America. It is Los Angeles. It is the patch of earth where you stand.

Where I AM, I AM the Son of God incarnate. And where I AM the Son of God, I AM the City Foursquare. Let none violate the twelve gates of righteousness![1] Let none violate the mighty sphere of pearl! Let none violate the diamond of the will of God out of which issues forth the threefold flame within the center of the city. Let this be your affirmation and your declaration of who I AM.

THE ALCHEMY OF THE SIGN OF THE CROSS

Thus when you go forth to conquer, make the sign of the cross in the earth! Make it in the air! Make it in the fire of being! Make it in the waters of consciousness! By making the sign of the cross you declare, "Where I AM, God is. Where I stand is Alpha and Omega. I proceed from that origin. By that origin I go forth to conquer in love."

Beloved ones, making the sign of the cross is not superstition. It is heavenly alchemy! It is the alchemy of Helios and Vesta, who have marked the sign of the cosmic cross of white fire and therefore involuted and evolved a solar system. Thus where you stand to be the nexus of the descent of Alpha, the integration of Omega, there consciousness is. There being is God-willed, and there I AM. For I, Jesus Christ, a Son of God, the fulfillment of the only begotten seed of promise, do stand at the nexus of every heart center.

I AM in the center of the Son of Righteousness of your own being. When you therefore commit to the cross of consciousness that I have become, that I have mastered by initiation, you therefore also stand by grace in the presence of that momentum of attainment.

It is as though the LORD God held the giant mantle over the earth, and without having earned the wearing of that mantle you come as little children and you stand under the mantle, and the Lord God holds the mantle until you are able to carry its weight. The weight is light. But if there be darkness in you, the wearing of the mantle of God is as a lead weight. Then it is that your body becomes as lead, and then it is that you must mark the sign of the cross.

God has ordained you to counteract darkness. He will not allow that darkness to overcome you if you remember to mark the sign of the cross where you stand. For every cosmic being of cosmic consciousness who has attained to the liberty of the sons of God has employed the alchemy of the sign of the cross. And therefore you not only stand in my presence when you are in the cross of white fire but you stand in the presence of Lord Gautama Buddha, of the World Mother, of the saints whom you love, and of many unknown wondrous manifestations of God who are the kindling light of a cosmos.

THE ARCHDECEIVERS OF MANKIND AND THE WOLVES IN SHEEP'S CLOTHING

I come, then, your Lord and Master, your servant, your brother. I come on a mission of the age. It is our Father's desire that none of these little ones should be lost.[2] Beloved ones, there is great fervor for the Holy Spirit in the Christian community this day in what is called the charismatic movement. Indeed, the Spirit of the Lord moves across the land, and we are gratified.

But we are the guardians of the race. We are the guardians of his consciousness in manifestation. Therefore, beloved hearts, we must always see the counterpoint of the fallen ones, as the great Spirit of the Lord does move across the earth.

Beloved ones, as the Holy Spirit would enter the temple, so the impostors of the Holy Spirit, of which my beloved Magda has spoken to you, are ever present, lurking in the garments that yet remain unclean, that are yet spotted with the world's consciousness.

And here now I unveil to you the plot of the archdeceivers of mankind and of the wolves in sheep's clothing.[3] It is to rally the children of God in their various camps and understandings of me around a focal point of that which appears to be the Holy Spirit but is in many cases the gripping of unclean spirits and the manipulation of the energies of the chakras of these children of God, which science they do not understand for they have not been God-taught in the sacred mysteries.

And so these children of God feel the release of energies untoward, uncontrolled. And not having the experience of the highest contact with the hosts of heaven, they are confused and they believe that their belief is sufficient to ensure their protection. And so, beloved ones, as their souls become more and more entwined with the archdeceivers and their representatives, the children of God will form alliances and will position themselves on a certain line of consciousness.

Since part of the self-awareness of the children of God will include the impostors, these impostors within their ranks will violently react to the coming of the reality of the ascended hosts and of the real Holy Spirit. Because of their conviction and because of the fanaticism of the demons of possession, these impostors will therefore muster a horrendous energy to oppose the coming of the ascended masters, our stepping through the veil—indeed our stepping through the very flesh and blood of your own forms as your countenance becomes transparent and your eyes as the fiery coals of the living flame.[4]

And therefore, beloved ones, although there is a seeming resurgence to the original forms of Christianity, those original forms also contain not the primitive light but the primitive and base elements of the carnal mind that must first be exorcised ere the devotee open himself to the great light and influx of the Holy Spirit, which the Lord God has prepared for his children in this age.

Do you see, beloved ones, that as there is division and as there is a greater and greater polarization between the representatives of the false hierarchy and the representatives of the Great White Brotherhood, there is planned by the fallen ones the hour of confrontation—the hour when those who represent the mystery schools and the guru-chela relationship will be in such great number that the children of God, as they are unwittingly seized by the fallen ones, will consider that this is the hour when for righteousness and for a holy cause they must wage war against those whom they consider to be in sacrilege and acting contrary to my directives.

Blessed ones, there are many pastors of the sheep of Israel who are the wolves in sheep's clothing. Unfortunately the uniform they wear cannot easily be taken off, as in a play on the twelve tribes, but it is inextricably interwoven within the aura and within the chakras. And therefore when these pastors stand in their pulpits, whether in the Catholic, the Protestant, or in the Jewish tradition, all those who are a part of the congregation receive, by the flow of attention and of allegiance and of a misplaced loyalty, that momentum of misqualification, of misunderstanding of the blind leaders of the blind.

You who run and read righteous judgment can see the cast of the eye, can see the deception. It is very clear. And even when the simplest disciple stands in the presence of one of these [wolves in sheep's clothing], the demons [of that one in sheep's clothing] begin to tremble. He begins to shudder, and he himself cries in outrage for no reason whatsoever, even before the chela has even opened his mouth in declaration of the Word.

I tell you, you are witnesses in this land even as you are silent in the shaft of light that you are becoming by your dynamic decrees, by your realization that I live in you always, that Christ lives in you always, and that you have the potential to be God and you fear not to declare it and fear not to denounce the ways of Satan publicly.

MAKE THE VIOLET FLAME WORK FOR YOU!

Thus, beloved ones, you have become a great threat to the hordes of darkness. And therefore this brings me to my topic—my mission with Saint Germain. Saint Germain holds the key to the alchemy of the deliverance of these children of God from the ploys of the fallen ones. For you see, they cannot stand in the day of the judgment, and the day of the judgment is the day when the first invocation to the violet flame is made by the child of God!

Blessed hearts, simply to declare "I AM a being of violet fire! I AM the purity God desires!" is a revolutionary cry. It is a battle cry because it completely upsets the fallen ones, who hide in the folds of the garments of the children of God. They cannot stand this light of the Holy Spirit. They cannot stand its presence. They cannot bear the heat. They cannot live in the presence of love that is the core of the violet flame.

Freedom is foreign to their nature. And therefore when one child, even the lisping of a little child, will give that statement once with the authority of the I AM Presence, it is the beginning of the end of the spiral of deception of the hordes from without and deception from the inner self—the self within that is not the Real Self but the self that has seated itself in the position of authority within the citadel of being.

The violet flame is the energy of transition into the New Age. The purple fiery heart of Saint Germain is the nexus of the figure eight from the Piscean dispensation unto the Aquarian light, the Aquarian cycle of the Mother and the Holy Spirit. I would that your heart would become a replica of the purple fiery heart of Saint Germain, that you might see the dazzling brilliance of amethyst crystal now in your heart, and above the crystal, eight points of diamond light—the eight points of the Eightfold Path of the Buddha, reminding you that it is how you live that determines how you will win.

Beloved ones, the purple fiery heart of Saint Germain is God's gift for transition. The next best thing to the child of God giving

Saint Germain's mantra is that you give it for him, that you declare it in the name of the I AM Presence and the Christ Self, in the name of the adorable soul of the child of God—whether he is Christian, Muslim, Jew, Hindu, Buddhist, or any other—that you give that call and you invoke it in his name:

> In the name of the I AM Presence, the Christ Self, the adorable soul of every child of God, I give the mantra of the violet flame. I sing the song of the violet singing flame. I release waters of the living Word from out the centers of my temple.
>
> *Flow,* O violet flame from my heart! *Flow* from my soul, from the All-Seeing Eye, from my crown, from my belly, from my bosom, from my heart, from my hands, from my feet. *Flow!* Inundate their homes, their families, their churches, their mosques, their temples and synagogues. Inundate them with the flame of freedom!
>
> O Saint Germain and Jesus Christ, in the name of the violet flame, I command you to go before me into the world, as John the Baptist, clearing the way for the coming of the Word, to which I shall be witness, and of the Christ that I AM and of the Saviour, who lives within me.
>
> Violet flame, go before me as a violet-flame carpet beneath my feet. Go before me! *Clear* the way! *Clear* the way! *Clear* the way! For lo, I come and I walk upon the waters of the astral plane. I walk upon the air of the minds of the people. I walk through the sacred fire and I stand in the midst of the congregation of the righteous.
>
> O violet flame, prepare the way of the coming of the messenger of God. O violet flame, prepare the way of the coming of Jesus and Saint Germain. O violet flame, go before every chela. And LORD God Almighty, place your Word within our mouth as thou didst unto Moses and unto the prophets of Israel and unto the gurus of the Himalayas.

Beloved ones, let this be your prayer, and continue this prayer in your own words, specifically calling to the violet flame to go before you in all that you do. I tell you, you can build a mounting momentum, a tidal wave of light that will inundate every circumstance, every knotty problem, every point of contact that you anticipate will be to you a problem in the next hour or the next day.

Beloved ones, make the violet flame work for you! It is waiting to be called into action. And let the ascended masters who ensoul it come forth. For when you call forth the violet flame to go before you, everyone in cosmos who has become one with that violet flame will personify that flame and will come and march before you as legions of violet-flame angels. Omri-Tas and 144,000 priests of the sacred fire will go before you.

Beloved hearts, you have heard that 1978 is a year when all of your good can be multiplied infinitely for the balancing of great karma, personal and planetary, and when your failures will also be multiplied upon the screen of life. This is because a greater concentration of the All-Seeing Eye of God is being lowered into manifestation through the devotees of this organization. And where the lens becomes greater, where there is greater magnification (as you very well know), the specks of dust appear and the stars are more brilliant.

And thus it is. If you would have the All-Seeing Eye as you have invoked it diligently in this year, then you must realize what is the power of that Eye and why God has withheld it from the people of earth for so many ages. It is because standing within that Eye, people are wont to become extremely irritated, as the grains of sand gritting in the gears of life cause them to misqualify energy. And therefore God removes his light and his eye, and men dwell in darkness and they are content in their darkness. And in their darkness they say, "We have light." Well, we say, "That is questionable. It is all relative."

And so, beloved ones, increase the Eye of God and you

increase your opportunity for alchemy. Increase the vision of the people, as this is taking place through the multimedia presentations and through the motion picture that you have begun.[5]

So increase the vision and you will increase the victory, soul by soul. You will increase your good karma, and one day, when you stand before the Lords of Karma and you see me as I stand at your side giving testimony of your life, you will say, "Thank you, Jesus, for teaching us the way. Thank you for showing us how to balance our karma. Thank you. For I have 51 percent [of my karma balanced] because I have listened and heard and followed the Word and not mocked the one who came in your name."

REMOVE YOUR DOUBT AND FEAR BY SAYING, "JESUS CHRIST, COME INTO MY TEMPLE!"

Beloved ones, the mockery of our message is always the horrendous fear of the hordes of night, who will enter the swine and gallop down the hillside into the sea.[6] They are the ones who fear the perpetual fire, the eternal damnation. They are the ones who fear the great lake of fire in which they will be dissolved.[7]

That event [of the swine galloping into the sea] that took place symbolized the fact that the entire momentum of animal magnetism[8]—and I did not say "animal life" but the entire momentum of animal magnetism—within the human consciousness, with all of its forms and manifestations inhabited by the aggressions of the demons, will at the command of the sons and daughters of God run into the lake of fire and be dissolved. And that energy will be returned to the Great Central Sun for repolarization and for qualification in worlds beyond worlds beyond worlds in which you, beloved twin flames Above and below, will one day be the Father-Mother principle of life, giving love, wisdom.

Realize, then, that the tormenting demons, the demons of aggression who pound your mind and who question our light, are about to enter into the flame of Alpha and Omega and be no more.

Their fear is the ultimate expression and the end expression of their rebellion against God.

Therefore deal with fear as an enemy of your inner conviction to pursue God. Disassociate your fear and your doubt from this messenger, from this organization. It has naught to do with what is taking place here but only that the fallen ones tell you that your doubt and your fear is centered upon this objectivity that you see before you. This is the lie of the archdeceivers.

That vibration of fear and doubt resides within your own subconscious. Exorcise it in my name! It cannot remain when you pronounce the name of Jesus Christ with full conviction and when you continue to pronounce that name until every last impostor of my name, who mouths that name perpetually in disguise, is removed.

Beloved ones, do not let the fallen ones mouth my name through you, but in your own conviction give that name with the power of the Son of God and therefore say: *Jesus Christ, come into my temple!*

[Audience repeats with conviction.]

Hear the difference, then, in the authority of my name and of my Word and the pleadings of the groveling of the demons, who have no salvation and continually say, "Jesus, Jesus, Jesus."* Does this sound like the Son of God? *Nay!* And we will not have it within our congregation!

Now I say, I am here to remove your doubt and fear! If you are attached to your doubt and fear, then I say, as a lead weight you will sink to the bottom of the astral plane because of it! And it will not be because of the Great White Brotherhood, of my presence, or of the presence of Saint Germain or of our messenger! Whether right or wrong, the messenger's manifestation has naught to do with your own human creation!

Therefore you who have tarried in doubt and fear for many a year, hear my Word! I tell you, this revelation is for your salvation!

---

*spoken in a slow, low, monotonous tone

You must win your ascension independently of what you think is right or wrong with this organization. You must see squarely that your human rebellion is your own fault and no one else's—not of your father, your mother, your children, your society, your economic level, your race, or your various aptitudes.

Beloved hearts, we have come to save that which was lost. We have come with the promised Comforter in the presence of the violet-flame Spirit, in the light of the Maha Chohan. We have come to deliver the children of God. Therefore say once again for the love of the hearing of my ear, *Jesus Christ, come into my temple!*

[Audience joins in.]

When the full belief of your heart and the pure motive of your desire accompanies that call, you will find instantaneous release. Let me define for you the meaning of "instantaneous release."

Beloved ones, it is the instantaneous release of that which binds you in that moment. Only so much energy can bind you in a single moment. There are coils of energy moving within your subconscious.

Do not say that the Law has failed if in five minutes from now you encounter another motion of fear and doubt or another spiral of that energy. *You* are the alchemist! And I lay upon you the entire responsibility for the proof of this law and dispensation of my name, which I promised to you two thousand years ago in the name of Almighty God.[9]

You have thousands of years of momentum of fear and doubt. Therefore have the courage to shout in the temple of your being my name with the command, *Jesus Christ, come into my temple!* [Audience joins in.] And want it enough to shout it moment by moment, hour by hour, as though you were wrestling as Jacob wrestled until the coming of the day, until the angel then overcame within him that same measure of fear and doubt.[10]

THIS IS THE AGE OF *YOUR* ALCHEMY

Blessed hearts, for the gift of your ascension is it not worth the effort? ["Yes!"]

Now let us *make the effort* and be on with our joint mission with Saint Germain! For without him the children of God will not come into the true Christ consciousness in this age.

I bow before the flame upon the altar of Almighty God and I say: May you make it your own! May it blaze also upon your altar!

With each call you make I will confirm the call, but I will not extend one portion of myself to you without the call. For this is the age of *your* alchemy, *your* proof, your living witness that *you* are the Christ, the Word incarnate, the only begotten Son of God, full of grace and truth![11]

See, then, that you are full of that grace and truth, and therefore be emptied—by the power of my name—of all that has invaded your temple! And hear when the Mother as messenger rebukes you for that substance in your temple and that consciousness of which you are totally unaware because in that section of your temple you yet abide in darkness.

I AM come in the light of the messenger! Know that by that transfer of word and admonishment you have the key to your union in this life with God. Once again:

Jesus Christ, come into my temple! [Audience joins in.]

Now stand and say it with authority!

Jesus Christ, come into my temple!

[Audience stands and shouts with authority: *"Jesus Christ, come into my temple!"*]

Amen! ["Amen!"]

January 1, 1978
Pasadena, California
ECP

CHAPTER 7

We of the ascended hosts have . . . prepared a feast of the sacred fire, a conclave of light, a celebration of transmutation of the waters of the human consciousness into the wine of your own God consciousness. . . . But alas, many have made light of it and gone their ways as it was foretold.

CHAPTER 7

COME TO THE MARRIAGE FEAST

*Jerusalem
In Pisces 1978*

Beloved of My Heart,

As we have been together over the millenniums, as I have held you in my arms, and as you have followed me in the resurrection, so we have communed together on the mysteries of the kingdom of heaven—the consciousness of the living Spirit where God is.

Many of the teachings which we shared in the Upper Room and in the Retreat of the Resurrection over the Holy Land were set forth in parable, that they might be sealed until the hour of your own resurrection at the fulfillment of the appointed cycle. It was then that I told you of our coming again, of the descent of the Holy Spirit through the sons and daughters of God already one with me in the ascension, of the initiations of Saint Germain, of Mother Mary, Archangel Michael, and the hosts of the LORD who would once again walk and talk with the people of God on earth.

When we were together in the last days before my ascension and since that hour as we have met again and again upon your going out and coming in[1] to the Presence of God, as your souls have incarnated, lo, these two thousand years, you have asked me "of things to come concerning my sons."[2] Even then you desired to be taken up from the earth with me to sup with me in glory and to sit with me upon the right hand of my Father.[3] And I gave to you my promise which I have kept to be with you[4] in the hour of death and the reawakening of the soul to eternal life. And I gave to you the promise of our coming in the "last days"[5] when you would experience the kingdom of heaven on earth as the marriage of your soul to your own beloved I AM Presence prepared by your own Christ Self, the *king* who holds the *key* to your *in*carnation of the *God* flame.[6]

One with that Christ flame within you, I have sent forth my servants, legions of angels of Alpha and Omega, magnificent God-free beings who have stood before you, bowing to the great light of God within you, bidding you to the wedding. The few have answered the call of the Son of God but the many would not come. And we of the ascended hosts have again sent forth other servants telling them which are bidden that we have prepared a feast of the sacred fire, a conclave of light, a celebration of transmutation of the waters of the human consciousness into the wine of your own God consciousness.[7]

And my angels have said, "Tell them which are bidden, Behold, I have prepared my dinner: my oxen and my fatlings are killed, and all things are ready: come unto the marriage."[8] Lo, I have prepared my table before you[9] in the wilderness of the last days. The ascended masters have come. I have come in the Second Coming through the power of the Word in the presence of the Lord's body. I have descended into your midst trailing clouds of glory accompanied by myriad angels, archangels, seraphim, and cherubim. But alas, many have made light of it and gone their ways as it was foretold: "one to his farm, another to his merchandise."[10]

And some have even held in their hearts for our servants the messengers that hatred which is as the sin of psychic murder—thinking they did God service.[11] Knowing not what they have done,[12] this remnant have actually taken the servants, the blessed angels, and by their fanaticism and the condemnation of thought and feeling have sorely abused their blessed presence. Denying them, they have both denied me and my Father.[13]

I quote to you from the parable of the marriage feast that you might understand that the first circle of initiates have been called to the consummation of love and to the opportunity of embracing the Christ not alone in me but also in themselves and in the ascended masters, that they might reunite with us in the glory of the ascension. The marriage feast is prepared in the four quadrants of being according to the cycles of the year—winter, spring, summer, and autumn—at our retreats in which our "servants the prophets"[14] have served as priest and priestess at the altar of the sacred fire to commemorate the wedding ceremony of your soul's reunion with your I AM Presence. Indeed, many have been called but few have chosen to come into the oneness of the Holy of Holies.

Since the beginning of this year of 1978, the Lords of Karma have reviewed the record of the lifestreams who have been bidden —the few who have come to the marriage and the many who have made light of it. And now is come the judgment. To them who have received our Word, our energy, our light emanation, more shall be added. And unto them who have not responded to the call shall be taken away[15] that which they think they have gained in their private interpretation of the Word, in setting themselves apart from the body of God through pride, ambition, the glamour of psychic phenomena, and the false Christs and false gurus who have declared the kingdom to be "lo here!" and "lo there!" when I have told you repeatedly that "the kingdom of God [the consciousness of God] is within you."[16]

The smugness, the selfishness, the utter contempt of the "carnally minded"[17] who have professed to follow me in the regeneration but have betrayed our best servants as well as the company of saints has been read from the record by the Keeper of the Scrolls before the Lords of Karma. And nothing can alter that record except the renewal of commitment to the Great White Brotherhood. This you may make known by your presence at our forthcoming retreat. For those whose circumstance in life makes difficult the journey in time and space I say, "With God all things are possible."[18] Nevertheless, you may fulfill the Law right where you are by the consecration of your energies through the dictations and lectures of previous Easter conferences that you might create a chalice in your home and community in which my angels may pour the yearly dispensation of the resurrection flame.

Let those who are sincere "followers of God, as dear children"[19] make known to the Lords of Karma, to me, and to Mother Mary your desire to be present physically in our midst at the quarterly conferences. And we will call upon the law of the abundant life for your lifestream even as you give your invocations to the sacred fire for the abundance of every good and perfect gift[20] and of the necessary supply that you might fulfill both your spiritual and your material obligations to the Lord of life.

Now the Four and Twenty Elders turn the page in the Book of the Law. The fallen ones, who have murdered the sons and daughters of God through the ages and who have slain the evangels who have gone before the archangels as messengers of the Word, are brought to the judgment—they and their works—to stand trial by the sacred fire. Those who were bidden and were not worthy, who failed to respond and still fail, will now have given unto them a wider circle of karma and they will take the path of their own karma which they have already preferred by free will to the path of the ascended masters and their karma of light and grace which they have offered freely to all.

Now therefore, as the cycles have turned and my messenger Mark stands with me "on this side of the bank of the river"[21] in the ascended octaves of light I send my angels with my messenger Elizabeth out into the highways to gather together as many as they will find, even those with bad and good karma, that the wedding might be furnished with guests. Let all who are bidden come to the marriage feast and to the celebration of the Lamb and the Lamb's wife.[22] Let all take care that they offer invocation to the Great God, the One, the I AM THAT I AM, in the days and weeks preceding our conferences so that they will not be found without the wedding garment—the auric forcefield necessary to receive and retain our light. For there is indeed "weeping and gnashing of teeth" in that plane of Self-denial that is called "outer darkness."[23]

I have written to you on this occasion that you might know that your presence is requested in the hour of my Second Coming, which accelerates year by year in each of the quarterly conferences. Now you have the opportunity to be one in the freedom bought for you with a price[24] by Saint Germain, sponsor of America and of the flame of freedom in every heart and in every nation. Know, then, that one day the opportunity to confirm your God-reality right in our very midst may be taken from you if you do not confirm it today in joy. Putting first things first in the zeal of the apostle Paul, you must forget those things which are behind, and reach forth unto those things which are before. In word *and* in deed you must press toward the mark for the prize of the high calling of God in Christ[25]—both in me and in you.

Now then, let us gather together concentric rings of light made up of souls who are hearing the word of the messenger for the very first time, souls who will seize the Word and run with it as the torch of liberty to an age. Indeed, "many are called, but few are chosen."[26]

As always I will stand upon our platform that the few have graciously provided both in Pasadena and at Camelot, and there I will raise my hands in blessing and in welcome to the many. And I will transfer to you on Easter Sunday that portion of the Holy Ghost which you are able to receive according to the strength of your wedding garment. The platform is necessary for your evolution, for the balancing of your karma, and for your ascension. The platform is your heart, is our focus, is America, is the earth. All of these must be sustained by the flame of constancy, by the call that compels the answer that ye may have your victory.

Work while ye have the light.

I AM
Jesus the Christ

A letter by Jesus
1978

CHAPTER 8

*Beloved hearts of light, expand your consciousness
to include the miraculous, the wonders of love,
the advent in this hour! Expand your consciousness
and shatter the shackles that have bound you,
lo, for thousands of years.*

CHAPTER 8

AS MY FATHER HATH SENT ME, EVEN SO SEND I YOU

Hail, O light within the inner heart of man. I salute the Inner Man of the Heart, the Real Self of each and every son and daughter of God.

I AM in the fullness of the LORD's Spirit on the LORD's day,[1] and I come in the sacred fires of the resurrection, as I have told you I would come—in the fullness of the judgment, in the fullness of the Word, and in the fullness of the promised Comforter.[2]

I stand in your midst as the testimony of light and the testimony of the victory of life, as of old. For I AM THAT I AM. I AM in your very midst that same Jesus who was taken up from you. And so I AM come by the same cloud of white fire. I AM in the light of the Holy of Holies. And seeing, ye see not; and hearing, ye hear not.[3] But not all. For in the very midst of your soul and the emanation of light therein, the cathedral of the heart is established, and there in the Presence of the One God we sup in the glory of his righteousness.

I come, then, to send that sword whereby peace shall be established forevermore—first the sword and then the fullness of the light of peace. For I AM come to bring judgment.

So it was as foretold in the Fátima prophecy of my own beloved, the Virgin Mary, who has come to you, though ignored by Church and State. Yet the message remains the clear call of the faithful within and without the Church to reestablish and reinstitute the original Church upon that Rock, and that Rock is the realization that I AM He.

So in the fullness of that "I AM He" consciousness, let those who would represent my office now understand that there is and there can be no compromise with the prince of this world. And no matter what the ordination or the prophecy upon those representatives that have come forth in the name of Peter, it is the judgment of Almighty God that those who cleave unto the Lord Christ shall be sustained and those who go out of the way, even as Peter once did, must have the reprimand that is forthcoming, "Get thee behind me, Satan."[4] Beloved ones, God is no respecter of persons,[5] and therefore in the very person of the one who was called Peter, God ordained the raising up of that community that would portray the effulgent light. And so by that apostolic succession, down through the ages the torch of the flame of Christ has been passed.

CHURCH IS THE ONENESS OF THE SAINTS IN HEAVEN AND ON EARTH

And what of the faithful who have been taken out from that Church by the going out of the way of the fallen ones who have lured them to alternate paths of righteousness?

Beloved hearts, the dispensation is unto the individual and not unto the organization. For it is upon the Rock of the recognition of the Christ that the Church is built, and this Church is community, the community of the called-out ones. And therefore upon the Rock of that commitment and that recognition—there within that commitment, there within the heart—is the white stone that is the foundation and the chief cornerstone of the building of the temple of man and of woman.[6]

Beloved hearts of light, there is no predestination that does not take into account the free will of man and woman, of those who are in the fore in Church and State and those who are tending the flocks of sheep upon the hillsides of the world or harvesting the grain and the wheat. The predestination of every soul born of God is to do that holy will, to see that holy thing born of thee that is called the son, the daughter of God.[7]

And so it is those who come into alignment with the inner will of God who are predestined to come into the glory of everlasting life. Many are called but few are chosen.[8] Wherever there is compromise, there is that unworthy and unprofitable servant, and so there is weeping and gnashing of teeth.[9]

Beloved ones, compromise with the fallen ones is at an all-time high upon earth, as predicted for the end times and the Second Coming and the coming of the kingdom. And therefore that spiritual wickedness in high places[10] has reached the deplorable state whereby there is the wedding between Church and Marxism and Communism and socialism and the compromise of the true Church and the breaking down of those traditions that are the sacred chalice of my blood and of my body. And thus there is schism within the Church and schism without, as the fallen ones lobby for their rights to pursue Antichrist and demand the ordination of that right, right within the midst of the temple.

And therefore I come. I come for the scourging. I come to chase out the moneychangers within the temple of Church and State.[11] Beloved ones, no matter what the person, if the individual attempts to combine the power of Satan and the power of Christ, that individual cannot stand but must be brought unto the judgment and therefore unto the promise, "of his kingdom there shall be no end"[12] and "the gates of hell shall not stand against that Church."[13]

Beloved ones, Church is not a mere institution. Church is the oneness of the saints in heaven and on earth. Church is the inner kingdom. Church is righteousness and consciousness, and every true believer who has contacted the real light of Almighty God is one in that Church. Many would be astounded to know that I personally answer the prayers of the Muslim, the Jew, the Hindu, the Buddhist, and those who simply cry out without the understanding of me as my person.

Beloved ones, there is a smugness, a self-righteousness, and a spiritual pride among those who have thought that they have held the keys unto the kingdom and yet have betrayed the very light and the very mysteries of my body. And what of the hour of the judgment, when those who are cast out fail to minister unto the body of God. For is this not the judgment—whether or not the individual servant has fed my sheep? Thus the feeding of the sheep and thus the judgment remains between the individual and his God.

And therefore there are saints who are born who come out from under the yoke of tyrants, and yet by submission to the tyrants' will they themselves are tried in the fiery trial. And so it has ever been that those followers of Christ have won their crowns and have been knighted in the inner courts of heaven, even though their taskmasters have been the servants of the Devil.

And so, beloved ones, the upholding of the office of the Vicar of Christ over the centuries has been with the understanding that it has not been by the limitation of the man occupying the office but by the mantle and the grace and the Spirit itself, which is able even to transcend and transform beyond the frailty of the human person. This is the great mystery of the incarnate Word—that the incarnate Word is not dependent upon the vessel but in itself is that Logos and is that Truth whereby all men are saved.

Beloved ones, do you think that the eternal God within you is moved, whether you turn to the right or to the left? I tell you, nay! But you indeed are moved and your soul is moved, either away from or toward the center of everlasting life. And thus it is not God who is compromised but the soul itself, who must by free will prove every jot and tittle of the Law.[14]

HUMANISM IS NOT THE WAY OF THE ORIGINAL CHRIST-MANIFESTATION

Therefore I AM come. I AM come with the fulfillment of that prophecy of the destruction of the temple in order that the temple might be raised up.[15]

Hearken to my Word, O ye saints, those who form the body of God within the Church, to whom I would speak. And yet there is not a mouthpiece through whom I may speak, and so I must call those other sheep that are not of this fold. And we must gather upon the hillsides of the world, for the cathedrals of this world belong not to these sheep who have come out of the highways and byways.

And so there is that Bishop Lefebvre,[16] who preaches in my name, who would move with the faithful, who would restore the Latin Mass and the ways of tradition. Beloved ones, I AM with each and every servant son who is sincere in following the law of God as he understands that Law.

Therefore, my ways are not your ways, saith the LORD.[17] And you must understand that even in those who have deserted the true faith and who have made their journeys hither and thither as the cardinals of the Church into the Communist countries, setting aside therefore the great light of Cardinal Mindszenty[18] at the request of the Communists, beloved ones—even these are yet on the path of understanding who is God and who is anti-God. And until the ultimate judgment, they have the opportunity to repent and to recognize that the reformation of an integral humanism is not the way of the original Christ-manifestation, which I brought.

Beloved ones, if humanism could save the world, then I tell you, it would have done so long ago. For the way of the humanist was not merely born in the Renaissance, but the way of the humanist is ever the raising up of the human being as being the highest manifestation, the alternative to the Son of God being raised up within the individual.

Do you understand, beloved ones, that when there are those partakers of the leaven of the Pharisees who declare that Christ does not dwell bodily within his creatures, within his offspring, within the mystical body, then, you see, there is no hope for salvation, and the alternatives of Marxism and of Communism and humanism must be exalted in place of the Church?

Those who do not believe in the great mystery of my coming will again and again set aside the Church and relegate it to a sub-position in civilization, when the Church *is* the cornerstone of life, the apex of individual fulfillment.

Beloved hearts of living fire, those who betray the essential message of Christ, those who betray the Law and the grace of that Law, are those who have not experienced God, have not seen me face-to-face. They have not seen me because they have not seen God within themselves. And they have not seen God within themselves because, beloved ones, they have not been willing to surrender the Antichrist. Blessed hearts, you cannot perceive the inner Christ until you have been willing to submit all unto the judgment.

How can it be that those who have risen to positions of power in Church and in the governments and economies of the nations have gone so far in the assertion of power and yet have not the living Christ within them?

Beloved ones, they have believed the lie. They have believed the lie of the Serpent that originally traduced Adam and Eve in the Garden. The lie that forms and systems and philosophies that have evolved by the fallen ones may sit in an equation with the eternal Eucharist, with the angels of the Eucharist, with the Blessed Virgin.

My beloved, those who persecute the followers of God within those countries where Communism has gained that foothold according to the Fátima prophecy, those who persecute these Christians in these nations, are not of God and yet they are treated with respect by members of my Church, both Protestant, Catholic, and by Jew and Muslim alike. All are my children.

My children, my children, you have erred, for you have lost all advantage by siding in with the fallen ones. And the advantage you have lost is the great company of saints and the emissaries of God standing upon the hillsides of the world. Beloved ones, the one who decides in fear to submit to the compromise solutions of the fallen ones immediately loses the reinforcement of the entire body of light.

THE CHRIST WITHIN YOU IS ABLE TO BEAR THE CRUCIFIXION

You will remember that I was alone in the garden pondering the great mystery of the resurrection and the mystery of the crucifixion. That aloneness was the aloneness that comes to every son and daughter of God, who must choose to be in God and in his will or choose a separate path.

Beloved ones, until the choice is made, "Nevertheless, not my will but thine be done," that son stands alone, suspended in the vastness of a cosmos that is absolute silence. The silence is awesome, almost frightening. For one perceives the awe of God and one's self suspended in the midst thereof.

And the choice to be God, the choice to move through the initiation of the crucifixion, to lay down one's earthly life that eternal life might be had by all, is that choice. And without taking that choice, beloved ones, there is a loss of the great light of God and a loss of a cycle.

Beloved ones, why have they not chosen to follow me in the crucifixion, those who are the shepherds who have been raised up in this age?

Lo, the false pastors that destroy and scatter the sheep of my pasture![19] Woe to them! Woe to them, I say, as unto ye lawyers who enter not into the kingdom and hinder those who would enter from entering in. They have not chosen the crucifixion, for they have never understood that it is never the outer self, the lesser self that is crucified, but always the Christ. And the Christ himself within you is able to bear that crucifixion, is able to walk through the fiery furnace and emerge without so much as the breath of smoke upon that one.[20]

Beloved hearts of infinite fire, when you believe that you are performing the work, then you will enter into fear and doubt and loss and separation. Then you will stand and receive the glory and the plaudits of this world, and you will forget that all of these are come to naught and that the only plaudit that you must seek is the Word of Almighty God, "Well done, thou good and faithful servant. Thou hast been faithful over a few things; I will make thee ruler over many."[21] "This is my beloved Son, in whom I am well pleased."[22]

THE LIGHT OF THE SAINTS IS THE EVERLASTING LIGHT WITHIN

I come, then, with the judgment of those who have usurped power, those who have thought that the ease of power was in the succession of a human lineage. Beloved ones, the priesthood of Melchizedek is not after human lineage, as I have so taught and as I gave to my apostle Paul. And therefore the priesthood and the priests of the Order of Melchizedek are those who individually come under the rod of Aaron and thereby submit unto the crystallization of the God flame within.

And so the outer Church and the inner Church must become one. And those who hold the keys in the outer Church must recognize that it is the inner Church of Mother Mary, it is the white-fire core nucleus of the Mother in the very heart of the Church that becomes the Bride of the Lamb. This adoration of the Mother is the adoration of the Son. Without the Mother, there is no Son. Without the Son, there is no Mother.

And so the oneness of life becoming life by the Father-Mother God is that portion of light that belongs unto all the faithful, and all who have ever ascended into the light of God are a part of the company of the L ORD. And therefore, let Jew and Muslim, Christian, Protestant, Catholic, Hindu, Buddhist alike proclaim the light of the saints as one with the everlasting light within. This, my beloved, is the strength of the body of God upon earth.

There is no need for you to judge, for the judgment is mine and vengeance is mine, saith the Lord.[23] And therefore the judgment is the separation of the chaff and the wheat, and that separation by the threshing floor of the coming of the messenger of God is prophesied as that coming of the one, the servant John the Baptist, who came to prepare the way of the Lord.[24]

And so we send our messengers in this day and age to go before the coming of the individual Christ Presence within you, to go before the teaching and the understanding that my coming is indeed the congruency of the Christ within and the Christ without.

PREACH THE GOSPEL TO EVERY CREATURE

So I say, experience God and be God, and stand fast for that salvation. For there shall be many signs and wonders and many changes and conditions, but those who endure unto the end, as it is written, will be saved.[25] This endurance is the challenge of life. It is the endurance of that which is within you as sin, as karma, and it is the endurance of that which is in the world. Herein is the patience of the saints—that tarrying in this plane of consciousness, you are able to be present with the LORD in prayer and meditation, in your perpetual calling upon the name of that LORD, and in the inner bliss of our oneness.

So in that joy and long-suffering, be the leaven of God. Go into the highways and byways. Go into Church and State. Stand before those who have stood in the light of my own flame and preach to them as I preached in the levels of hell during that passion week after the death upon the cross. For I went forth to preach to those beloved ones who to outer appearances did not have the light or the response.

Yet it is the requirement of the Law to preach the Gospel to every creature.[26] For by your preaching of the Word and your witnessing of the Word, I AM in you and I stand before the accuser and the Adversary, before friend and foe alike. And therefore, he that receiveth you, receiveth me.[27] Blessed is he that cometh in the name of the Lord.[28] Blessed is every follower of God.

Beloved ones, let there not be self-righteousness, condemnation, or judgment. For the dividing of the Christian body into sects and into various beliefs is the weakening of the light of the eternal God and the weakening of your resistance unto the monolith of the dragon that has sown the seeds of that conspiracy that is amalgamated East and West. Now let the faithful rise up into the fullness of joy within every church. And within that joy, let them realize that their reason for being is to challenge injustice, to let my people go, to set the captives free.

I come in the great mystery of the saints robed in white. I come, then, to challenge the pride of the wicked who have donned the apparel of the Good Shepherd. So they will be exposed, but leave it unto God. Only bear witness. For by your witness of the light, those who have not the light are forced to choose.

And in this day and age, beloved hearts, the wicked are outraged against those Christians who have had the courage to stand and still stand. And so all of the powers and that wickedness in high places does not have the power to detain or delay, even an hour, the rapture, the reunion of the soul that is wed to God with my everlasting life. Be comforted, then, that the hour of the resurrection is the hour when you yourself may enter into that eternal light body.

YOU ARE THE LIVING CHURCH

The seven archangels, who serve the Lord Christ, stand with me, and I AM in that body and that company, even so the mighty cherubim who keep the way of the Tree of Life and who guard the flame of the ark of the covenant.[29] So I send these. And unto every son and daughter of God, every tender child, I send two flaming cherubim to keep the way of the ark of the covenant.

Therefore know that in the body of God upon earth the altar of the Church is within the true temple made without hands, the altar of the sacred fire that is within you. So let it be the fitting habitation of the Lord God.

So now, each and every one of you who is one in God, by the requirements of the grace and the Law, receives these flaming cherubim to keep the way of the Tree of Life, the I AM Presence, and of the threefold flame of the Trinity within you. So be the fullness of the living Church. You indeed are the living Church, as is each and every one who is seized with the passion to become one with God.

I AM Jesus, your Lord and Master. Be not astonished that I should be in your midst. For it is the fulfillment of my word to you that my Father and I would make our abode with you and in you in the last days.[30]

And did you think that in making our abode with you, we would not commune with you and talk with you and contemplate with you and also rebuke and denounce all error?

Did you think that the great Prince of Peace would be forevermore silent because the fallen ones have decreed it? Beloved ones, those who silence God in the least of these my brethren so do it unto me.[31]

Ever be, then, the witness of my flame, and let the glory unto the Lord be easily passed from your lips as a perpetual prayer of righteousness, as the affirmation, as the sound of the rushing of waters, and as the sound of the wind of the Spirit.

So let the perpetual prayers of the righteous form the angelus and the rosary of Ave Maria, that the entire planetary body might be sealed in the swaddling garment of your eternal light body, your seamless garment that you weave, one by one. And in the sealing of the earth, so is the wrapping of my body in the grave cloth. So in that sealing of the earth, the sons and daughters of God will have the opportunity in this hour of transition to put on and become the fullness of everlasting life through the resurrection flame.

THE KINGDOM OF GOD IS WITHIN YOU

What I say unto you, I say unto all: Watch and pray, for ye know not the hour when the Son of man cometh.[32] I AM coming here and now. I AM coming in the fullness of the light and the cosmic initiations of Alpha and Omega.

Lo, I AM in Alpha and Omega, the beginning and the ending, the first and the last.[33] I AM that which was and is and shall be forevermore within you, the eternal light.

Only choose and discover your life hid with Christ in God. Only choose. For I come through many manifestations and many individuals. And so it has been said, "Be not forgetful to entertain strangers, for thereby some have entertained angels unawares."[34]

I AM the fullness of the joy of the angelic hosts, and I come in many guises, even as the Virgin Mother has appeared here and there in the garb and in the apparel and in the mien and countenance of the people to whom she has appeared.

So it ever is that the LORD God adapts himself and allows his children to hear his voice within their own language, within their own understanding, and to see his face according to their own inner image of the eternal Christ, out of which they are fashioned.

Beloved hearts of light, expand your consciousness to include the miraculous, the wonders of love, the advent in this hour! Expand your consciousness and shatter the shackles that have bound you, lo, for thousands of years, when you have walked following the blind leaders of the blind instead of recognizing in the fullest dimension of your being that lo, the kingdom of God is within you.[35]

I AM the priest, the minister, and the rabbi standing at the altar of Being. I officiate at the altar of the Holy of Holies within you. Come unto me, all ye who are heavy laden, all ye who labor, and I will give you rest.[36] My yoke is easy, and my burden is light.[37]

THE LAYING DOWN OF YOUR LIFE FOR THE FRIEND

Beloved hearts, on this celebration of Easter 1978, I offer to you the cup of joy and the cup of sorrows. I offer unto you the cross and the victorious crown, in the order of their appearance. I offer to you the cross of world karma as I bore it. And therefore the angel of my Presence will knock and will ask of each and every one of you, "Are ye able to bear the portion of that world sin that he bore?" And the answer will be forthcoming from you according to your free will. And in answering yes, be certain that you ask for the initiations of the cross that must precede your carrying of that cross. For the LORD God does temper the wind to the shorn lamb.[38]

And so you see, before the angels will give unto you the cross of world sin, they will place upon you those testings of your soul whereby you may be tried, purified, whereby you may prove what is that light you may bear, what is that darkness you may counteract.

So let the saints who yet breathe the air of freedom, let the saints who yet walk under the blue sky of awareness, let them carry the burden of those who are in the trial and tribulation of the persecution unto the death. But fear not, for their souls are not touched. Their souls are sealed beneath the altar of the living flame.[39]

I stand before you to transfer to you my light, that in that light your love might be the receiving point whereby you rise in the understanding of laying down your life for the friend.

Beloved ones, the friend is always the Christ. The friend for whom you lay down your life is the eternal Christ within me and within every child of God.

Is there any other way, any other calling? For me, there is not. For you, there is yet the freewill choice.

I AM with you alway, even unto the end of the cycle of the age.[40] Amen.

March 26, 1978
Camelot
Los Angeles County, California
ECP

CHAPTER 9

I AM the Eternal Christos!
I send forth my Word as a sword of living flame.
I send it into the air, into the earth, into the fire, into the water.
And it shall not return unto me void!

Jesus releasing his Judgment Call "They Shall Not Pass!" on August 6, 1978 through his messenger Elizabeth Clare Prophet.

CHAPTER 9

THEY SHALL NOT PASS!

Lo, I AM Alpha and Omega! Lo, I AM come the risen Christ, the living proof eternal of the victory of life over death—death that is unreal.

O my beloved, I come into the very midst of the circle of our oneness. Lo, I AM Jesus! Lo, I AM in the flame of the Holy Spirit within you! Bear witness unto my coming, for I AM the resurrection and the life[1] within you in this very hour if you will receive me as the Christ who lives within you ever, as the Christ who speaks throughout the vast ages by the power of the Lord's Spirit unto the prophets of the people.

Lo, I AM come! Lo, I AM here! And therefore, let the demons and the fallen ones who would procrastinate my coming be bound! Let the doubt and fear that has been perpetrated year upon year now be bound in the very midst of the lightbearers! And let the eternal quest of the soul not be the eternal questioning of the Word incarnate. For lo, this mystery of the LORD God he would form in you, each and every one of you—every man and woman and child and babe in arm. Lo, the mystery of the Word incarnate is now and ever was and ever has been. For lo, I AM THAT I AM!

I AM the Eternal Christos! I send forth my Word as a sword of living flame. I send it into the air, into the earth, into the fire, into the water.

And it shall not return unto me void!
And it shall not return unto me void!
And it shall not return unto me void![2]

I STAND WITHIN THE HEART OF EVERY TRUE FOLLOWER OF GOD WHO WILL RECEIVE ME

Therefore, let those who dabble in the black arts, who practice the practices of Satan, know that I AM the living Christ—not removed into heaven, but here upon earth I AM. And I stand within the very heart of every true follower of God who will receive me, who will in joy prepare me room. For my coming in this hour is for the judgment of those who assembled even at Pharaoh's court, even the black magicians of Egypt who would practice their death upon our messengers and our disciples north, south, east, and west.

I hurl, then, the challenge of the Cosmic Christ, Lord Maitreya, the beloved Guru of the incarnate Word! I hurl, then, the challenge of Lord Gautama the Buddha, who would unfurl the banner of righteousness in ye all this day! I send forth the challenge of the Virgin Mother unto those fallen ones!

So we declare: let those, then, who would move against this light of our coming in these little children, in the holy innocents, in each soul of love, as well as in our messenger hearken, then; for I speak by the authority of the Almighty. I AM his Son! By the Trinity of Father, Son, and Holy Spirit, which I touch within you as three-fold light expands, I, Jesus, declare that those who send forth this darkness upon our chosen ones, our little ones, and our best servants receive, then, the hand of the Lords of Karma and the judgment.

Therefore know, O children of the Sun, that in each twenty-four-hour cycle it is your opportunity to raise your right hand as I raise my right hand even now, to place your left hand to your heart, and to release the sacred fire of my Word for the judgment and the challenge of the black magicians upon this entire planetary body in the earth plane, in the astral plane, in the mental plane, and those who would usurp the light of the sacred fire in the etheric plane. For they have declared war against the Woman and her seed,[3] and by that malice they have determined the death of the lightbearers.

And therefore I, Jesus, place my Electronic Presence within you and upon you and my mantle for the hour when you raise your right hand and you declare within me: They shall not pass! They shall not pass! [Audience joins in.] They shall not pass! Beloved ones, let me recite my prayer, I bid you.

For the hour when you recite with me, then: They shall not pass! They shall not pass! [Audience joins in.] They shall not pass! Beloved ones, I desire to recite my prayer! Will you keep silence, then, as I speak?

I will place, then, my Electronic Presence upon you for the hour when you recite my prayer as you raise your right hand and as you place your left hand to your heart, saying: They shall not pass! They shall not pass! They shall not pass! By the authority of the cosmic cross of white fire it shall be that all that is directed against the Christ within me, within the holy innocents, within our beloved messengers, within every son and daughter of God is now turned back by the authority of Alpha and Omega, by the authority of my Lord and Saviour Jesus Christ, by the authority of Saint Germain. I AM THAT I AM within the center of this temple, and I declare in the fullness of the entire Spirit of the Great White Brotherhood that those who, then, practice the black arts against the children of the light are now *bound* by the hosts of the LORD; do now receive the judgment of the Lord Christ within me, within Jesus, and within every ascended master; do now receive, then, the full return —multiplied by the energy of the Cosmic Christ—of their nefarious deeds which they have practiced since the very incarnation of the Word. Lo, I AM a son of God! Lo, I AM a flame of God! Lo, I stand upon the Rock[4] of the living Word and I declare with Jesus, the living Son of God: They shall not pass! They shall not pass! They shall not pass! Elohim. Elohim. Elohim. [chant]

By the light of the Virgin Mary, I have spoken unto you. I have given to you, then, a call that is yours to set before the altar of the living God. May it proceed from your temple each day that you may reenact the judgment of the Four and Twenty Elders before the Court of the Sacred Fire upon the God Star.

THE PROPHECY IN THE BOOK OF REVELATION

Beloved ones, you who count yourselves as initiates of the sacred mysteries of the body of Christ must understand that the prophecy that is given in the Book of Revelation for the judgment of the dragon, the beast, the false prophet, the great whore, and the Antichrist[5] is a judgment that must be reenacted and spoken daily. And that Revelation is not simply a revelation to be contemplated. It is a living Word. It is the doctrine of the Holy Spirit. And those who are the Christ incarnate, those who wear the robe of my Electronic Presence, are expected to give forth that Word for the binding of the fallen ones each and every day as they present themselves anew with their affrontry, with their boldness, with their manipulation of energy lo here, lo there—in the Congress, in the schools, midst the little children, among the aged, in the midst of the drug uses.

Beloved ones, many nefarious practices are being attempted against the children of God and many seeming manifestations that be harmless, even promising great good. I call to your attention, then, that drug which is now being experimented with and even pushed among Keepers of the Flame as a life-saving, life-prolonging drug —that GH3. We desire it not to contaminate the temple of our children, of our Keepers of the Flame. I say to you, go not[6] when they declare the coming of everlasting life by chemistry. Beloved ones, the only guarantee of life within you is the life of the living God that you espouse. Beware, then, of instruments and objects and all of those fanciful concepts and those who then purvey and sell pyramids and tell you, "If you will only have this pyramid or this instrument, it will guard you from all evil." Beloved ones, it is the everlasting Presence of the Lord God, it is the I AM THAT I AM, it is the Saviour *within* you who is able and only able to give you life.

Precious ones, we deny not the science of the Great Pyramid. But the Great Pyramid is your very life, it is but the outer symbol of the great temple of your being and the resurrection flame that even now is kindled and does burn as the threefold light upon the altar of your heart. Do not mistake, then, material objects for your salvation; for one day you will be called upon by me, by the Lord Christ within you, by that Jesus who I AM, to stand alone robed in white without assistance from any other source save that light that burns upon the altar of your heart. And by that light and that light alone you, too, will prove the victory of life over death and hell.

Beloved ones, therefore do not clutter your path with all of these objects and do not run here and there. For salvation is not of flesh and blood[7] nor is it of the perfectionment of this human temple, but the perfectionment of the virtue of the soul. And therefore, take all other exercises—physical or mental—in moderation. And do not think that in any exercises—whether of yoga or of pranic breath or any other form—that you will succeed in perfecting that soul. But by virtue, by the sacred labor, by grace and good works, by faith and hope and charity you will win the path of your ascension.

THE MYSTERIES OF GOD ARE REVEALED IN THE HIDDEN TEMPLE OF THE HEART

Beloved ones, let all other things, then, come into balance and perspective as the minimum necessity for the sustainment of balance within the four lower bodies. This temple, then, is the temple where the mysteries of God are revealed in the hidden temple of the heart by the secret of the hidden man of the heart.[8]

O beloved ones, I stand then to *heal* the body of God of all superstition, to *heal* you of dependence upon other individuals and those who tell you you are sick and those who tell you that you are maimed and those who tell you that you are infested with dreaded diseases. Beloved ones, however well-meaning, they are pronouncing their judgments, and these are the curse of death. I say to you, look up and live and take only the prognostication of your own mighty I AM Presence, your own Great God Self, and your Christ Self.[9] And all else take, then, at the level that it is given where it has no power to deter you but where you act wisely and with dominion observing the alchemy of the sacred fire taught to you by Saint Germain, observing the chemistry vouchsafed to you through the Lords of Karma and by the mighty arm of the healing sciences.

Beloved ones, let the psychic practices of the pendulum and all sorts of nefarious deeds be now routed from those who would be the practitioners of the healing arts. And let those who would convey the mighty flame of healing of my life know that the requirement is not more and more instruments but more and more Holy Spirit. And let those who would set themselves up to be a part of the Center for the Disciplines of Wholeness know that we set our requirements at the level of the cosmic honor flame and we will not tolerate deception, insubordination, or disobedience from any among those who have set their hand to the healing arts.

For, beloved ones, the only permanent healing that will ever come by any means must come from the white-fire core of being of the one who holds the Alpha polarity—the one who places himself in the position of the Lord Christ and the one who, then, is the recipient holding the Omega polarity. And each one has equal responsibility to hold the purity of the Holy Spirit that only the energies of the Holy Spirit be allowed to pass into the temple.

Beloved ones, therefore take care not to place yourselves in the hands of those who by handling your temples steal your light while pronouncing your illnesses. Beloved ones, go rather to the field and eat the grass of the field. Go rather to the waters, the cleansing waters of the seas. Go to the ritual of fasting. Go, then, to the ritual of prayer. Go to the mud of the earth. And discover how God himself has provided for thy healing in joy.

Without joy, beloved ones, there is no healing but only a psychic interdependence; and I will not have this psychic interdependence entering into the body of God upon earth. And therefore, let those who would walk in my footsteps using the hand to convey the current of life know that there is a price to be paid when you allow psychic energies or your human consciousness to flow forth from you. Your position is only privileged when you retain it in absolute adoration of the Trinity within.

"BE THOU MADE WHOLE!"

O beloved ones, if you partake of those substances that are provided so lovingly for your healing, know that the power lies not in the substance but in the qualification of that substance within your own hand, within your own heart. Therefore when you take whether of the food or of the concentrations of the food or of the elements that are prescribed, know that first you must hold them in your right hand, placing once again your left hand to your heart and calling forth the infinite blessing of Almighty God and the charging of that substance with a concentrated light that is the specific for your healing.

So thus you may charge your water, your food, and all of which you partake. And one day, one day you will come to the place when you will not need to charge that secondary substance, for you will find that by the invocation unto the Lord Christ you will find the command "Be thou made whole!" resounding within the temple of your being, resounding within the secret chamber of your heart. But, beloved ones, when you lack that attainment you ought to have a realistic assessment of your life and not jeopardize your life or the life of your community by doing those things which only bring shame upon the teaching of the abundant life when you have neglected the glorious dispensations that have come forth for the saving of life through the hands of the Lords of Karma.

Give not power, then, unto the energy veil—whether that energy veil manifests as sickness or as the drugs to cure that sickness—but understand that all energy and all Matter is designed to be infused with the flame of the living Spirit. And therefore diseased Matter may be made whole, and you may charge that which is given for the transfer of the energy also with the Holy Spirit. Without the infusion of God, neither the practitioner nor the patient has the fullness of the glory and the joy of the coming of the Lord Christ into the temple. This is the purpose of all treatment. And if it be not present, then let those who partake of it go their separate ways and to the mountaintop, commune with the Lord Christ and find the sacredness of the transfiguration, and then return to the resolution of the problems of karma that find manifestation in the physical temple and that must be resolved by the practicality of life.

Beloved ones, seek balance, know balance, and be that balance. But let your leaning be the leaning upon the rod and the staff—the rod of Aaron[10] and the staff of righteousness, the staff of the Good Shepherd, the staff that is the raising up of the Kundalini fires within you.

Beloved ones, when you pursue that exercise of the breath given to you by the three wise men, when you pursue Djwal Kul's exercises[11] you begin the process of the balancing of the temple for the raising of that sacred Kundalini. And when that fire raises, it consumes the cause and core of karmic conditions at certain levels within the chakras according to the Great Law of the Lords of Karma, only according to that which the Great Law will allow. If you, then, do not take upon yourselves the mantle of being the physician, being one with your Christ Self unto your temple, how can you expect us to work through another who is less understanding and less dedicated unto the teachings and to the decrees?

Beloved ones, have you not understood the incident when the woman touched the hem of my garment and I perceived that virtue had gone out of me and she was healed of the issue of blood which she had had for twelve years?[12] Beloved ones, many practitioners of the healing arts bear greater karma than that woman, and when you place your bodies in their care you indeed take on that karma and they indeed take on your light and thus perpetuate within you their very judgments which declare that you have chronic conditions. Indeed, the fatigue that follows convinces you that you have heard the correct diagnosis even while the full momentum of our flame has flowed from you because you have placed your trust outside of your own regeneration—rejuvenative fires of the Holy Spirit that are as a fountain of living flame bursting within you.

Let the student body, then, be moved to a greater practicality and a greater spirituality, and let each one be unto his God a chalice ready and willing to receive the wholeness of perfect health in body, mind, and soul. And let all be willing to surrender upon the altar of my life that which they retain as point of manipulation, that which they retain as disturbance and discord in the subconscious that may, then, come forth at any hour as disease or disturbance—as an excuse for service.

Those who would rather not serve, who understand that which is the requirement of the hour, may very easily then come up with patterns of emotional disturbance, mental disorder, and physical difficulties. Beloved ones, when these manifest they are very real—they are very real manifestations of selfishness and an absence of true caring for the body temple over many centuries. Therefore we must always deal compassionately yet firmly; but the responsibility of the healing, beloved ones, always lies within you.

You may take the hand of the practitioner of healing and you may walk awhile with that one. But, beloved ones, you may not blame the practitioner or place upon that practitioner the responsibility for your health as some have said when they have arrived at their offices: "Well, what are you going to do about me now, doctor?" Beloved ones, we have had enough of this dallying.

THE CALL THAT ALLOWS THE INTERCESSION OF MILLIONS OF COSMIC BEINGS

We come to tell you that this day we draw close about ourselves and about our messenger the chelas who are of the light, the chelas who are determined to be of the light and to concentrate that light. For I tell you, beloved ones, the fallen ones have indeed placed their challenge upon you and upon the Mother of the Flame, and they are determined to move unto the death.

Beloved ones, the death will be their own if only you raise your right hand to roll back that energy. But if you do not, you will find yourselves becoming the passive recipients of nefarious forces from the astral and physical plane and we will not be able to intercede for you. For the call compels the answer, and the call must come forth in each twenty-four-hour cycle *from this octave*. Therefore the price that is paid for the path of Christic initiation is to come into a more intense and intimate association with our love through our messenger, through the Path that we place before you. And those who desire that inner walk must know that they will also face the Adversary who is the adversary of the ascended masters and of the Christ from the beginning.

And so, beloved ones, we release the fullness of love necessary that you might be God-victorious, but it is *you* who must hold the sword! It is *you* who must use the sacred Word! It is *you* who must defeat the Adversary in this octave by God's grace and by the call that allows the intercession of millions and millions of cosmic beings who have come for the deliverance of earth and her evolutions!

Beloved ones, the time to entertain fear and doubt and human questioning is long past. For when you come upon the energy of this darkness—projected as a frenzy, as chaos, as confusion, as insanity, as sudden illness—you must be ready to leap in the sacred fire, to roll it back! You must be absolutely certain of who you are, of who I AM, and who is this messenger who stands before you. For if you will enter into the doubt and fear and human questioning, you will find that that will be the very inroad to unseat you from your horse. And as we have seen in the past, these unseatings have for many been permanent; for they come in the hour of your greatest opportunity for victory, and the victory cycles are wide and they do not come often in ten thousand years.

Therefore, beloved ones, heed my warning and receive my joy. For in the fullness of love, in the fullness of truth and the certitude of truth, you will know your God-victory here and now. Be not dismayed; for as I have told you, "Greater is he that is in you, than he that is in the world."[13] Practice this science and be the proof of the true religion. For there is no projection, no instrument of black magic, not one perpetrator of black magic upon this entire planetary body this day who can stand before the Lord, the living Christ that I AM within you!

Beloved ones, if you attempt to defeat these fallen ones alone, there is no guarantee of your survival. For it is by the armies of the Lord, by the coming of the Faithful and True,[14] by the coming of the Holy Spirit in the entire Spirit of the Great White Brotherhood that the children of light will escape—yes, clean escape these perpetrations of darkness. Beloved ones, they are many. Their name is Legion.[15] They practice their arts from the darkest jungles of Africa, they practice them in the Bayou, they practice them from coast to coast.

Beloved ones, there are always the rivals of the true servants of God—some who have left from among you, some who have never been a part of this circle whose gossip carries on as the carrion crows from without. And therefore to seek to name them becomes an endless naming. And thus I commend you to the Law of the One.

The Law of the One makes you invincible, God-victorious. For within the hallowed Circle of the One, no thing that is apart from that One may enter.

Invoke the Law of the One! Invoke the Circle of the One! And know that unless you are one with God, you will be vulnerable, you will be found wanting.[16] The hour, then, of the testing of the ascended masters or the testing of the messenger is past. Those who then have not yet the proof of our witness, let them look within. Let them look to Almighty God who has placed a flame upon the altar of their heart. And let them look at the twenty years of service of our witnesses in this life alone and many thousands of years.

Beloved ones, it is the hour of the summoning of the elect into the white-fire core where there is safety and habitation and solace and compassion and love and the true teaching that you require for your ascension and the great mysteries and the initiations. Lo, this is our table that we have prepared in the wilderness[17] for those who elect to be the will of God.

I seal you in the name of our Father, in the name of the Son, the true Light within you,[18] in the name of the Holy Spirit that leaps and rejoices and kindles anew your own eternal Selfhood. I seal you in the light of the Woman clothed with the Sun.[19] I seal you in the light of the Law of the One. Amen.

August 6, 1978
Camelot
Los Angeles County, California
ECP

CHAPTER 10

*O my beloved, this is the hour of the reckoning
of your own God consciousness and your own freedom.
And therefore I say, follow me in the regeneration!
Follow me in the regeneration!
Where there is no regeneration, there I AM not.*

CHAPTER 10

THE COMMUNICATION OF THE WORD

The Word goeth forth, and by the Word is the staying light of the LORD God. By the Word of the Holy Spirit is the transfer of our love unto the evolutions of light throughout the galaxies.

I come with my own Beloved* as we stand together here to hold the balance of the flames of Alpha and Omega and to restore, by example unto America, the light of the family, the light of the Circle of the One, the light of the binding together of Alpha and Omega according to that cosmic law that is reflected in the law of the union of twin flames, the union of souls who have come to serve in my name.

THE MARRIAGE VOW

Blessed be the name of the Law, I AM THAT I AM. For by the Law and its fusion, by the vow unto the Law is oneness sealed in every octave. And therefore understand that the marriage vow is the vow of the soul unto the beloved I AM Presence and unto the I AM Presence of the twin flame. And the vow is this:

> *I will walk the path of initiation with the blessed soul that thou, O LORD, hast anointed unto the oneness in earth as it*

---
*the ascended Lady Magda, Jesus' twin flame

is in heaven. I vow to be in the honor and the love and the obedience unto the Lord Christ, and I vow to keep the faith of the Holy Church Universal and Triumphant. And therefore I accept the sacrament of marriage as the blessed daily celebration of the communion of our Lord, the body and the blood.

Even as the husband is the bearer of the essence of his blood, of his light of Alpha, so is the wife the carrier of the body, of the very flesh, of that light of the eternal Logos, of that light of Omega. Therefore this communion, this partaking of oneness, is the dedication of life unto the inborn Christ, the indwelling Word that now comes, *that now comes* to rest in the very cradle of your heart.

Therefore I stand now on the west side of the City Foursquare and I chasten the children of God who have not sealed their love by the vow before the altar of God. And I commend those souls who have walked the path of the eternal lovers, therefore to come before the altar of God for the sealing of their vows, that the fruition of the Holy Spirit might be the use of the sacred fire in the bringing forth of children of the light. This violation of the Law in America is one of the fundamental causes for the disruption of the flow of light in her society, and, my beloved, it cannot be!

Therefore, preach the gospel. Therefore, preach my Word. Therefore, deliver my sermon. Therefore, go to those who are ignorant of the Law because they have gone before the false Christs and the false gurus, who have told them that they could do away with the great tradition of the Law. For I AM come not to destroy the law of God or of the prophets but to fulfill that law.[1]

THE CONSECRATION OF THE SACRED FIRE

And therefore that law of the eternal One, as in heaven so in earth, must be fulfilled by stalwart souls who recognize that the very role in marriage is the holding of the office of Alpha and Omega and far transcends the earthly personality, the earthly sensuality, and all of the desecration that the fallen ones have made by their exposure* of the uses of sex and their exposure of the inner-temple experience within the secret chamber of the heart that is the eternal union in all octaves of the Father-Mother God, of the flaming sacred fire.

I therefore stand and I bring judgment upon those who have desecrated the body of Alpha and the body of Omega in their pornography and in their exposure, in their destruction, then, of the magnificent rising flow of the caduceus light unto the crown of each individual.

So let the consecration of that light be for the scepter of victory. Let it be the caduceus of healing. And let healing be the goal of those who unite in marriage, and let them consecrate that sacred fire unto the wholeness of the family, the community, and America. Let them set aside that unnecessary overindulgence, and let them recognize that the fruit of the Spirit is indeed the union of souls. And the union of souls is for one purpose—the path of the ascension and the service to life in the very process of that ascension.

O my beloved, let, therefore, the family be consecrated, and let the daily rosary be consecrated to the Holy Family and to the raising up of the Manchild within each family, that those souls of light who have been aborted might now, therefore, be brought into manifestation and be received and honored as the coming of the LORD, which indeed they are. They are the coming of God into manifestation as the LORD God Almighty disguises himself in each and every one of these little ones.

THE PATH OF THE ALCHEMICAL MARRIAGE AND OF LOVE WITHIN THE FAMILY

I, Jesus, stand before you, and I call for the soul to commune with the Great Shepherd of life, to seek the alchemical marriage. For upon the foundation of this path of those who are one with the inner Beloved is the holding of the balance for those who are

---
*The word *exposure* in this context might mean "exposure as violation of."

torn and tormented and dismembered and tempted as they have failed to understand the meaning of their marriage vows, as they have not had quickened within them the cloven tongues of fire of the Holy Spirit and therefore do not know that state of holy matrimony within the Holy Ghost.

The wedding, beloved ones, is the wedding of heaven and earth, of Spirit and Matter, and of the Word made flesh. It is the very fusion of life, which God has ordained and celebrated in all octaves of being.

O my beloved, there is not a nation or a family or a community where the cancer of World Communism or of world deception through the manipulations of big business can enter—no, there is not a place where they can enter when the family is sealed in a higher light and a higher purpose.

Let there be the alchemy, therefore, of the transmutation of the water unto the wine, and let the watery, vapory consciousness that has not understood the great presence of love within the family now give way, now be forgiven, now come to the altar to receive the sacred fire of transmutation, and let fathers and mothers consecrate life unto the wine of the Holy Spirit.

Oh, this alchemy must be sought and won and you must preach it as Saint Francis did in the very squares. You must understand that the Word that is not conveyed, that is not spoken, that is not delivered with a diamond point, with the pen of the diamond and with the sword—the two-edged sword—is as though it were stillborn.

RING OUT THE PRAISE OF THE LORD!

Beloved ones, in the transfer of the Word is the victory. And therefore the open door of the translation of the Word by the prophets, by the messengers, by the Mother of the Flame in this age is the transfer of our energy for the judgment, for the dividing of the way, for the summoning, for the conversion, for the resurrection. And as you receive that Word and transfer it, so you become a carrier, so you become a transformer as effective as the One.

Therefore, deliver that Word. When I cannot hear you speak, when the souls of light cannot hear you because of that false pride and that false humility that withdraws, that mutters, that does not give the Word that is to be transferred, then I am burdened, for you have aborted my very own presence.

Beloved ones, without communication the hordes of darkness run rampant upon the planetary body. And therefore the lines of communication from God to man, to woman, to child, and to one another is the perpetual vigil of the holy angels, of the blessed voice of conscience within, of the ministering angel. The perpetual singing of the hosannas of the angels and the saints in white is for the sustainment of the vibration of the Word as it ripples across the cosmic sea.

So in its mighty rippling it passes through the chakras of those who are attuned with it, and therefore they can no longer keep silent. They must ring out the praise of the LORD and sing the Magnificat[2] and sing the words, "Let God be magnified!"[3]

O the magnification of the Word! It is by your seven centers. And therefore the perpetuation of the dynamic decrees is the acceleration, is the raising of a lost continent, a lost soul, a lost twin flame, a lost community, and a lost chalice of the Holy Grail.

THE COMING OF THE COSMIC CHRISTS

I come, then, to announce the mission of the Cosmic Christs who come with Lord Maitreya. For beloved Lord Maitreya comes not without a retinue of angels of the Cosmic Christ and magnificent God-free beings who have that attainment of the eternal Logos. And therefore with the coming of Christmas Eve there will be the penetration of earth of Cosmic Christs who come to make their abode wherever there is the forcefield and the love of the Holy Family, where vows have been made before the altar of God. So within that home and household and within that family a magnificent cosmic being, an ascended being, a Cosmic Christ will hold the Electronic Presence, and that Cosmic Christ will also hold the Electronic Presence for those who are keeping the flame on the path of the alchemical marriage.

Therefore, whether as disciples unto the flame of the ascension, whether alone or all one in earth and in heaven, one and all in that love-flow will know the Electronic Presence of the Cosmic Christs. And this magnificent illumination is the purpose of their coming, as the Four and Twenty Elders and the Lords of Karma have seen that it is the very ignorance of the masses—the insanity and the vanity, the ignorance of the Law, the unawareness, the asleepness of these masses—that is to a large extent the cause of the absence of the penetration of the light of wisdom and of the difficulty of the transfer of the teachings of the ascended masters to greater and greater numbers.

Therefore these Cosmic Christs will be here for the stepping up of that Cosmic Christ consciousness, and they will be here for the pushing back of the barriers of ignorance. And they have come for illumination, and they have come for the preparing of the way of the messenger and of the going forth of the two by two.[4]

These magnificent Cosmic Christs come as the initiators of mankind. They come in the person of your messenger and yourselves, O beloved sons and daughters, to challenge the Antichrist, to challenge the false prophets and the false Christs, who must be flushed out from their forcefields, from their lairs, those who have siphoned off the children of God and even some from among the 144,000, into their communes, into their cults, into their groups where they have denied the LORD God.

Beloved ones, this action of the light must come. And I tell you, when that judgment is delivered by myself through the Mother of the Flame, there is the gnashing of teeth, there is the crying out, there is the accusation, there is the condemnation as the demons who possess so many in a fanatical Christianity know that their time is short.

THE JUDGMENT OF THE FALSE PROPHETS

I, therefore, stand in the midst of the temple. I stand in the midst of the temple of the righteous and in the midst of the temple of the people and I declare judgment upon the fallen ones who have taken up these children of my heart.

I declare the judgment, then, of that one, Jim Jones, and all who are with him.[5] I demand the judgment of the false hierarchy and the fallen ones and the hordes of night who have perpetuated this heinous crime—all the more heinous when it is done in the name of the LORD, causing the evolutions of this earth to tremble and to fear and therefore to be cut off from the true spirit of prophecy and to throw the children of my heart back into the very grips of the wolves in sheep's clothing, who occupy positions in the churches of tradition, and within their strongholds do no better than those who come with their warped teachings.

Therefore my blessed children have become as a ping-pong ball. And as they have gone forth from out of those temples where they have seen and heard that their ministers have not taken a stand for truth, so they have gone forth in search of a higher truth and they have been led astray by the false Christs and the false prophets. And therefore their reaction is to go back once again to the old bottles, and these will never, never suffice.

I therefore call to stalwart men and women of truth to defend freedom of religion, freedom of speech, freedom of assembly, and freedom of the press as never before so that the holy light of freedom may be known and so that there might be the protection of that true word.

I therefore stand and I declare the judgment of the false prophet Reverend Sun Myung Moon,[6] and therefore let the children who have come around him be set free! I declare the judgment of the false prophets [impostors] of the Lord Krishna and the Lord Maitreya and the Lord Buddha! I declare the judgment of the false prophets [impostors] of Guru Nanak[7] and of all the great saints and lights of the Himalayas, whom I have known for aeons and who are my own brothers and sisters on the Path!

I declare the judgment of the false prophets of the true Church! I declare the judgment of the false prophets of the Holy Spirit, of the Father! I declare the judgment of those who say they are Jews but are of the synagogue of Satan![8]

I declare their judgment within the Protestant movement, within the World Council of Churches, within the National Council of Churches! I declare their judgment within the Roman Catholic Church, within Judaism, and in the councils of the Sanhedrin! I declare the judgment of that one, Caiaphas![9] I declare the judgment now! And each and every individual who has been a wolf in sheep's clothing, so let them wail and bewail and wag their heads as I am on the cross with the Mother and her seed!

Therefore I AM the resurrection and the life of truth within America, and I stand for the binding of the hordes of night and death! I stand for the judgment of that cult of death and that religion of hatred in World Socialism and World Communism! And I exhort the souls of light who have gone after other gods—who have gone into other nations, who have left America in search of other gurus—to come home! To come home! Come home to the City Foursquare! Come home to that table that is prepared for you in the wilderness, here in that very place of Camelot, where the Mother dispenses the teachings of the ascended and unascended masters of all ages.

I speak to souls of light who are caught with this or that would-be teacher. When you are denied the table of the Mother, you are denied the very freedom of your own soul. And therefore follow not those false gurus who have not permitted you to use the science of the spoken Word or to come under the teaching of all of the hosts of the Lord or of your own I AM Presence and of your Christ Self.

I call and I summon those twelve legions of angels from the

heart of the Father. I summon them now, as never before, and I call for the rescue of my children. I call for the rescue of my children from the brainwashing and the fear of the fallen ones and their psychology. Beloved ones, each and every one [of these fallen ones] is a rebel against the cause of freedom and the cause of Saint Germain! And as you watch, you will see how the false gurus have sent their hatred and their vituperation against my very own father, my very own Saint Joseph, the very own principal of life who bore the great light of the Maha Chohan and of the Holy Spirit.

I KNEEL IN HONOR OF THE GREAT GOD OF FREEDOM

I bow before the light of Saint Germain and I acknowledge him as the father, even as my Father in heaven is come down unto the earth. Therefore my Father is in heaven and on earth, even as my Mother is in heaven and on earth. And therefore I defy the fallen ones who have desecrated the great masculine ray and all who bear it, and therefore those who have the hatred of Saint Germain will bear that karma of hatred against my very own father!

And therefore those who bear the hatred of the Mother will bear the karma of hatred against my very own mother, for I AM born in Spirit and in Matter out of the mighty flame of Alpha and Omega through those blessed lifestreams who sponsored my incarnation. Indeed, they were of the virgin birth and of the virgin consciousness, being the direct lineage of Sanat Kumara, the Ancient of Days, and therefore they brought together the mighty pristine purity of the flame of Alpha and Omega, even as I sponsor you to do, O my beloved, for the bringing forth of the holy family.

Therefore I say, those who sin against the Holy Ghost as the cloven tongues of the Father-Mother God do far greater sin than even those who sin against my name. For those who sin against the origin of the Christ do therefore sin against the Almighty God. And I say to you, there is not one of those would-be gurus and teachers, those would-be Christs and prophets, who has bent the knee to confess that he [Saint Germain] is Lord, that he is the Lord of Freedom.

I kneel, therefore, in honor of the great God of Freedom and the light of the blessed ascended master Saint Germain, who himself is hanging upon the cross of world hatred in this hour. And I am grateful that you, my beloved, in every corner of the earth, understand that that crucifixion of Saint Germain is the hatred, the mass hatred of the fallen ones, who see in his coming the very liberation of all souls whom they have manipulated by their perversion, their diabolical perversion of the light of Alpha and Omega.

They shall not pass!
They shall not pass!
They shall not pass!

TRANSMUTE HATRED BY THE SACRED FIRE OF LOVE

I, Jesus, stand within this nation, America, and I release my Word! And it is for the rolling back of those individuals who in my day also came with their tormenting demons, who cried out my name day and night because they were not of God and because they would tempt me in the very laws of salvation to save them because they spoke my name.

Beloved ones, they are not of the seed of Christ! They are not of the seed of God! And therefore those demons who inhabit the temples of my children—they cannot be saved merely because they repeat my name! They are cast out this day! And I say, everyone who is innocent may choose to be free! But I tell you, they will have to bind their pride and their ambition, for there are many in the Christian churches this day who have the ambition to have the Holy Spirit.

Therefore they enter not by the door but they repeat only the mere words, and they have never, ever contacted the living Word and they are leading the children of light astray. They are betraying the community of the Holy Spirit, and they do betray the coming of the New Jerusalem, that Holy City. Therefore they are judged! Therefore I give them the opportunity to be cleansed!

Beloved ones, I summon you to go forth in the very name of your own messenger—who is worthy, who is worthy before God to stand in the very midst of these offenders and to cast out those fallen ones. For I have stood in her very temple and I have spoken through her and I have challenged those fallen ones. And therefore they have cried out because they have known that *their day is done! Their day is done! Their day is done!*

And you are worthy, O my children! You are worthy to go forth in my name! I anoint you as the other seventy,[10] as the other one hundred and forty and four.[11] I anoint you two-by-two, for only by this Word and by this judgment, only by the direct confrontation will these fallen ones be bound!

I tell you, they stand in the way of the mighty progress of Saint Germain for America. And if they are allowed to continue in their hatred and in their prayers of malintent, which conjure up the fallen ones and therefore cause an astral Armageddon that is so unnecessary, they themselves, beloved ones, will figure in the destruction of an age!

Therefore do not take lightly my Word, for the misuse of the light of the Christ is indeed the greatest abuse in America today. And well may you understand, then, the cynicism of those who have never even touched the hem of my garment, when they see so many misrepresenting the path of freedom and of my flame.

These things ought not so to be, and therefore understand that persecution comes as the outrage of the demons who inhabit the temples of the people. And that outrage that comes to you must instantaneously be transmuted by the sacred fire of love as you have no anger, no animosity, but only the living flame that therefore calls a halt to this infamy.

YOU MUST ACCELERATE!

Therefore let those who understand the need to accelerate stop absenting themselves from our services, from our ministration within the Chapel of the Holy Grail.[12] Let them be attentive. Let them be present on Sunday morning. Let them understand that when you come and you face the altar dedicated to Alpha and Omega and when you sit before the messenger, you therefore sit before the entire Spirit of the Great White Brotherhood. And the very tenure of your attention gives to you the increment of fire whereby when you go back into the world you become the summoning presence, you become the presence of the judgment.

This dipping into the sacred fire is a ritual of creation. If the seraphim, my beloved, who are already living flames themselves, must go back to the Great Central Sun and dip into those fires in the cycle of the twenty-four hours and in the cycles of the creation, and if Naman himself had to dip seven times in the Jordan River,[13] understand that the mere knowing of the Word is not enough to meet the world in this hour of the intensification of hatred. It is the becoming of the sacred fire by ritual, by devotion, by the regularity of the day of rest, the one day in seven when you come for the recharge.

And when you go forth, my beloved ones, there is never any danger to the individual who stands in our flame, and that very flame itself is the all-consuming fire. But when you go forth out of balance and therefore enter into the very same spirit of fanaticism that you are attempting to dispel, then you will be vulnerable. And then you may say, "Why, the ascended masters' teachings have failed me. The angels have failed me."

Therefore I warn you that the failure is within yourself to apprehend and to understand that the law of Alpha and Omega, the law of the transfer of the body and blood of the Lord Christ, is indeed a science. And when you neglect the points of that science, you leave yourself in want, absenting yourself from wholeness.

Each and every one of you will be called upon to face these hordes of darkness, and so, you see, there is no escape. You have put your hand to the plow. You must accelerate the wheels within wheels.[14] For you are on the track of cosmic consciousness. You are on the path of your ascension, and the cosmic computer of the mind of Christ is preparing your initiations.

And so you see, beloved ones, God has honored your word. Your word is your very life, your person, and your presence. You have asked; now you receive not merely a day-by-day descent of light but an entire path that is open to you. If you fail, therefore, because you have become fainthearted, you will find that it will require many long cycles to begin again. And this, of course, is unthinkable!

But I give this teaching for every child of God and every son and daughter so that you might understand that there is no other purpose to life on earth than the rescuing of my children. I kneel before the altar of Alpha and Omega each and every day for the rescue of my children, who are so filled with demons and with their false consciousness and their false awareness that even when the Word comes, they persecute that Word. They know it not. They understand it not. And they have become in such a frenzy and such a fear because of what they have been put through by the fallen ones that, beloved ones, the angel of the LORD must wrestle with them until they come into the light itself.

FEAR NOT TO TAKE A STAND FOR TRUTH AND FOR THE CHILDREN OF THE LIGHT

I speak, then, for I come this Thanksgiving Day with gratitude to God that there is a home of light, that there is a Camelot where I may send the tattered and the torn, "the homeless, tempest-tost,"[15] all those who know that God is and yet have not found that representation upon earth that is worthy of their love.

And so I send my legions, the twelve thousand, and they come and they go into every psychic activity, every group of fallen ones. They go into Ecuador, to that false prophet Johnny Lovewisdom.[16] Let him be bound as he impersonates the light of Maitreya, for Lord Maitreya himself delivers that judgment this day! And all impostors of the God and Goddess Meru and all impostors of our retreat of Lake Titicaca[17] who have drawn those children apart from the Path—let them be judged, therefore!

I send my ray, and I report to you this day that those episodes that have taken place in South America, in Guyana,[18] are a repeat of a horrendous and heinous crime that occurred upon that continent many thousands of years ago at the hand of the black priests, the fallen ones of Lemuria. It was a desecration of life, and those who are a part of it again have also been led to the slaughter once again.

Beloved ones, now is the hour of the judgment. Now is the hour of the purging of South America of all of these ancient records on behalf of the Great Divine Director and the incoming seventh root race. And therefore as the light descends it brings out the darkness, and this is the very purpose of our stump[19] and the stumping of Shiva and of the Darjeeling Council. And so as the light was released consecutively in the power of the nine in these twenty-seven stumps, given freely by all of you and by our Mother, so that light has been for the purging and the penetration of astral planes heretofore not exposed.

Therefore you can anticipate the exposure of more and more darkness, and you can anticipate that as that exposure is come, you also must perpetually invoke the call to Archangel Michael for the protection of the victory of light, for the protection of the victory of those souls who have heard the Word, that they are not tempted to leave the Word of the Mother because of their suspicions, because of all the falsehoods that are going abroad. All of this must pass into the flame!

Beloved ones, we send our Word. We do not qualify or compromise that Word. For only when the fullness of the truth is spoken do the sons and daughters of God know my voice. They know my voice through you and through our messengers because they hear the unqualified truth. And if you fear to speak that truth because of loss of popularity, you will not only lose the children of the light who then do not hear the certain sound of the trumpet but you will lose your popularity as well. You will lose your popularity with Almighty God, who has said, "Thou art neither cold nor hot, and therefore I will spew thee out of my mouth."[20]

Fear not, then, to take a stand for truth and for the children of the light, never condemning the children of the light but only exposing the error of their indoctrination and leading them gently by the mercy hand of Kuan Yin, of Mother Mary, of Portia, and of all the ministering angels of my bands back unto the living flame of their own God Presence. Therefore each and every day that you compromise the full expression of the truth, you fail to create an arc. You fail to send out a lifeline whereby that one lost sheep will be drawn in.

THE CRUCIFIXION IS THE BIRTH OF THE GLORIOUS RESURRECTION OF THE WORD INCARNATE

Fear not, I say. Fear not to arouse the fallen ones and the demons. Let them come out! Let them come out with their shoutings and their screamings and their accusations, for by that very defilement of the Word they are judged and the planetary body is cleansed.

You see how the earth's atmosphere over the Holy City reflects the great crystal clarity of the clarification of the mind of God. It is a sign that the judgment has come, that the earth has been purged of many forces on the astral plane, of black magicians who perpetrated the crime through the insanity, through the drug entities, through the vanity of the ego of that one Jim Jones and many others like him who are scattered abroad on the earth.

Beloved ones, without the black magicians operating behind these individuals they would have no power. They have no power of themselves, and therefore the fallen ones use them. They will use every individual who allows the ego to remain with its pride, with its ambition. And so even unto Peter I said, "Get thee behind me, Satan!"[21] For he was also used for the declaration of that ultimate falsehood that states that the son and daughter of God is not required to pass through the crucifixion.

Beloved ones, if you are tempted to believe that pseudo-mystical statement that denies the crucifixion, you have lost the entire meaning of the path of Alpha and Omega. And only the sons and daughters of God may pass through the crucifixion. The fallen ones have no right to that honor! Theirs is the judgment!

And so, my beloved, the fallen ones know not that supreme moment of union by love in the giving of the body and blood of the living Christ within you for the salvation of the earth. The crucifixion is not the hour of the death of Christ. It is the hour of the death of the human consciousness and the birth of the glorious resurrection of the incarnate Word.

And therefore Christianity has been invaded by a cult of death all of these centuries, and I come to cast out that vibration of death and to tell you that it has no part of my Word or of my life! Beware, then, of the annihilation of the soul by brainwashing, by dependency upon the false gurus instead of the utter independence within you unto your own Christ Self!

Beloved ones, never, never, never in all eternity will my representatives or the organizations of the ascended masters be allowed to contain these vibrations whereby the souls of the people assign their free will and their thinking and feeling process to another.

CARRY THE TORCH OF FREEDOM

O my beloved, this is the hour of the reckoning of your own God consciousness and your own freedom. And therefore I say, follow me in the regeneration![22] Follow me in the regeneration! Where there is no regeneration, there I AM not. And therefore go not there. Tarry not in that plane of consciousness.

We stand for a mighty people, the 144,000 who are my own, whom I call in the name of the Ancient of Days. In this hour of thanksgiving, our Lord Saint Germain has summoned together and has called together all of those sons and daughters of freedom who are on the etheric plane who have given their physical lives for the cause of freedom on earth in the various nations of the earth within this century and beyond.

Those, then, who are on the etheric plane who are the unascended ones are in a mighty hall with Saint Germain, with Portia. They gather together in thanksgiving, offering unto God in this very hour thanksgiving for the life that they were privileged to give so that you might live, so that you might celebrate your Thanksgiving on earth and yet carry the torch of freedom. It is a mighty assembly and Saint Germain is there, loved and applauded, for he has been their leader. He has stood beside them in the hour when they have counted not the cost of the defense of freedom.

Beloved ones, the great master strategist of freedom, Saint Germain himself, takes the opportunity upon this occasion to speak to these souls about the plan of freedom for this decade and the coming century. He shows them now, as the Great General[*] would, the entire plan of the battle of Armageddon—with charts, with that chalkboard, and with explanations. Mighty angels of freedom stand with him, and they are showing these saints robed in white that they must yet come in another hour to reincarnate for their final incarnation. And in this incarnation, he explains to them, they will be bearers of his flame, his violet flame, and he guarantees to them, beloved ones, that they will be taught the use of the violet flame.

Beloved ones, Saint Germain makes this guarantee because he trusts in your word and in your commitment and in the messenger. He therefore trusts that by the time these souls are of age the violet flame will be a household word in every nation. And these little children will recognize the name of God, I AM THAT I AM,

---
[*]Jesus is likely referring to General George Washington.

and they will recognize the violet color and the flame. They will see the violet-flame angels face-to-face. This is the dispensation of beloved Saint Germain unto those patriots of freedom, patrons of the Law, patriarchs of the ages who will come again. Because they have given their life to him, he gives his life to them.

Beloved ones, you see how the decisions of the cosmic councils and the Lords of Karma, as they are transferred by the ascended masters, do always hinge upon hierarchy, the hierarchy ascended and unascended whereby that grand cooperation of the entire Spirit of the Great White Brotherhood, heaven and earth, makes possible the calculation of the future with a certain certainty that does not depend on human whimsy. As Saint Germain has said, the human is entirely unpredictable, and therefore he makes no predictions based upon anyone's human self but upon the God flame within you, which has been sustained centuries upon centuries.

THE QUICKENING OF THE INNER CHRIST SELF

Beloved ones, as lovers of freedom commune in America today, as many are in prayer for this nation, as many are concerned and pause to give thanksgiving, they are also being inspired by the very Electronic Presence of Saint Germain within their midst and they feel the fervor of his heart as he gives to them his heart.

Yet, my beloved, if they heard his name and understood his person, many would rebel against this vibration, which they accept now as children. They would do better, beloved ones, if you would make a concentrated declaration and consecration of your daily services to the transmutation of the hatred of Saint Germain, of the flame of freedom, of the United States of America, of the Woman clothed with the Sun,[23] of the Manchild, and of the Constitution, which guarantees the freedom of all. It is against these that the forces of darkness have pitted their hatred, programming the children of God.

So many of the people merely speak what are the various

vibrations of the mass consciousness. Do you see? Their minds are not their own. They repeat what they have heard or have been told. They repeat it in the elections, and they do not have the original tie to the I AM THAT I AM, which Saint Germain sought to guarantee in this nation of freedom.

Let us clear, then, the opposition to the light of Aquarius, the light of creativity that overcomes the boredom, the monotony, and the sameness of socialism and socialist states. My beloved ones, when there are those who go to certain socialist nations and say, "All is well," they must realize that socialism is not a religion or an economic system or a government for the children of God or for the sons and daughters of God. Those who acclimatize themselves to it are therefore either soulless ones, robots, or they have made themselves mechanized automatons by the betrayal of the threefold flame they once had. All is well for the automated individual within a socialist state, but all is not well for the son or the daughter of God!

And so, where the gift of the Christ consciousness has not been conveyed, where I have not been able to stand in the midst of the people to call upon that conversion and to make of them sons of God, so where there have not been the ministers and the pastors of my Word to affect this transfer of light and through whom I might reach the people, so there are those who have never received the quickening of the inner Christ Self. And without that quickening, therefore, they have no need of independence, individuality, or a government or an economy or an education that allows for that freedom. Do you see? Socialism comes only where there is the mechanization of those who are asleep.

Your own Gautama Buddha anticipated the hour of the cult of death and its coming in this age, and therefore he demonstrated supremely the decree "I AM Awake!"[24] It is the sleeping millions who prefer socialism and Communism, and this is why that cancer moves across the earth—because in their sleep they have not the quickening of Alpha and Omega. And those cloven tongues of the Holy Spirit, Alpha and Omega in the Person of my own Father-Mother God, does not enter into their temple. And without that quickening light, the life of the cells is not quickened—the life of the brain, the life of the heart!

And so you see, without that presence there is no deterrent to the mass brainwashing of the cult of death. They are dead because they have not been quickened, because there is no life in them and they prefer to be herded about as cattle! And so, you see, to defeat World Communism and World Socialism you must begin at the beginning with the flame of conversion.

Therefore this is my gratitude this Thanksgiving Day, that here in America there are sons and daughters of God of the supreme vision to see that they must first be converted through forgiveness, through penance, through redemption, through regeneration, finally to be carriers of the Holy Ghost and to transfer that light so that every sinner, everyone who yet has the weight of karma upon him, may be called to the same penance, to the same repentance by the flame of forgiveness and therefore to receive me into the temple.

THE HEALING LIGHT OF THE HOLY SPIRIT

I come quickly into the temples of my children, but I cannot enter in until I am bidden. And, beloved ones, my children are not bidding me enter because they prefer their demons of fanaticism and their dark, dank doctrine and dogma, which they spout and which they use for another type of conversion. For you see, when they preach their word with their emotionalism, with their weeping, and with their energies that are impure, then those who know not what they do, who are a part of the circle of the congregation, receive a transfer of the discarnate entities.

And those demons enter into the temples of the innocents, and because so many of those innocents have been users of drugs, you have that group that has been called "the Jesus freaks." They have become "freaks" because they have first punctured their blessed seamless garment by the drugs given to them by the false gurus of the Holy Spirit, who are the pushers of drugs in the streets and in the high schools and in the grammar schools of the nation. And then with that vulnerability, they have sought me! They have entered the churches! They have come in! But because they were already vulnerable when they came into the presence of the false pastors that lead astray my people, so they have had leaping into their temples these demons of fanaticism. And these blessed children, then, are in need of healing!

My beloved, you must understand that the day will come when because allegiance is given, even by those who are sick and possessed, I will stand in the midst of you and I will deliver through you individually and through this messenger the healing light of the Holy Spirit!

You must prepare for that day, for you can understand that through the drug culture they have destroyed the very elements of the physical body and the etheric body. And only the restoration of Alpha and Omega can affect—by my body and by my blood and by the body and blood of your own Christ Self—that alchemy in Matter and then the healing by exorcism of the fallen ones.

Therefore the healing is twofold. And therefore, you see, there are thousands of churches, and so many of them, by compromise, have allowed the desecration and the abomination of the temple. Therefore my children have sought help! They have gone into these churches! They have sought me! They have not found me! And they have gone forth and they have committed suicide, and I have greeted them on the other side of the river, only to hold them in my arms and to promise them another opportunity.

Beloved ones, if there could be sorrow [in heaven], then I would tell you, I weep! As I wept for the death of Lazarus, so I weep in the hour of the death of my children. I come before you, charged with the light of hope that has been given to me this day by the blessed archangels and their archeiai, who have comforted me as I have wept for this generation and for America. And the great light that they bring from the altar of God is unto me a great gift.

Beloved ones, you may not understand how the ascended beings can weep. Beloved ones, it is the very alchemy of the Holy Spirit itself. For we know and we see far more than you could be aware of. And if you would see, as we see, the torment of these souls who pass from embodiment who are caught in the astral plane, you would also understand. And therefore we show you not, but we summon the mighty archangels to transfer to you the mighty fervor of the Son of God, for it is this fervor that becomes the preaching of the Word!

THE DELIVERY OF THE WORD

Beloved ones, there is a difference between the *preaching* and the *teaching*. The preaching comes forth by the mighty power of the sixth ray of ministration, service, devotion, and the desire body that flows with a mighty River of Life. Do you see, then, that it is the very fervor of the sixth ray of love that carries the gold and the purple of the cloven tongues of the Holy Spirit? And this is the very capacity for the conversion itself, when the Word is transferred thusly.

But, beloved ones, the congregations of the people cannot always take the intense fire of the preaching of my Word, and therefore we come as the World Teachers in the love and the tenderness of the golden flame of illumination. We break bread. We sit at table with you. We share Holy Communion. And we give you the instruction of the Word gently, and yet with a mighty fiery, yellow lightning that penetrates ignorance and density. And then when you are fully armed with the teaching and you pass through the ritual of the third ray of love as the Holy Spirit, of the purification of the fourth ray, of the science of the fifth ray, you are finally ready again for the delivery of the Word with that mighty fire.

And so, you see, there are some who cannot even receive me in the preaching of the Word through our messenger, and they think that the release of light as the Holy Spirit is a monotone, when actually it is the great cosmic tone of a concentrated and controlled release of the sacred fire that is even measured word by word in its rhythm so as not to burn but to tenderly enfold the hearers.

Beloved ones, I have stood upon the lecture platforms. I have delivered my preaching as a mighty cosmic fire, and the people have stood still. And those who have not stood still are those possessed, those so dense by their own lack of awareness of Self that in the pitifulness of neglect they have actually left while I stood within a foot, within ten feet, within twenty-five feet of them. And your own messenger has held back her desire to cry out to those people, "How can you leave when you are standing in the presence of Jesus himself?"

But, beloved ones, they have gone their way, not knowing— not knowing my voice or my light and accusing the messenger of fanaticism or any other accusation that has been leveled against the prophets because they cannot take the Holy Spirit. And when the true Holy Spirit comes, beloved ones, it is something that is absolutely unbearable to those who are the impure and those who are the seed of the wicked. They cannot sit in the temple and receive such a concentration of light.

IN GRATITUDE

And so I stand. I stand with beloved Magda before Alpha and Omega and before this altar, and I give gratitude unto God this day for noble sons and daughters of God, for you, Keepers of the Flame, who keep on receiving that light as I deliver the Word to you and who have become the receptacles of that light.

I give gratitude for my messenger Mark, who stands with me, and for my messenger Elizabeth, as their twin flames stand together without any concern for the opposition to the Word, without any concern as to their person or their popularity or their life.

You would do well to emulate the two witnesses, for your time and space are coming. For each of you has a twin flame, and you and your twin flame are required in this age to witness. Some of you will not meet your twin flame in this entire life because it is not ordained, because your twin flame has other service in other spheres or is perhaps an ascended master. But it matters not, for you witness together, you communicate together. And the reality of your twin flame is in your own Christ Self and in the purity of your soul, one with the I AM Presence. We stand to sponsor you in that witness. We stand to call you to speak in the congregations of the world.

I, therefore, release that cosmic flame of gratitude unto my beloved friend, Kuthumi, who began the revolution as Saint Francis, who dared to be the lover of the Mother. O beloved ones, the lover of Mother Poverty understands the coming of the Virgin into this world, that the Virgin is not received. Therefore, is poverty. Therefore, the Mother comes only with a flame, and her self-sufficiency is that flame and her joy. And out of that flame the Mother brings forth the eternal light of the Christ, her perpetual gift unto millions.

I dedicate this band of sons and daughters of God and beautiful children unto the revolution of my beloved Francis and Clare, who gave their vow of marriage upon the altar. It was a marriage unto God, and they held the twin flames of our life, of the Lamb and the Lamb's wife.[25] And without those flames held in each and every endeavor by the two-by-two, there is not the wholeness and the fulfillment of the dispensation. This is our dispensation to you, that you also are arcing and holding the balance, one with the other.

And so we ordain the holy night of Christmas Eve as the celebration of your union. Let it be a mighty union for the victory.

In the name of the Father, who gives birth to the Mother, in the name of the Son and of the Holy Spirit, in the name of the cosmic cross of white fire, I send my legions out into the world for the acceleration and the healing of our youth and our children in this hour of the spirit of the Christ Mass.

Will you join us, Magda and me and the holy angels, in our vigil of prayer for the youth and for Saint Germain's flame of freedom? [Audience replies, "Yes!"]

I thank you and I bless you, as you are already blessed by the Word of God who lives in you. Amen.

November 23, 1978
Camelot
Los Angeles County, California
ECP

CHAPTER 11

Beloved ones, there is not a condition...
that is of greater concern to Mother Mary in this hour
than the protection of children awaiting birth and
the protection of those in embodiment who are sent
upon a regal and a rightful mission for the LORD.

CHAPTER 11

DEDICATE YOURSELF TO THE ISSUE OF ABORTION, FOR UPON THIS ISSUE HANG ALL OTHERS

Into the temple most holy, I am come. I am Jesus. In the flame of the Holy Ghost, I transfer to you the message of my love and my living presence among the people of light. This day, in the celebration of the Christ born again, I bow to the Ancient of Days, who is upon the throne, and the Son of God does sit on the right hand of that flaming one.

I and my Father are one,[1] and you who have seen me have also seen the Father. But if you have not seen me, then you know not the Christ within yourself or the Father who is the I AM Presence of each one.

Therefore I speak to you this day on the knowing of the Lord who dwells within your temple. I speak to you on the knowing of the Person of Christ as that Christ was revealed to me and as the blessed Father revealed to you that Christ through me.

I come to send a sacred fire unto the earth. I come with that descending light, and that light is the principle of the Law, which must be maintained as the cube of consciousness that remains the cube and is not scattered, is not misaligned. So as the light descends as Law, it is also the Person of Lawgiver.

Beloved ones, the fallen ones pretend to be on the path of initiation, but they have set themselves up as a law unto themselves. And they have distorted the cosmic cube, even by microseconds of consciousness of their individual rebellion. And they have rebelled against the great Person of the Lawgiver within, and therefore other gods, other astral masters, have come into the temple of being because they themselves have been without the standard of truth and without humility before the person of that standard—the standard-bearer, the messenger of light.

WHEREVER THE LITTLE CHILD IS THREATENED THE CHRIST OF ALL IS THREATENED

Beloved ones, the messenger may take many forms. The messenger is always God hiding behind the mask of this or that one. Therefore, take heed that ye hurt not one of these little ones, that you do not offend one of my children.[2] For the offense of the little child is symbolical of the offense of the Christ Self in all people.

When you see the little child and you can turn back and condemn that child, it is a sign that you would do this unto the Manchild or the Christ. And as you look here and there in the world, you will see children abused by parents who use them to transfer their momentums of darkness, their frustrations and their anger, to ground them because they themselves have not the courage to contain that anger and to put it into the fire of the Holy Ghost. Wherever the little child is threatened, there is the Christ of every part of life threatened. And so I desire to see my disciples within this community raise up a greater awareness of the ministration of myself in the little children.

The priority given unto the children is given to me as a priority, not as a coddling or a favoring or a spoiling of the outer self, but in the great spirit of the Magi, the adoration of the threefold flame, which they bear. Their light is a great light because it is a part of the new dispensation. And so you see how the child is persecuted East and West, even before it is born.

The angels play a tune in minor key upon their harps. It is a mournful tune, for it is the mourning by the light of the secret rays of those children who have passed once again into the octaves of light because there has been no room in the inn this Christ Mass. The millions of souls who have been deprived of life this year would give testimony to a victory for the Herods. That victory must be unto the hosts of the Lord. It must be a physical victory of souls come into life because there is the defense of the Word and of truth.

A GREATER PRAYER VIGIL ON BEHALF OF THE LITTLE CHILDREN

Now I announce to you the desire of the Blessed Mother of my life, the beloved Mary, to initiate in you an activity of service unto the child in the Order of the Holy Child,[3] conceived by the messenger Mark Prophet in communion with the ascended masters. The Blessed Mary bids those Sons and Daughters of Dominion[4] and all who aspire to that order to a new vigil for youth, for the holy child and for those coming to earth. This service of the Mother of the Flame for the youth of the world must be taken up by those who are the sons and daughters, the shepherds of my sheep. It is through this very service that you will transmute the karma that you bear with the children of the world from previous indulgences of error in other incarnations.

Let the karma, then, of all who would be chelas of El Morya and disciples of the Christ, the karma which they have retained on record as the karma with children, be put to the torch in this year. This is my Christmas prayer to you—that you heed the Word of the Blessed Mother Mary, that you heed her Word for a greater prayer vigil on behalf of the little children, all that besets them. And therefore you must study the conditions of their life and that which prevents them from receiving me as their Saviour on the Path.

Beloved ones, great souls can come to earth through you and through many wonderful families of light in all religions in this year.

But the drive toward abortion, the drive toward the taking of the life of the Messiah before it is protected by the fullness of consciousness' descent, that is on the increase. And therefore, it must be exposed—by enlightenment, by love, and by a God-determination that invokes the judgment, that confirms the judgment, and that is absolutely determined that the will of God shall prevail in this issue. Beloved ones, there is not a condition of earth that is of greater concern to Mother Mary in this hour than the protection of children awaiting birth and the protection of those in embodiment who are sent upon a regal and a rightful mission for the LORD.

So there is a disturbance in the balance of the planet, and the concern of the Mother is that the Great White Brotherhood will no longer be able to stay the hand of the descent of the karma of abortion, propounded and extended throughout the earth from this nation of America. The time has come, then, when the earth will reap that karma which they have brought upon themselves by the murder of the holy innocents. Therefore let *The Feast of Saint Stephen*[5] and let the day of the holy innocents be celebrated as a vigil for these souls and a vigil for an ignorant, manipulated humanity who have responded to this doctrine of death instead of to the culture of life everlasting.

EDUCATE THE PEOPLE ON THE ISSUE OF ABORTION

Beloved ones, we see the education of the people. But now we must say again, this is the year when all must become physical, when you must see that any impediment to the manifestation of the Holy Spirit is removed from you. For you must pass into the line of reality, into the line of tangibility, into the line of credibility among your peers of light upon earth.

And so let the Coming Revolution* begin with the lightbearers, and let it cross the lines of separation in organization or doctrine. And let it be a uniting of hearts who see the great need for a massive education, in spiritual matters and material as well, to precede the

---
*the Coming Revolution in Higher Consciousness

coming of the great flame of freedom in the heart of Saint Germain and a new order of the ages.

Let enlightenment go forth. Let those who have diligently prepared the exposé on abortion be commended and also receive the impetus to the finish, so nobly begun in Alpha, now concluded in Omega. That book, that handbook on abortion,[6] is most necessary for the Virgin Mother to plead before the courts of heaven for more mercy and more dispensation and to show that some upon earth have responded to her call.

SETTING BACK THE EVOLUTION OF SOULS

Beloved ones, we cannot speak of Elysian fields and other glories and other realities while there is one lost sheep. Today there are many, many lost sheep who have strayed from the flock, not by their own doing but because they have been deterred by those who have willfully prevented their birth in life. So great is the upset in the United States today in the balance of those lifestreams who have been sent for the victory that the major subject of discussion before the Lords of Karma at the conclusion of this year is how we will find entrée for these souls of light and how we will then allow them to accelerate and to take their place, which has been blocked now for many years, even unto a decade.

And so the setting back of evolution by those days and hours and years, that becomes the great dilemma. And of course, beloved ones, the shortening of the days for the elect,[7] the acceleration of cycles, is in our hands. But how can it be that all of these souls who have lost opportunity for preparation and development can suddenly be expected to come into life fully apprised and aware, perhaps arcing through necessary periods of development to suddenly come into an age of responsibility, whereas they ought to still be enjoying the great freedom of childhood? This will be the case when souls are late in arrival and the cosmic timetable will move on.

And so it will be necessary to accelerate the program of Montessori International[8] as a blueprint for many schools throughout the earth. And therefore let the most qualified teachers of excellence, of humility and devotion come forth. Let them understand, it is not the children you teach alone but all who will be coming who must have the program, the outline, and the very best opportunity to rise up into the native awareness of their individual Christ Self in those very early years.

Beloved ones, I behold many souls of light simply tarrying on the very edge of the threshold of time and space, already, as it were, in a consciousness of embodiment, already about their Father's business, yet missing the very necessary lower vehicles to be of influence upon those who have yet the need to see and hear and feel and taste and smell the manifest Word of God.

JOIN THE RANKS OF THOSE WHO HAVE HELD THE BANNER FOR LIFE

Beloved ones, those who have nobly held the banner for life and against abortion throughout the nations require your intercession, require your entering into their ranks for the giving of the invocations to Archangel Michael, the giving of the rosary, and the calling forth of those dynamic decrees that will bind the fallen ones and their attempts to avert the freedom and the liberation of life. And so, beloved ones, I commend the students of Montessori International and of Summit University to join the ranks with all of those who are speaking and who are delivering the Word on this issue. These children of the light must have reinforcements.

And let this year, then, be dedicated by the teaching centers to this issue, to its exposure, to the explanation of the family, that it not be destroyed by the beast of socialism, and to the correct teaching on community as the extension of the family and God-government as being ordained to represent that family on behalf of the incoming Christ.

And so, beginning with the soul aborning in the womb, we see the logical conclusion of a ministry that gives the outline of life, that explains the meaning of love and the opportunity to balance karma within the family by love that intensifies and has a greater and greater commitment, year by year, to the Person of God in the souls who are found one in that hallowed circle.

THE DIVIDING OF THE WAY OF THE TARES AND THE WHEAT

Beloved ones, let, therefore, the sons and daughters of God take this issue as the one in which they determine to be God-victorious, for upon it all other issues hang. And, beloved children of God, you who are pursuing the fullness of your own Christ Self, understand, then, that those leaders who will not take their stand for God and for life must also be accounted for, those to the right and to the left of the law of being.

And so, you see, the very issue itself is a dividing of the way of the tares and the wheat[9]—those who are of God and know they are of God and will defend the right of God to aborn within them, to be born, to come forth. Those who are not of God know they are not of God and do not desire to perpetuate their own seed, their own anti-God Self, and therefore they are the ones who have promoted abortion. Beloved ones, those who are of the seed of the Murderer and the Liar from the Beginning pursue their policies of abortion simply because by nature they are murderers.

The question is, then, who among the children of God have been indoctrinated by the Liar and his lie, and who among them are not the children of God but the wolves in sheep's clothing who have not the light of Christ in them and, therefore, will never succumb to the great Logos—the great reason of the Word that life is God from the moment of conception until the hour when the breath of the Holy Ghost returns to the Father and the crystal cord is cut and the threefold flame ascends to the etheric plane.

Beloved ones, those who deny life will not listen to reason. They will not accept facts and figures. And thus they stand exposed when you call forth the judgment and you bring the light of truth.

Go not after these, then, but go after the lost sheep of the house of Israel[10] who have lost their way through a false indoctrination and through the brainwashing of Zero Population Growth.[11] Go after the children of God who are making the karma and who ought to be liberated from the Liar and his lie. Draw them into the sheepfold. Give them the teaching and, above all, the comfort of life.

SEALING THE CHILDREN IN THE LIGHT FOR THE VICTORY

I am Jesus. I stand within your temple. I release a great sacred fire that is my meditation throughout this day upon the light of the little child. I walk the earth and I minister to children, and all children of earth this day will see me as I AM, will know me as I AM, and will know who they are in God. For I, Jesus, have determined that my Christmas Day will be with the children of the earth so that that promise of their own victory may be sealed.

My own heart trembles with the heart of Mother Mary as we look upon those things that will shortly come to pass upon the earth. And therefore we look to the protection of the children, to the sealing of the children in the divine plan and in the light that will be the protection of all in coming changes. It is the light that seals every part of God, the light that cannot be taken away. Pursue that light and guard it in these little ones and you will move forward into the victory.

Let your joy and your celebrations this day be in honor of the children around you and those throughout the earth. And remember to give a prayer now and then, as you join in fellowship, that my presence shall be unto these children a quickening fire, a baptism of the Word, and the opening of their individual mission.

I have come in Mighty Cosmos' secret rays. I have come speaking to you from within your own secret chamber of the heart. I have spoken from within that you might now go within and accustom yourselves to receiving me each day, and more frequently, in that inner chamber.

I desire, then, to breathe upon you the breath of the Holy Ghost and to leave with you the great message of the Word which I have delivered through our messenger in the great tribute of the prophecy of Isaiah.[12] Surely he came to deliver to you the message of your Christhood. Run with it, my flock, and set the captives free.

In the name of the Father, in the name of the Mother, in the name of the Son and of the Holy Ghost, I AM with you alway.

December 25, 1978
Camelot
Los Angeles County, California
ECP

CHAPTER 12

*I carry you in my arm as the blessed Lamb of God,
even as I AM the Lamb upon the throne of your being.
So I AM the shepherd in your midst.
I have been with you always.*

CHAPTER 12

THE SYMPHONY OF THE RESURRECTION FLAME

I give you my peace, a flame enveloping your soul. The mighty sound of the resurrection flame is all-engulfing. Standing in the eye of the flame, you hear only the great symphony of your soul, my soul, as one.

I AM the Saviour of the soul of the devotee of light. I AM come, joyous in this momentous release of resurrection light from out the Great Central Sun.

Our Father has sent the extraordinary symphony of the resurrection flame. Oh, see how all pain and hurt of this life and every other life cannot be remembered or heard or felt or revolved or experienced anymore. This is the meaning of the resurrection.

I carry you in my arm as the blessed Lamb of God, even as I AM the Lamb upon the throne of your being. So I AM the shepherd in your midst. I have been with you always. And in those hours of darkest, darkest night that you have also tasted as the bitterness of the myrrh, so I have been there. And the sound of my flame has resounded to your soul, all-enveloping, so drowning out the darkness, unfortunately to increase the anger of that darkness.

Nevertheless, I did wrap your soul in the swaddling garment out of which my own tomb cloth was made. And thus from your inception in my arms to the proving of your victory in the tomb, I drape upon you the mantle of white linen that is the sign of the saints who gather together now in the crucible of love.

Our love is born of the longing we share for one another in our Father-Mother God, our longing that is increased by the span of the cross of time and space upon which our own Reality is crucified by our own unreality.

And so there come players to the scene implementing the great drama of life again and again. Let the players to the drama of your life enter. Let *all* enter. Receive them as friend because they bear a cup of energy that you must then repair. Sometimes you must repair [by going] to your cloister to pray. And then on another day you must repair my house and then repair each fragmented stream of consciousness that renders the image of the Christ most fractured and not understandable to the innocent eyes begging for wholeness and purity of visage.

THE TRUE PAIN OF OVERCOMING

I come with a clean countenance that I would make your own. I bid you, then, do not descend to the levels of psychic astrology, calculation, or manipulation of karma. Do not count your beads, willing God's will to be your own so that you may manipulate persons and circumstances and then call them the divine plan. Enough of this psychic fantasy in our midst!

Let the chelas of the will of God hear the real and living scripture of the daily bearing of the cross, of the forsaking of the life so that one may gain a higher life!

Hear the Word concerning the cross, the persecution, the trial, the temptation, and the victory! For the message of victory is there, the logical conclusion of all that must go before.

Let us, then, cease within the midst of the body of God the desire to constantly be anesthetized from the great beauty and the glory of the very implementation of pain as a measure of the balance of light.

Perhaps it is a pain of the heart or of the soul. Perhaps it is the pain of knowing that at some point you defied the goal or that an angel ministrant came to tarry and to ask you to visit one who was sick, and perhaps you did not go. Perhaps you realized only too late that God had deigned to send you a high and holy being, an angel of light, and yet you answered and went your own way. This is the true pain of overcoming.

I speak not of the pain of the ego and its paltry suffering as it is deprived of the wants of this world. Those who experience life in this breadbasket yearn for crusts and receive only the dry crusts. But I speak of souls who would become saints—those whose pain and only pain is in every moment of separation from the Holy Spirit, those whose pain is to be more of God, whose pain is in the suffering of humanity and in a sense of inadequacy to heal that pain. Among these I would walk, and not among those who murmur at the call for labor and prayer without ceasing.

I come not to those who murmur against the brother or sister who gives the full measure and cup of devotion and then has as their reward the pointing of the finger by another who would say, "These are fanatics. I will not be as they are. I will not follow their example. I will lead a balanced, sane life. *I* will show and demonstrate the Path for millions to follow. I will not remember the path of my Saviour, who gave to the uttermost and did not care for this life nor its friends nor its compliments."

For, my beloved, I saw clearly your day and your coming. I knew that each measured footstep of my life would be measuring the cycles of your own. I saw the New World. I saw the New Atlantis of my father, Joseph.[1] I saw the new birth and the oncoming new race, and I knew that there must be a foundation laid whereupon the great pyramid of the seventh ray might come forth.

And oh, how I yearned that my life might be a perpetual healing presence, the healing of the people of that human propensity to idolatry. The disease of the ages is the worship of this or that self. And how it destroys the single walk! How it destroys the light!

LET NO MAN TAKE THY CROWN

There is the great parable of the one who established the vineyard and then absented himself, and by and by [that lord of the vineyard] sent his servant to receive the reward. And the servant was not received but destroyed.[2] And the lord sent another and still another and another servant, and again and again the servant of the master of the vineyard was denied the fruit of the vine. And finally the lord sent his heir, his son, and the son therefore did they murder, thinking thereby to gain the son's inheritance.

My beloved, let no man take thy crown.[3] Understand, then, that many servants have come in the name of the LORD bearing the good tidings of the oncoming Christ. If, therefore, the prophets, the patriarchs who declared the coming of Messiah were themselves denied by the people to whom the LORD sent them, how then would you expect that the apparent heir should be received? And the Pharisees and Sadducees knew whereof I spoke, but they were afraid of the people.

How are the high and the mighty afraid of the people? Is it their numbers? I tell you, nay! It is their light and their light-potential and their oneness with God. They fear their union. They fear their enlightenment. They fear their praise and acclamation of my coming. Therefore they enact laws against the people's assembly, against their freedom to come together, to worship, to speak, and to write freely.

And thus around the world today the four sacred freedoms enshrined by my father and your own prophet Samuel[4] are envied in those nations where they dare not worship together except under the auspices of the State and its puppets planted in the Church, in the economy, in the government, and in the school systems. O my beloved, the four pillars in the temple of America are for the sustainment of the contact with the Coming One!

WE WILL NOT LEAVE YOU COMFORTLESS

See how the numberless numbers of saints robed in white parade before all the world through the pages of the Book of Revelation, which I delivered to John. Yet see how all the world will deny their very presence though they were nigh, even at the door of consciousness of John, who himself did not taste of death before he entered the kingdom of God.[5]

Thus among the highest and most holy of all devotees of Christendom, my own beloved John—chosen to leave the record of my most intense love—is denied by those who have protested against the Holy Church and arrived at zero, nothing—no awareness of the Person of God despite the very Revelation itself, preserved intact by guardian angels of Archangel Michael, who have stood guard with their mighty flaming swords to see that the message could not be broken. In it are not only the keys to the age and to the psychology of the soul but the keys to all of the mystery teachings of our Brotherhood.

We will not leave you comfortless.[6] We will come to you, as beloved Sanat Kumara comes. And you will know, before our mission by our witnesses is fulfilled, the meaning of every word and the Word behind the word. Many dispensations, sphere upon sphere, will be required before the final awareness of the great geometry that becomes the majesty of music itself is revealed in the mighty formula of that Holy Book.

Thus, John did commune with my angel. He saw the Lamb. He saw the oncoming tide of light. He saw the depths of hell. He saw the Final Judgment. He saw the second death, the Book of Life, and the armies of heaven. He saw the Four and Twenty Elders, the ascended masters, the four cosmic forces[7]—all that you have understood for many a year.

Why is there, then, this controversy, this apostasy, this heresy among the very ones who profess to keep my flame, when the very literal penetration of that Word would preclude the denial of the hosts of the LORD?

My beloved, you can clearly see that the seed of the wicked have cast a spell over the minds of the sheep, have clouded the image and the ability to see. How have they done this? It is because of the tolerance of those who have succeeded in securing positions of leadership—their tolerance for human good and human evil. And you already know which of the twain I consider the most deadly.

How hard it is for the little people of the earth to ever perceive or understand the nature of human goodness to be the casket itself whereby even death becomes the goodness of life!

THE SANDS IN THE HOURGLASS

My heart pains this day for the youth of this land and every land —these ones, so young, such tender vines, who are pushed upon the battlefields of Asia, of Africa, who must bear the weight of war and the hatred of their overlords, being taught to kill and murder before they are taught to know the sweet face of my Mother's love. My heart pains when I see their lives destroyed by the fallen ones, who are even now the hordes in embodiment seeking to devour all whom they may devour ere the last trumpet call sounds, compelling them to the judgment.

I have come to you with a special prayer that you might be relentless in overturning all laws facilitating abortion in the earth. Now I come to you and I say, spare me! Spare me—your brother, your friend, and your Master—the incalculable, imponderable grief of seeing life aborted in these stages when the most creative potential of the Cosmic Christ is about to blossom as the flowers of the field among the youth. My heart burns within me not only for their suffering but for the imbalance in the foundation of the City Foursquare.

Indeed, I weep as I stand upon ascension hill over Jerusalem and I say, "Father, must it surely come to pass as thou hast told me and as I have told the disciples? Must all these things come to pass? Can they not be averted by the faithful? Can they not be passed into the flame, that life might continue without interruption?"

And the Father has answered my prayer this very day as I have communed with him just above your heads, in that place where I often go to view the souls becoming more of the light here and there across the earth. And so the Father has said to me, even as I say to you, "While the sands yet fall in the hourglass, all things are possible unto the one who is one with me through thy name."

Thus he has shown to me alternative visions of that which may transpire according to the free will of those who are the real leaders in the earth. And so I have seen numbers of panoramas of the movement of history and of life on the continents of the earth depicting the possibilities for the coming decade and the next unto the year 2000. I have seen the alternatives at hand, and I have seen that not until the sand passes through the nexus is the determination made as to what life will be.

Thus I have chosen to come and place in your hand a handful of sand and an hourglass. For I would like you to experience the placing of that sand in the upper sphere. I would like you to experience what it is like to be in the eye of creation, in the eye of the Lords of Creation and the Elohim as we also, in the consciousness of the Cosmic Christ, must release the energy as that spiral that does flow as a crystal clear river of water of Life.[8]

We know that we are but instruments of the creation. We must let go of the energy. We must let it descend. We would like to perform cosmic acrobatics and descend immediately to the lower sphere and become the one who holds the chalice to catch the sand that we have just released. But, you see, it is not permitted by the law of polarities. There must be the giver. There must be the receiver.

You stand in a position to have the chalice upraised. Now for a moment stand with me [Audience rises.] and realize how you would feel if by cosmic law you knew you had to release the oncoming light, the oncoming cycles and dispensations. Thus you are in the upper sphere and you release the sand, and you watch it descend as you look for the upraised chalice.

Now and again there comes a righteous man or woman, an innocent child, and the sand is perfectly received, safe and sound, and all will be well in that hour and in that day. Then comes the agony of seeing that for a particular moment of dispensation there is no one with upraised chalice.

THE CRUMBLING OF THE TEMPLE WALL IS COME

We have gone to a number of nations on the continent of Africa this day, as you have called us to do. My beloved, we have not found in some nations a single soul who had the capacity of even an equivalency of cosmic consciousness, as some of our chelas here have, to hold the balance of light against the hordes of darkness that would destroy the opportunity for millions to even begin their path of evolution.

This was the reason for my weeping over Jerusalem. For I saw that even though the Father had given to his children two thousand years to put on the great mastery of life that I gave in just three years, yet the hour would come when all of that mastery would be required, would be essential, would be indispensable to the guarding of the flame of freedom of my father, Joseph, who had by then preceded me into the octaves of light.

And thus I saw what I see this very day—that where there have been those who could have risen through service to all to be rulers over many, they have dallied, they have played, they have abused the light. And suddenly they expect wonders and miracles and angels to appear. And when we send our prophet and no miracles are forthcoming, they malign, they condemn, they accuse, and they direct their murderous intent toward her, toward the flock of the faithful.

My beloved, this has happened. Why, souls of millions of

people in the nation of Ghana, who received the great light of our coming through our witness,[9] were yet influenced and burdened by those among the Communists and those who again have taken their positions and bastioned themselves in the towers of the Church to defend an unholy doctrine.

Thus Church and State always unite against the living truth. And thus the crumbling of the temple wall is come,[10] and you see that not one stone is left upon it as the collapse of the government and the economy of such nations is imminent—all because of the denial of the Christ in the simple servant.

Can they not see your sincerity, your transparency? Must their own filthiness of soul discolor every servant that we send forth? It has ever been so, but it need not continue. For I send my cosmic honor guard before those who will stump in my name. I will not leave you alone before the wolves of this world. I will be with you.

Each one who will open his mouth in my name will know such joy of the presence of angels that it will become now a race among you to see who will be the first called to represent me unto the cities and the nations. For you will have such eagerness to receive that cup of the heavenly angels and of the holy joy that you have seen upon the countenance of our messengers these many years.

I desire to make it your own. I will multiply the great scenario of the drama of my victory of the resurrection and the people will say, "Lo, here and there we see the shining faces. We see the two angels.[11] We see the hosts of the LORD. We see the pilgrims of peace filing to the nations with their relentless, shining swords of peace as sacred Word does flow, intensify, and guard the Holy of holies."

How will the wicked, then, destroy in all my holy mountain as I build my mountain, a great pyramid of souls? Simply, they will not! *They shall not pass! They shall not pass!* But rather, our shadow will pass upon them. And with the coming of our shadow through our saints there will be the precipitation of our robe of judgment. So it is come.

So, then, I would show you in my retreat of the resurrection flame[12] (as you come with me this very night) the succession of murals of life, and I will ask you to choose. You, then, will have the privilege of performing your cosmic acrobatics, for you will indeed dive back into the earth, seize the chalice, upraise it, and receive the grains of sand that are indeed become within you the great Rock of Christ.

THE PURPOSE OF THE RESURRECTION FLAME

Lo, I AM come. I AM come to the little children. I AM come to the tender vine of our youth. With the understanding of the little child that I AM in the arms of God, so I know each little fear and trembling that requires only a gentle word, a quiet assurance, and it is dispelled.

How fortunate are you, mothers and fathers, to have the opportunity to express tenderness toward these tender vines. Let your tender hearts become a mighty focus and magnet of love. For we would see the harshness expressed to the little children set aside so that they are not marred but raised up with the rod of firmness that emits from the blessed fire of the Kundalini of father and mother, and never from anger or insecurity or a lashing out because of ancient memories of having been lashed out at.

This is the purpose of the resurrection flame. I show you the history of your soul. I show you how I have been with you, not allowing what you have accepted as negative records upon your subconscious. These impressions you must let go of. For from the very beginning I have enveloped you in my flame of peace, the flame of the resurrection.

Do not seize an excuse, then, for a sense of injustice about life. Do not seize an excuse for self-pity because of your past, in this life or another. For though it may have been done to you, remember that in reality I have already spoken it: "Inasmuch as ye have done it unto one of the least of these my brethren, ye have done it unto me."[13]

My beloved, I was with you in those hours of torment and pain.

I was there. My Electronic Presence was upon you. What they seemed to do to you, they did to me. And that mighty flame of my life has long ago discharged that energy into the violet flame. Therefore in reality it has never touched your soul except in those instances where you chose to personalize that which was directed only at the Person of the Son of God.

Thus, though it may seem a hard saying for you to receive, in reality the only persecution and torment that could ever affect your life is that which you yourself received in a state of incompleteness and acceptance based upon your own incomplete sense of life.

Therefore in this profound knowledge you may accept the healing this hour, in my presence, of all psychological imbalance, emotional disturbance, even physical diseases based upon your interactions of early childhood even to the present.

You may then know that in the power of my present flame, which I release to you in this moment—*if* you will it so; *if* you are determined not to harbor a single excuse any longer for incompleteness—you may accept your wholeness as my wholeness, for we are one. You may accept my flame as I give it, and then relentlessly pursue the immaculate image until every one of your four lower bodies and your chakras truly reflects the wholeness that you are, that you ever have been, that you always will be.

I now release a mighty whirlwind action of the light around you. It separates you from every human opinion, every condemnation, every accusation, and in this moment you *are* healed! I declare it! I AM it! My Mother holds the immaculate vision of your wholeness.

BEHOLD, YOU ARE PERFECT IN GOD!

Now learn, then. Learn the mystery of the healing that is made, that is done, that is sealed, and the healing that you become because of the necessity of learning how to accept that which in reality is done at inner levels. My beloved, it is clearly a message that you must ponder.

It is first learning to receive healing as a blueprint that enfires your etheric body. Second, it is learning to accept the mental concept, the matrix itself, by the power of the reason of the Word. Invincible mind of God it is! And it must become your own awareness!

Then there is the acceptance within the feelings. How Peter yearned to have that acceptance. But unfortunately he did not always have the dominion over the untransmuted substance of fear and doubt. Learning to consume it, to make way for the healing that is already yours, becomes the challenge of the hour. And finally there is the clearing of the physical vehicle so that it might be the chalice for that healing.

God has never given a stone when asked for a crumb of bread.[14] My beloved, the prayers for healing are answered. Pray, then, for understanding and love to be the fulfillment of that healing that is already yours by the resurrection flame. Behold, you are perfect in God! He has never rescinded his vision that is upon the very screen of cosmos itself!

My beloved, learn the way of receiving the grain of sand into the chalice. Learn the way of penetrating the nucleus of every atom in a grain of sand. And realize that in that and that alone is a sufficiency of the resurrection flame of Helios and Vesta to seal you in the very light that descended from out my own heart and the heart of my Presence for the resurrection on this morning, which you commemorate.

The mystery of life is in your hand. Release the sand and now descend, and never be without a cup—a cup to receive the sacred fire.

I AM with you alway, even unto the end of the age![15] I AM! And I AM forever and forever your Jesus Christ, Saviour of the soul and its return unto God!

In the name of my Blessed Mother Mary and my father, Joseph, in the name of the Holy Ghost, I AM the eternal Christ forevermore, worlds without end!

AUM.

Now, most beloved, bring to me the newborn children, for I would touch them by the fire of my heart.

[The sacrament of Baptism follows.]

April 15, 1979
Camelot
Los Angeles, California
ECP

CHAPTER 13

*Come with me, my children, lambs of God.
For I would be with you in the hours of your initiation
unto eternal life.*

CHAPTER 13

TAKE MY CUP, AND DRINK YE ALL OF IT

I have desired in the desiring of my soul to be with you in the hour when you seize the mighty cross of the resurrection and prepare to meet resurrection's goal.

I receive you, then, my disciples. I receive you in the name of my Mother, Mary, who moves among you in answer to your call. I extend the flame of my resurrection unto all who enter the spiral of Saint Germain's Mission Amethyst Jewel.[1]

I send forth the golden-pink light and the white-rainbowed-aura hue of my own resurrection as a mantle upon those who sing the violet flame in the twenty-four hours of the day and the night. I come, then, to infuse the flame of freedom with all of the glory of my own victory.

I hold you in my arms as the lambs of God. I move in you, midst the people of earth. I am the challenger of the seed of the wicked, and they move here and there in their usual attempts to thwart the resurrection of the Son of God within you.

Let us, then, concern ourselves with this mighty event and with the transfer of this light of my sacred heart to you who are my own and to all who shall believe on me through thy name and through thy witness.

So it is my desire to see you be that living Son of God in the world, a living testimony, and [following] after the teaching of Gautama, that you not be so concerned that the Evil One or his cohorts should suddenly conform to the mysteries of the Holy Grail but that *you* should conform to the inner will of God and make your calling and election sure.[2] It is certain, for it is the prophecy of God that the angels will come to bind the tares and remove them, inasmuch as the judgment is in his hands.

Let us more so pursue *with diligence* the victory of the individual incarnation of the Word. For this purpose I am come so that your joy should not be dependent upon the outer sign or symbol but upon your own heart's fullness of the Holy Ghost.

Prepare, then, for the hour of the celebration of my ascension, for in this year I shall dedicate it to your own and transfer to you a very special and most extraordinary light of my finer bodies. Prepare also for the day of Pentecost. For the world shall be filled with a holy light when our disciples prefer, then, one another, and prefer the worship of the living God.

Thus the tides of darkness, they roll in and they roll out. But the coming of the Son of God in the person of your blessed Self is the greatest event of the twentieth century. With this event secured, then the world must come into alignment.

Let our chelas assemble as I will come to celebrate the great victory of the freedom flame in the name of Saint Germain at the celebration of the summer solstice.[3] The victory conference of freedom scheduled for this year[4] will have the blessed mounting joy of the resurrection of all of the saints of God who have gone before you. They will come for an extraordinary and most blessed transfer of light to the body of God.

Let the initiates on the Path hear my call and know that I desire to be with you, even as I desire to be at the home of Mary and Martha and Lazarus. That special home of light for me on earth in this hour is where you are—you who have entered into the real and living communion cup, the wine of the Holy Spirit that courses through you as the violet flame of my father, Joseph.* He taught to me so much more than the sacred labor of carpentry. He taught to me the sacred labor of the alchemy of the Holy Ghost —the changing of the water into wine.

Truly I am the son of Joseph, the great miracle alchemist of all time, and truly my works show forth his handiwork and the blessed grace of my mother. So, parents of the New Age, impart and endow your children with the very essence of your soul's communion with Saint Germain and Mother Mary. So transfer the light of the Holy Family.

LET THE VIGIL BE KEPT OF THE FLAME OF FREEDOM AND OF MY RESURRECTION LIGHT

I come and I tarry with you at Camelot today so that you may receive in the level of your souls an understanding of the challenges that are ahead for each one of you on the Path, even unto the opening of the way of the teachings unto all of the nations of the earth.

Let the vigil be kept of the flame of freedom and of my resurrection light. Let it be kept in every hearth and home where there are Keepers of the Flame who understand the signs of the times and who live with John the Beloved in the inner message of the Book of Revelation unfolded by the Father—my Father and your Father, my God and your God, the blessed Ancient of Days.

I am here, then, in the sweetness of the springtide to anchor the continuing flame of that resurrection. Hear, then, in the mighty account of the resurrection of Lazarus,[5] that which shall be your portion and your opportunity.

Let the cosmic timetable roll! Let the souls of light come to the altar of invocation, where I send forth my Word, and my Word returns unto me.[6] Let the souls of light go forth from the sanctuary

---
*Joseph was an embodiment of Saint Germain.

of the Holy Grail and be my witnesses in Jerusalem, in the four corners of the earth.

So witnessing unto me, you will know the fullness of my cup. And you will rejoice to see that in the resurrection of the soul of America, the intended divine plan of Almighty God is that your own resurrection should anchor you firmly in the earth plane for the ongoing and continuing victories that shall culminate in the presence of the ascended masters, the glorious Second Coming of the living Christ moving among the people as the true teachers of the age.

So occupy till I come.[7] So tarry with me today. For I desire to rest with you on the Sabbath and to take up on the morrow the continuing and mounting challenges of the flame of peace in America and the earth. Thus we shall see how the Darkness shall mount and be pierced by the Light.

Come with me, my children, for my desire is to be a part of each one of you as you take my cup and drink ye all of it. No matter what shall befall, know of a certainty that the coming of the Son of God, as the lightning that cometh out of the East and goeth unto the West,[8] shall be the sign of your victory and the manifestation of myself. Come with me, my children, lambs of God. For I would be with you in the hours of your initiation unto eternal life.

In the name of the blessed Guru Maitreya, I bow before his chelas on the Path and I take your hand for the fulfillment of the cross and the crown of life.

May 6, 1979
Camelot
Los Angeles County, California
ECP

CHAPTER 14

*I have come to infire you, then,
with the fearlessness of the prophets,
the great love of the avatars, the living truth.
It is a piercing message. It is a cup to drink.*

CHAPTER 14

THE WORDS OF MY FATHER

I have held consort with the many cosmic beings who hold the balance of light in the outer universes, where the soul evolutes and follows its course to the stars. I have held consort with the few in the earth who hold the balance of my star, yet remembering that we are one, that the Father hath made us one, and that we are made one by his love.

Love was the sealing of our hearts in the hour of my ascension, and to the present hour I have held consort with the many and the few, and light kindles the universe! Light kindles the earth! Lo, I AM come!

Do you see me, O my souls of light? I AM before you! I move in your midst! I AM here to deliver the Father's Word. Lo, this is my Father's house, and the earth is my Father's, and all who dwell therein are my Father's.

And so the divine plan of Gautama Buddha, of the Ancient of Days, of Lord Maitreya unfolds as a scroll read by the Keeper of the Scrolls, who stands next to me in honor of this day when victory has been assured me by the Father for many souls of light, some now dwelling in the inner retreats, some within the earth.

I come with a gift of a dispensation of light of ascension's flame. I *charge* it forth into the earth! I *charge* it into the heart of the Mother and her children! I *charge* it into my community of the Holy Spirit worldwide! And those who are the sincere followers of God, no matter what the burden of their life, shall receive the impetus of my victory in the hour when the clock strikes twelve according to this longitude.

I AM here. I AM centered in the City Foursquare, and I have come to be with you for the conveyance of a greater light. When the greater light is come into the world, so is judgment come. And so until all have received that judgment, you will hear me speak again and again.

The sweet prayer of love of all who are the blessed rises as the rising petals of roses or rising raindrops or rising snowflakes. As God sends love to you by the beings of nature, contemplate how you will send love to him.

Can you imagine a world where snowflakes and raindrops and rose petals rise? Well, you ought to begin, because you *are* the snowflake, the raindrop, and the rose petal, and you will soon rise higher and higher in that spiral of my love. Your acceleration, defying all gravitational pull, as did my own, will be the only living proof that can be known—that the ascension is the only open door to immortality and hearts to restore.

When your life has been lived in love and all is said and done, it is the victory won that will leave that proof, that real proof that I AM Real, that God is Real, that the Holy Spirit descends to seal you in the light, to heal you by the cloven tongues of fire, and then to steal you for a higher home and the goal that I have won and that you too shall now win.

I have come to infire you, then, with the fearlessness of the prophets, the great love of the avatars, the living truth. It is a piercing message. It is a cup to drink.

SACRIFICE AND SURRENDER TO THE FULLEST

Beloved ones, now is the hour of intensity. Therefore prepare. Prepare your heart and soul. When you are prepared for every eventuality of the battle, then come what may, you will go forth in joy, in firmness, your heart and mind set for that victory. But if you should go forth unprepared and unawares, not ready for whatever may beset your path, then you will not laugh when a big bear or a gorilla crosses in the way. You will be taken, then, by surprise, and perhaps led astray from the straight and narrow course.

I see the lives of many of you as I have read the storybook of your doings these two thousand years, and even the best among you have had frivolous years of forgetfulness. And how easy it is to enter into all sorts of diversions within the earth plane.

And so we are together again. We are one in the sacred fire, and this is all that matters now. But see that you do not repeat a little of this embodiment, a little of that one, mixing together a potpourri of your own stew—your stewings brought forth from the past when you and your mewings cast a long, long feline shadow across the earth.

Beloved ones, come out from among the members of your past incarnations! For some of you yet suffer from those temptations that rise like the odor of an overcooked stew from the subconscious and allow you to view those past doings with a certain nostalgia until you desire to go back and experience them again. And so, therefore, though you are the devotees of light, sometimes your lives are all mixed up with a little bit of this and that as you somehow seek to re-create a security out of the past that is no longer a choice. For before you lies the future vast.

Therefore I say, shed every layer of outworn garments! And recognize those tendencies of personality, those desires and those traits that will lead you astray as certainly as you have led others astray in those former lifetimes when you indulged those tendencies to the fullest.

There is not a problem that you have today, I can tell you (almost all of you), that was not one day in the past full blown, tormenting, overcoming you, and in some cases utterly destroying a lifetime and taking you and your vow out of the way from the central theme of purpose.

During the centuries since my ascension, many have been the devotees, as Morya says, for a lesser cause. Now I would call to your attention the great sacrifices that so many have made, and yet the victory is not yet won.

I AM here to tell you that I expect sacrifice to the fullest, and surrender! I expect service up to the final hours of your lifetime! I expect you to stop your doubt and fear and compromise, your going there and here! I expect an intensity worthy of the Holy Ghost, who desires to descend into your temple but waits until you sweep that temple clean of that residual substance!

My beloved, I offer you all that I have offered unto the first apostles. I offer you that which I gave to Paul.[1] I offer you my life as the instrument of the Maha Chohan in order to give to you everything that you need to perform those works of light.

I directed the reading from Ezekiel[2] so that you would understand the sacrifice of "a mere prophet." A mere prophet, you say? He was God incarnate! He was willing to be the instrument of the Ancient of Days!

Now I have come to ask every soul upon the planetary body who has ever crossed the ascended masters' path, who has ever heard of our activity, who has ever sat in our conferences: Are you ready for the sacrifices that the Great Law demands of you in order to transfer this light to the world?

This is my question, and I expect that answer in action! Therefore you may keep silent, lest in thinking that because you have given your word, you have truly answered.

WHAT MY FATHER SAID TO ME

The state of the world is not good, as you observe. And the acceleration of Darkness, side by side with an acceleration of Light, can only produce cataclysm of one sort or another unless a greater intensity of light be anchored swiftly.

You have the mechanism. You have the teaching. You have a temple already prepared. You have the chakras. You have the knowledge. You who have heard my voice since my Second Coming in this manifestation of the Church Universal and Triumphant, since my coming in the very beginning with Godfre and Lotus, with the beloved Mark: *Lo,* I AM here! *Lo,* this is my Second Coming! And when I speak, I AM here!

Therefore let all who have heard me know that I demand that my disciples shall give answer, even as the Ancient of Days demanded answer from Ezekiel.[3] It is all or nothing! I cannot work with you when you give me half a pie, your eye on other desires. Either we save the earth now or it is questionable that it can be saved at all, preserved as a habitation of dwelling for the present population.

I do not say that come what may, we cannot preserve a remnant. But if you desire to be that remnant, believe me, you will require all of your light, every erg of it, and all that you can muster of courage and will and endurance and skill, should that become the eventuality.

I have stood before the Father this day. I have kept a twenty-four-hour vigil prior to my coming before you. I have listened to his words. Some of them I may tell you, and some of them I must withhold. But he said to me:

> My Son, go and tell the Mother and her children, who cluster together, that I AM come. Now as always, I AM determined to save the earth. I have sent forth my edict through my son Gautama for the judgment of the seed of the wicked.
>
> Now on this day, thy ascension day,[4] I send forth the Word for the summoning of the righteous. Too many upon whom we have counted for the victory have gone astray and have allowed other activities to take the place

of the living Word. By the scales of their eyes they have not beheld how effective is the dynamic decree, the coming together, the service, the joy, and the literal sacred fire circle of our communion.

Therefore, go and tell them how effective is that Word so that they will know it is not absurd but truly the fulfillment of the Word to come together and praise the Lord I AM. Tell them that I, the Father, thou the Son, and the very Person of the Holy Spirit do stand wherever that Word is given by a single soul in a single decree. Tell them that that Word circles the earth by the power of Infinity and sets up a satellite of God-energy that will counteract every darkness.

Tell them of the power of the Word and the playing and the replaying of my Word that I have sent through my sons and daughters, the ascended masters, unto the two witnesses. Tell them that their service counts for grace.

Tell them that they yet run in the race and that their ascension is not yet sealed, therefore *intensify!* Tell them that they must *intensify!* Tell them that it is in the very nature of love to discover oneself in the final course, racing a race of life and death.

This is not unusual for the overcomers, my beloved. For the Father has shown me time and again that the acceleration unto the finish must be an intensity of sacred fire love in one's being so as to literally propel one to meet that God Presence in the air, to catch the very descending light of the ascension current!

Beloved ones, in the hour of your ascension you will be required to propel yourself upward into the arms of God, not to be borne there by angels who have borne you in previous hours of your transition. This time you will be the rocket on your own, fired by your own love and service. And all will count in that hour, whether you balance [your karma] or whether you do not; whether you make your ascension at the conclusion of this life or whether you must return for the leftover stew that you failed to transmute and to commit to that flame now; whether you ascend from the inner retreats (if you ascend in this life) or whether you ascend from ascension's hill,[5] wherever that hill might be, wherever you are.

I SUMMON THOSE UPON WHOM I WILL PLACE MY MANTLE

Let us see renewed fervor and dedication. Let my Word be published abroad as a challenge to Christian and Jew and Muslim and Hindu and Buddhist and those who have not known the living God but yet worship the unknown God. For I desire to speak to the people of this earth and I will witness, by my messenger, to my own victory and my own light. And therefore I challenge those who worship me to worship God within themselves, to fall down before the great fire infolding itself, and the bow and the rainbow round about, and the four living creatures who will appear as surely as they appeared to Ezekiel,[6] if you will invoke them in God's name.

Prepare, then, for your commission, you who call yourselves my disciples. For I AM here! I AM come! And this is my Second Coming! Do not wait to be flattered by your own interpretations of my prophecy as a dead doctrine or ritual.

I tell you, the Second Coming is come! And it comes in the person of the Christ, in the ascended masters who are even now in the earth! And you have not seen them descend in clouds of glory because of your own density and perversion and stubbornness and the blindness of your eyes!

If you would wrest yourselves from your television sets and your entertainment and go out at night and look unto the stars, you might see the sons of God descending. But you can scarcely take your eyes from the stock market or your business enterprise!

How can you know when the Son of God is come? You have

not received me in my messenger or in my disciples! *Woe to you! Woe to you! Woe to you!*

I AM come in the very midst of Israel a burning fire, a burning and a smoking lamp![7] I AM here! My Word is here! My salvation is here unto those who meet the full requirements of the law of love that I have taught.

Let there be a rallying, then. Let there be an intensity, then. For I summon my own to our Freedom Conference 1979, here at Camelot. And I summon you to two weeks of Upper Room training following that conference. For I will be present with my own Saint Francis, and we as World Teachers will transfer that mantle to those who would be shepherds. This is when we will do it, in these two weeks following the July conference.[8]

Let all who hear, come. This is the hour and this is the Call. Let those who desire the Holy Ghost be willing, then, to meet the requirements of the Holy Spirit. And *shame* upon you who have admitted the foul spirits and impostors of the person of the Maha Chohan into your churches! *Shame* upon you, I say, with your unclean spirits and your cavorting with demons—being so dense that you know not that you have not the Spirit of the Holy Ghost but of Beelzebub!

You have no part with me unless you leave this dark and wanton condemnation of my light! I summon my elect! I summon those upon whom I will place my mantle! And I will not tell you when I will come again to give you this dispensation or this offer!

CONTINUE! ACCELERATE! BEAR WITNESS TO THE TRUTH!

You who have known me in the heart of our circle, do not take for granted the ascended masters, their presence, or their messenger, *but heed the Word!* You have been served abundantly with our dictations and our light. Now we expect answers and action and giving and supply.

This Church, *my Church,* the one I have filled with my light, *needs* your support, *needs* your contribution! And it ought to be forthcoming as a just and lawful tithe without you having to be reminded that we are about the task of saving a world and we use all that is given to that purpose!

Beloved ones, I AM here. And never mind those who criticize my manner of speech. I will use what I will use. I AM one among my children, and you are my brothers and sisters. Now God has determined to save the earth! I have determined to save the earth! And I am looking for those instruments who have determined to save the earth and will finally measure the price, the personal price that must be paid!

The first price is harmony. I demand that you give it unceasingly. The second is love manifest by obedience to the Word, to the Law, to the embodied messenger. All things then follow when you have harmony and loving obedience. Then you are filled with wisdom and faith and hope and light and understanding and creativity and ingenuity, and you are the instruments of the Divine Mother.

I come in her name. I was sent by her flame in the Beginning and I returned to her flame in the ending. She is my Mother, now and forevermore. Therefore I preach her word and I go before her as the herald. I demand that the Word of Mother Mary be received in the marts of the world. I demand that you release that word and that you see that it is known.

All that has been done to the glory of God and to my light in my children is wondrous indeed. I praise the works you have worked in the LORD. I bow before you to express gratitude, for gratitude is due. But now I say, it is not enough. You know it and I know it. It is not enough and it will not be enough until the earth is safe, until the people of God are free, until the mockers in office are removed and the children of the light take their lawful place.

I am ashamed of those who would represent me in the government and yet have denied the word of my messenger. One by one by one they make themselves unavailable for the outpouring of Elohim that is necessary for the saving of the earth.

Therefore the Father has promised me, "We will raise up all necessary servants from those who are the true chelas. Now go and report to me within a fortnight who are the true chelas, and I will work through you, through them, for the victory."

Beloved ones, I shed a tear for the chelas who are not here by conscious choice and for those who are in the world serving me with the most intense love of their being but who have been denied their chelaship by the false hierarchy and its false doctrine—those who serve in perfect love without enlightenment and therefore have not the whole armour of God to meet the enemy in the hour of Armageddon.

Therefore I have sent you forth, you have gone forth, and some who profess to worship me have attacked you with their vehemence and their hatred, have torn down your posters, have sought to block your coming. Yet the Word has gone forth. They have been warned. You have preached directly in the very midst of those who profess to follow me.

I say, continue! Accelerate! And you who have not yet opened your mouth to bear witness unto the truth, try it! You will find that I will speak through you. You will know the Spirit of the Lord coming into your temple as you have never known it before. It is my assignment to you, and I am well pleased for your very trying, which has prompted your crying unto God for help. [You have said,] "Help!" And help has come forth. Never has it been denied except when your own pride has stood between me and your call. Cry out to me again, for I will come.

I have many messages to speak to the people of earth, and it does not matter if you or your speech are perfected. They will get the message, for they will feel the vibration pierce them to the quick and to the heart.

THE RESCUING OF SOULS OF LIGHT
FROM THE ASTRAL PLANE

Yes, this is the hour of the celebration of the ascension. My ascension was not for me alone. It was the opening of the door. Let us celebrate opportunity—renewed, enhanced, and increased by God the Father this day for many souls in the inner retreats.

And I would tell you that in these past two weeks I have sent my messenger personally into the astral plane with my legions, for it was required that the One Sent in embodiment go into the very core of the astral plane of this city Los Angeles for the rescuing of souls of light caught there for decades and centuries.

Beloved ones, these souls have been cut free by the call of the messenger and yourselves, and those who two weeks ago were crying out to me from the astral planes of Los Angeles now stand clothed upon with their white garments in the retreat of the God and Goddess Meru.[9] This is the offering that I have brought to the Father this day—the tangible works of my disciples, what they can do when they stand staunch as one and keep on keeping on.

No matter what you have heard about descending into the astral plane, I can tell you that it is terrifying and it is dangerous. That assignment given by my father Saint Germain will be given again and again, for there are many pockets of the astral plane where souls are imprisoned, where souls must be freed. And this is only the beginning.

As Morya has sent the messenger, as Shiva has sent her to stump, so Saint Germain sends her into the astral reaches of the earth. And I desire your support in the giving of the calls to Astrea and to the violet flame so that every last soul whom God the Father has assigned to these two witnesses will be cut free from out the astral plane before this dispensation has been fulfilled.

These souls have been waiting for the coming of the Mother—the Mother Mary, the Mother Omega, the Mother in you, and above all, the Mother in our messenger, who has returned to the shores of Lemuria.[10] There are souls, beloved ones, that only you as individuals can liberate. And there are more, many more souls that only the two witnesses may liberate because it is the dharma, and the dharma is set, and you are all links in the chain of being. And the cutting free of souls is a mighty science. There are many who wait for you until you have the attainment to go in places where today it is not lawful for you to go because the membrane of your protection is not strong enough.

SOULS CAUGHT IN THE MOTION PICTURE AND TELEVISION INDUSTRY

Now the Mother has seen the souls who have awaited her coming. Now they are candidates for the ascension. Some of them call [to me] to embody here in Camelot. They have asked me, "Will Camelot be there when it comes our turn to incarnate and to give our service and make our ascension?"

This I have asked the Father this day. And his answer, bless his heart, is the only answer that the Father could give: "I have committed all judgment unto the Son." This means that the judgment, as the decisions of life, rests with the Christ Self in you—your discernment, your discrimination, your decision. The soul, one with the Christ Self, makes the judgment and the determination to build a New Jerusalem.

Therefore the Father has said to me, "Go and ask the souls to whom life has consigned the judgment, whether Camelot will be there, whether America will be there when these souls are ready to incarnate." So I have come with my fire of the ascension glory in order to give to you the old, old story of the love of the Christ in me and in you.

I AM here. And when your lives, by your action, give to God the answer, I will relate that answer to those now working very intensely at Lake Titicaca, preparing to come. Their gratitude for your presence here knows no bounds. They know that by the presence of every one of you and not alone the messenger, they are now in a retreat, when they have for so long been in the grips of the toilers and the spoilers and a darkness so great as to be beyond your imagination.

Among those who have recently come are the ones who have sung for my coming, Jeanette MacDonald and Nelson Eddy.[11] They have come out from a long, dark night, where they have been with others who once reembodied in the seat-of-the-soul chakra of a nation[12] to deliver to the world the image of the inner harmony of God. And those souls of light—trapped by the laggards and their horrendous perversions of the All-Seeing Eye—have now been freed in great numbers.

Those in embodiment serving in the theater and the motion picture industry and in television yet need your call and your rescue. They have also been contacted, and these souls of light, now four hundred in number who live within this city, may be reached by first being cut free by the calls to Astrea relentlessly given.

We have an image of a new order of the ages of Saint Germain to portray to the world, and we find an abomination of desolation in all the houses of the industry in Hollywood. We find the drugs, the rock music, the sensuality. It is *hell* that is being portrayed to the youth today! It is psychic thralldom! It is lust! It is darkness, the gyration of demons!

We have not seen purity or the pure stream, and we are determined that if you will build a Camelot, we will send the souls. And we will raise up in the midst a pyramid, and the All-Seeing Eye upon that pyramid in the seat-of-the-soul chakra will be the illustration to the world of the entire path of the ascension, from the first incarnation unto the return to the I AM Presence.

We will deliver the music. We will deliver the history and the stories of love that are real. All of this is on the drawing boards of life. And the ones who will determine whether or not it will come forth today, my beloved, are the chelas of the ascended masters.

By your work and service in my flame and in my vibration, wherever you are upon earth, you will decide whether America remains, Camelot remains, and the earth remains in its present order.

I GIVE THE FULL MOMENTUM OF MY FLAME

You who have talent in many fields know the job that you must do. But do not forsake the vibration of light and love. Do not lower yourself to a worldly vibration and think that because you once had the teaching or give to it lip service, we can work through you. We can work better through those who have never contacted us than we can work through you who go away from the flame and allow it to be compromised and misused. This is a truth that you will one day understand when you come to understand the inner workings of the Law and the chakras.

Therefore, let us hear from the chelas. Let the chelas be present. Let those who have not answered me and my call through the *Pearls of Wisdom* now give answer. My ascension is not for the few; it is for the many! And it is not for the many in heaven; it is for the many who are left in the heart of the earth.

To you, my beloved, I give the full momentum of my flame. Wherever you are, my beloved, you who carry the vibration of my heart, you have my love. You have my ascension.

I AM Jesus. I AM with you. And I AM with you alway, even to the fulfillment of the cycles.

May 24, 1979
Camelot
Los Angeles County, California
ECP

CHAPTER 15

*Why does God allow injustice?...
He allows it so that the children of light may learn
from the nefarious deeds of the seed of the wicked
that which is the true course and that which is the false....
They, then, will put on my garment and do those things
which are most important.*

CHAPTER 15

WILLINGNESS TO CONFRONT THE ADVERSARY

Hail unto the beloved who are my seed! Hail unto the light of the Ancient of Days! I AM come into the earth. And lo, I AM come to do thy will, O God!

My beloved who are my true shepherds in the earth, I salute you in the light of Sanat Kumara. Before his flame I bow, and in his name I come to give comfort to my brethren. Won't you be seated.

The light that I bear is the light of the Father, conveyed to me as a taper before the throne of grace. I am come this day as the Lamb on Mount Zion. I come as the Lamb in the very person and the office of that one to seal in the heart of the earth and in the souls of my children the awareness that I am in the earth, that I speak my Word in this hour, and that I am present for the deliverance of the Woman and her seed.

I have come for the fulfillment of the vow that I made so very long ago when I beheld the turning aside of my father and my mother by Serpent and his seed[1] and the long journey into night that the children of the light must bear. Many, many souls in that Lemurian epoch responded to the very same testings of their path. And therefore there is a collective burden of karma that now we lay upon the altar of the Lord, that you might claim the burden of the Lord. His burden is light. His burden is also the very creation itself. And thus you might call the burden of the Lord the Lord's karma, for the light that he has set in motion is the effect of primal cause. And therefore, you claim the burden of the Lord, and it is the burden of light that transmutes the burden of karma.

This very mystery of the Holy Grail was given to me in those very hours when I submitted myself to Sanat Kumara, to Alpha and Omega. Following my death at the hand of Cain,[2] I went before the LORD God, seeing full well what would come upon the generations of earth. It was then that I volunteered to be the one who would redeem them from that fall. And I was placed under Lord Maitreya, who overshadowed me in each succeeding incarnation.[3] And through him I knew the Lord Gautama, who preceded me in the manifestation of the light of the East. And through him, I was constantly aware of the Ancient of Days.

CHALLENGE THE MOMENTUM OF ANTI-GOD IN THE PLANETARY BODY

My beloved hearts, the vow to defeat the fallen ones is a serious vow. Not many have made it. Certainly you could not expect children to take on such a responsibility. Of whom do I speak when I speak of children? It is those who have enjoyed the playground of the universes for aeons. They have enjoyed it so much that they have not elected to become joint heirs with my mission, with the eternal Christ. They desire to be cared for rather than to care for. Thus, beloved ones, you will not hear them knocking at the door of the Ancient of Days and saying, "I will go and confront the Adversary."

What do you think the test was like when I stood as David before Goliath?[4] What do you think—with sling in hand, my only defense, a single try at that third eye of the fallen one?

Beloved ones, I had prepared long. I knew that if I would one day confront Satan directly, I must now confront him in the flesh in this fallen one and overcome the fear of his size and his roaring and his momentum of all of the hordes of death and hell who accompanied him on that day.

My beloved, Sanat Kumara, through Lord Maitreya, gives to us the preparation for our tests one by one in useful order, and always the preparation is full and complete. And yet, so many, my beloved, who are called cannot be chosen. For after they have received the Word and the teaching, when they must face one of these fallen ones, I tell you, often they are defeated by a minor devil, for the false hierarchy does not even deign to send a superior member to many of these individuals. When, then, will they confront the Adversary?

Justice in the earth must come through those who know they are joint heirs, who have had enough of the round of human pleasure, who realize that life is short, that the comings and goings of souls are swift, that time is elusive, space a compartment of consciousness, and all that matters is the Reality of God, God, God.

The joint heirs of my mantle must drink the full cup. It is the cup of world karma. It is the cup of joy. And it is the cup of the betrayal of the fallen ones. Willingness to bear the burden of the little ones who are yet children is the bearing of world karma. Willingness to bear the spirit of the resurrection to offset that karma is the cup of joy. Willingness to confront the Adversary is the cup of betrayal.

My beloved, I will not tell you that the Path is easy or simple. But I will tell you that it is sheer joy and the wonder of the stars, that it is intense love that would almost cause your heart to break for the sacrifices it requires you to make. But just before it breaks, lo the descent of the ruby ray! And your heart expands and a new capacity for love enables you to transcend former attachments. And you press on, and by the very pressing on, you have eliminated entire legions of darkness and contingents of fallen ones. They are behind you. They are no longer in your class. You have outclassed them.

And so as you approach the light of the absolute God, remember that he, too, has his adversary, his counterpoint. And therefore, you will challenge the anti-God in the beast that was and is not and yet is,[5] the beast that was not, yet it was. That beast is the entire momentum of anti-God in the planetary body.

Precious hearts, I come with a very simple thought, a thought which must dawn upon those who will by and by realize that they are indeed called to be avatars. And the thought is this—that inasmuch as these serpents have plagued our Father's children for these aeons and inasmuch as you have attempted to defeat them halfheartedly while yet compromising with the world and have not succeeded, would it not be better to give to this life and to a few short years the ultimate of God consciousness to consume the anti-God, so that these little ones may come out from under the boulders of their condemnation with the joy of new birth and discover that they, too, have the intrinsic worth to be joint heirs, as you are with me and with my light.

Beloved ones, we have spoken of the failure syndrome. I would awaken you and quicken you from a momentum in which you have become accustomed to trying and then to failing and then to saying, "Well, at least we tried." To this you have often heard El Morya reply, "It is not enough to try. You must *will* to win! You must accomplish and *that* without the stain of sin."

Do you see, beloved ones? There are many in the earth today who are forlorn. They expect to fail. They expect the fallen ones to win. They expect that their voices will not be heard. And they carry on the lamentations of the prophet Jeremiah.[6]

Beloved ones, the days of lamentation have passed. This is the day of joy—joy in the Lord that a son of God *can* be born under the protection of the angels and the aegis of Alpha and Omega, that a son of God can pass through the initiations of the sacred fire in the very midst of the laggard camp, the Middle East, the very forcefield of the fallen ones.

THE CUP OF THE POISON OF SERPENT

I was not sent to an island in the South Seas. I was sent into the very midst of Armageddon, and that Armageddon was being waged long before I journeyed to that point. And the Armageddon of earth is always against the Mother light. For the light of the earth *is* the Mother. The light of the earth *is* the light that the Woman places in the heart of her seed.

Understand, then, that the great white light in the cube of Jerusalem, in the very place of that holy church which now commemorates the place of my birth—that light of the incarnation, that light of the Woman—is the forcefield in Matter that interacts, by the figure-eight flow, with the Temple of the Resurrection and the Holy City over Jerusalem.[7]

That light is coveted by the fallen ones. They camp upon its doorstep. They bask in its light. But they can never assimilate it until they bend the knee and confess that because a single son of God is victorious, so can they be God-victorious.

They have drunk of the cup of the poison of Serpent. They have believed the lie that that poisonous philosophy is sufficient unto their salvation. Beloved ones, you must understand that it is a deadly cup, able to turn the mind and heart of unbelievers entirely to the path of the fallen ones.

Precious hearts, the healing of the earth from the poison of Serpent would be more important to us, if it could be, than the judgment of Serpent and his seed. But it cannot be, for we must root out the cause and core. But, beloved, we do not rejoice in the judgment of the fallen ones. We rejoice in the salvation of the lost sheep, and they are lost because of the poison of Serpent. It manifests in all levels—chemically, alchemically, on the astral plane and the mental plane, even penetrating the lower etheric body.

Now you will understand how some can be so turned out of the way. There is literally a venom, which is why these fallen ones have been compared to snakes. Their poisonous venom, insidiously penetrating the rational mind and the corrupt astral levels of consciousness, polarizes the individual to the anti-God momentum of the beast. And thereby they pursue the work and the word of the beast. And they are brainwashed and they have become automatons to the beast. But some of these once had a soul and a free will and once stood before the Ancient of Days petitioning opportunity for life in the earth.

THE WHOLESALE JUDGMENT WILL COME ONLY WHEN GOD'S CHILDREN HAVE BEEN RESCUED

Beloved ones, if it were so simple that all who do the works of the Devil were of him, then the judgment could descend and divide the tares and the wheat. But as a matter of fact, the LORD God has spared this planetary body generation after generation because of the falling away of the children of the light. And if they were to be judged in this hour, they too would go the way of the seed of the wicked.

Our Father is so concerned with the salvation of the children of the light that it does not concern him to allow the tares to go unchecked or the seed of the wicked to increase their practices of wickedness. For he is looking to the day when not one but many sons of light will come and judge them and rescue his children. And only when his children have been rescued and separated out from among them is he willing to allow the descent of the wholesale judgment of the seed of the generation of vipers. Understand, then, that it is not mercy to the seed of the wicked but compassion and limitless understanding of the children of God who are lost.

Think of yourselves, any one of you, in this or a previous life when you might have been caught up in even a portion of this poisonous philosophy and way of life. Think if when you were in that situation suddenly the worlds were to have been judged. Where would you have stood without the knowledge of your mighty I AM Presence? Where would you have stood were the light to have suddenly descended and said to the entire evolution: "It is finished; as you are, so shall you be as you transfer from earth to heaven; he that is filthy, let him be filthy still"?[8]

WHY DOES GOD ALLOW INJUSTICE?

And so, my beloved, the question is asked: Why does God allow it? Why does he allow the injustice? Why does he allow enough war and murder and crime and outrageous behavior to cause such a burden upon God's people?

He allows them free rein so that the children of the light will wake up and realize that life is not a game, that unless they act, and act swiftly in time and space, evil will go unchecked. He allows it so that the children of light may learn from the nefarious deeds of the seed of the wicked that which is the true course and that which is the false.

All around you the wages of sin and of the works of the Devil are obvious. And therefore, you do not have to experience their way to see its end result—debilitation, degeneration, the loss of mind and heart and soul. It happens everywhere in life so that the children of light will wake up and choose a better goal.

God allows the injustice to spur on his sons and daughters, who would rather perhaps engage their talents in art and creativity and noble sculpture and literature, who must be called from their meanderings in his Great Causal Body as they experiment with truth and enjoy the vast contents of his mind. These sons and daughters must be quickened to the understanding that unless and until the fallen ones are judged, there is no surety of salvation unto the children of the light and there is no fulfillment of the path of their initiation.

Therefore putting all these things aside, the sons and daughters of God in the earth who truly assess the times and the signs of the seasons, they, then, will put on my garment and do those things which are most important. This is why God allows it. God allows it because of their own free will.

In the bliss of communion with him, they have not chosen the light. And therefore, they are placed in a planetary body where there is great darkness so that by contrast they may know what is their heart's desire. This simple understanding is a comfort to all of the ascended masters, but it has not been understood by many. The people do not understand why there is not simply a reign of peace, for I have come and I have come as the Prince of Peace. They do not understand that were this to be true before they had exercised free will and gained their wings, they themselves would descend into a not-peace—a *not-peace,* which is the absence of the disciplines of peace, a neutral zone which gradually degenerates into war itself through the departure from the necessity to forge and win the victory of life.

My beloved ones, our Father has waited for the coming of this seed. I have foreseen your coming. The events of the coming year and of the decade will rest upon the sons and daughters of God upon earth, the children of the light who have moved into their niche of cosmic responsibility. According to your implementation of the will of God unto the judgment of the fallen ones, so will there be the acceleration of light, so will there be the shortening of the days for the elect of God.[9]

RECEIVE THE GRAIL THAT I AM

The authority of God in the earth is always vested in the Son. And so it is that I place my mantle once again upon you as my apostles and overseers and true shepherds of my people.

My heart is yearning for my flocks to return to me. Feed, then, my sheep with the food that they are able to receive. But keep the sacred mysteries for the inner service, which they do not understand or perceive. Let the sacred mysteries be for those who understand the meaning of the Holy Grail.

> *I AM the Grail presence in the midst of Israel. I AM the Holy Grail in the advent of life, life aborning within my children. I transfer the Grail that I AM to my sons and*

daughters in the earth. I elevate you to assume the mantle that all who hear my Word, whose souls quiver with the Word of the Son of God, receive, then, my Call! Receive my Word! Receive the Grail!

I AM come. I stand in your midst. I stand for the rebirth of my own flame in your hearts.

Now, my beloved, I take my leave of you. For wist ye not that I must be about my Father's business[10] throughout the earth and the solar systems and the galaxies?

I bid you, be about our Father's business as we together span the highways and, from across the universes, catch one another's eye and say:

All is well. I AM the watchman of the Lord where I AM. I AM THAT I AM. I AM the Son of God on earth and in heaven. I AM the Holy Grail. And I give to all who will follow me in the living Word to drink of my blood that is the ruby ray. And to them I give to eat of my body, which is the ascended master light body of all worlds.

Lo, I AM come! I AM the light of worlds! I span the starry bodies! I magnify my being to hold within my garment all of the sheep of my pastures and all of the true pastors of my sheep.

In the name of our Father, in the name of my Mother, in the name of the Holy Spirit, in the name of the Son, whose light I AM, I AM with you alway, even unto the end of the world that is unreal and to the beginning of the world that *is* Real in Israel this day.

I AM your Jesus, always in the Christ.

December 25, 1979
Camelot
Los Angeles County, California
ECP

CHAPTER 16

*By the labor of the hands is there the flow of the Holy Spirit
and does that flow increase. By the labor of the hands
is grace measured, whether the devotion of the heart
be unto the Person of the Comforter or whether it be upon
lesser conditions and circumstances.*

CHAPTER 16

REKINDLING THE ESSENTIAL IDENTITY OF EVERY LIVING SOUL

Hail, children of the light, sons of God! Hail, threefold flames that ignite the fire of creation in all the earth in the hearts of my own!

Ye are the salt of the earth. But the salt that has lost its savor, wherewith shall it be salted? Therefore if the light that is in thee be darkness, how great is that darkness![1]

Light, my beloved, is the essential resource of life. Come down from the Father as the crystal clear stream of immortality, men have fashioned out of it their mortality—their sense of limitation and their correspondent limitations. Therefore if the essential light be compromised, where is that light but covered with a shroud of death?

For this cause I AM come into the world[2]—to give birth once again to eternal life by rekindling the essential identity of every living soul.

I take this Easter to call sinners to repentance worldwide,[3] for the preaching from the pulpits is either an intense fear tactic of hellfire and damnation or it is the whitewashing by sympathetic magnetism of the misdeeds of my children. Therefore where are the prophets in the land and where are the preachers of righteousness who will deliver to my children that light in its original intensity—that sacred fire that is the salt that has remained pure, that light that has not been misqualified into darkness?

We are come—the saints in white, the Lamb and the Lamb's wife,[4] beloved Mary, Saint Germain, beloved Magda. We stand to bear witness of the path of the ascension, of which the resurrection spiral is the natural and essential fulfillment. And from that beginning unto that ending the sacred fire must be nourished and tended, and the sheep of my flock must be led and God-taught in the way and the truth and the life of the light itself.[5]

Ye are children of the light, therefore walk in the light. And do not consider that transgressions are overlooked because someone is a chosen one. My beloved, our devotion is to the very first principles of the essential ingredient of the spark of life, and there is no compromise with compromise. There is no compromise of the eternal law of life. Yes, strait and narrow, strait and narrow is the way and the gate that leadeth to everlasting life.[6]

THE MIGHTY RHYTHM OF COSMOS INUNDATES THE WORK OF THE HANDS

Let those, then, who believe on the One Sent[7] understand the perpetual wave of light that comes as the mighty rhythm of cosmos to inundate the work of the hands. For by the labor of the hands is there the flow of the Holy Spirit and does that flow increase. By the labor of the hands is grace measured, whether the devotion of the heart be unto the Person of the Comforter[8] or whether it be upon lesser conditions and circumstances.

Therefore within the community of the Holy Spirit, my beloved, the sacred labor is accelerating sacred fire. It is not the projects that consume the man, it is the man who by sacred fire consumes the projects.

I wish to say, therefore, that the intensity of light begets the work that is ongoing—the work of the ages and the mighty cause of life.

And those who bear the light up the mountain are those who have the vision of those greater works which are done because ye believe in me[9]—that I AM the living Christ, I AM the living Saviour in the earth because I dwell in the hearts of my true disciples.

Therefore I come and I admonish you to contemplate the greater works, for by these the wave of light intensifies in the earth. And that sacred fire pulsating from the Sacred Heart of the Mother is a fire that impels you to precipitate the diamond of my heart for the crystallization of the mist. For unless the mist be crystallized, wherefore shall a mighty work appear? And wherefore shall the words and works come for judgment? After all, life is not the idling of the motors of Be-ness.

Beloved hearts, let those who have light and life and the knowledge of the sacred centers of being, let them spin the wheels of the chakras! Let them engage the gears of the chakras with the gears of the mind of God! Let them accept the fiat to let that mind be in you which was also in me![10] After all, these words read over and over again from carefully prepared Bibles, gilded edges, and all that which goes with the preservation of the letter are no more alive than the pure in heart, are no more alive than the love brought to them by those who commune in love.

My beloved, take care that you do not mistake the recitation of the Word for the doing of the Word. A simple message of Eastertide, yet how many are resurrected with me this day? I tell you, all too few upon the earth. They are much more concerned with outer awareness and have not the essential meaning of the resurrection flame. They have abandoned the path of fasting and prayer. They have not understood the raising up of that light or what it can do to transform a civilization and a single heart aflame with love.

My beloved, the hour is urgent and the urgency is unto the quick and the dead.[11] And the dead sense the urgency as they are in the consciousness of death. And therefore those leaders of the nations assemble, solemnly deliberating the fate of the planetary body and concluding that all is already lost and therefore they will make a pretense and a pretext for attempting to do something about the economy, something about war, something about Communism yet in their hearts they have not the ability nor the light nor the love to work a mighty change for God. For the work of their hands has never been blessed by the grace of God, for they never have consecrated that work unto the grace of the Almighty and therefore they are found wanting.

Yet they prance about, looking as though they were the wise ones when they have displaced the children of the light because the children of the light have allowed them to displace them, and therefore the earth is in a sorry plight. And there are those who lean upon the hollow root, and the hollow root can provide nothing but a stream of air unqualified by the sacred fire breath. Thus it is to the Holy Spirit that I direct your attention this hour.

DRAWING SOULS OF LIGHT UNTO THE LAMB IS THE WORK OF THE AGES

This moment of the resurrection flame and its rising tide in the earth must not be, after all, a mighty wave and a river that is parted by individuals standing in the midst who are not moved by it, who do not receive it, who do not allow it to pass through them. But this mighty wave of light must then be for the quick who understand the urgency of the hour and are not in a state of anxiety.

Do not fear and tremble as the devils who are brought to the Final Judgment, but let the sons and daughters of God who recognize the appearing of Messiah come to the fore and realize that all is not lost. All indeed can be saved, but it must be saved by the essential light of the native divinity of the sons of God!

By the flame that I AM, I charge you with my light and I challenge you to no longer be content to watch this stream of events and not to set yourselves up as that focal point of that light of which I declared, "And I, if I be lifted up, shall draw all men unto me."[12]

The drawing of the souls of light unto the Lamb is the work of the ages—of Sanat Kumara, of most blessed and beloved Maitreya, my very own sponsor and Guru. It is the very light of Gautama.

O essential hearts beating with the heart of God, the very purity of your heart-fire and your devotion to God is a sustaining principle in the earth, whereas all of those who gather together as those who are already the dead cannot, cannot contain the light—not to save their own souls and not to save the nations.

Therefore let us not lean upon the hollow root or the reed, but let us turn our attention to the fire of John the Baptist and see his prophecy of the coming of the fiery baptism of the Holy Spirit.[13]

Why do you think that I breathed upon them the Holy Ghost?[14] Because without it there is no life. And in the absence of the Son of God incarnate to sustain life by the Guru-chela relationship, those disciples who are left must have the Holy Ghost. Therefore I said, "Tarry ye in the city of Jerusalem, until ye be endued with power from on high."[15] For within that city the sustaining forcefield of my own lifestream would keep them until they might be filled with the fullness of the descent of the white fire of my own being.

And therefore if you have not the Holy Ghost, God the Father and the Son are not indwelling in you and the Spirit is not in you. And dare you say that you, then, are counted among the dead? Or dare you say that you are counted among the quick? Or are you somewhere between?

THE SOUL'S SALVATION IN GOD IS DIRECTLY DEPENDENT UPON ITS OWN APPLICATION OF THE LAW

There is an urgency in seeking and finding the Lord Maha Chohan, and some of you do not sense that urgency as though somehow you were held in a cradle or a swaddling garment and all would be well if you just sort of move along with the crowd and follow a certain ritual. Well, the Path is for striving and not for entertainment. The Path is for a sacred ritual whereby the individual infuses a flame into the exercise of the Word. Those who do not engage their hearts into the service therefore cannot reap the sacred fire of the heart of God.

Who do you think will win your ascension for you if you do not? By cosmic law I cannot. And if it were not so, I would have told you and long ago demonstrated for you the great drawing up of the saints into the ascension current. Therefore listen to me, my beloved.

You are preparing for the dark night of the soul and the dark night of the Spirit where your messengers have gone before you and the saints have walked. This is the sustainment of the threefold flame and the momentum of light within your temple in that hour when you must be tested to see whether or not you will turn away from all temptation and all temptation to do the anti-will of God and by the momentum of your own God-mastery and threefold flame so sustain the Principle and the Person of the Trinity without reinforcement from the heavenly octaves.

This surely is the necessary path and it will come to all. And in that hour you will not be able to call upon this or that friend or upon the messengers. Not even the angels of heaven could intercede with me as I went through the dark night of the Spirit upon that cross. Not until I had demonstrated that victory could they gather again and surround me with their healing love and their balm.

My beloved, there is a moment of aloneness when the soul must understand its salvation in God is directly dependent upon its own application of the Law. And this is the lie of the fallen ones that they have put abroad in the land, convincing all of Christendom that the mere acceptance of my name is salvation. Truly it is the beginning of the Path, but it is not the ending.

Therefore seek the fulfillment of the whole law.[16] Seek the fulfillment of the Law, my beloved, I adjure you. For the understanding of what is coming upon the earth—what I have set forth and what has been written in scripture—must surely make you to understand that the need for survival and salvation must be placed squarely upon the shoulders of the individual soul's application to the personal Christ within and to the mighty I AM Presence.

In each day, therefore, be satisfied when you have established the mighty current and flow between your heart and the heart of God by love and by devotion. Do not put your head to rest at night when you are in a state of disquietude, anxiety, when you are not conscious of the biding Presence of God. You can establish that contact in a moment, a microsecond, or perhaps it will take longer if you have wandered farther from the center of your being during the day. Do not think that sleep will take from you the cares of life; sleep will only multiply and augment those cares, as you are not in God-control when you are absent from the body. This is a great travesty against the Godhead and ought not to be tolerated by the disciples of the light.

There is a certain self-discipline on the Path. And when you think that no one is looking or watching or telling you what to do, you must not go into a passive state of simply allowing life or nature or circumstance to be the bulwark of your protection. There is no protection in Matter. There is no protection outside of the Holy Spirit.

Therefore seek the LORD. For the Comforter is come, is among you even in this hour—the mighty Person of the Holy Ghost. And therefore that Person must be your companion until you are so prepared and cleansed that at any hour of the day or night that Person of the Comforter may enter your temple, coming and going at will and finding habitation in earth.

YE ARE TEMPLES DESIGNED TO BE THE HOUSE OF THE LORD

Thus may the just be made pure by love. May they live by faith and hope and the good works of charity's love. Thus may your heart be perfected in love that the light of the eternal Saviour may enter in, that the Guru may come and go and find that habitation.[17] For he is most blest whose temple is prepared and the fitting habitation of the Holy Spirit and of the Guru. Therefore strive, for ye are temples designed to be the house of the Lord.[18]

As I contemplate the sweet mystery of life, the mystery of love in all of its multiplication of the inner radiance of the Father and the Son, I am mindful of the endearing relationships of my many incarnations—speaking first and foremost of Lord Maitreya and Gautama and of my Father, the Ancient of Days, speaking of my beloved and so many of you whom I have never forgotten who have stood by me in each of these successive incarnations leading to a greater and greater intensification of the spiral of victory.

I would commune with my friends. Therefore I have come to the place prepared—to Camelot, my home, to a sanctuary openly, unabashedly consecrated to the mysteries of the Holy Grail. I have come, for I have sponsored many knights of the flame and ladies ministering unto the heart of God. I have sponsored Arthur and Merlin, Launcelot, Guenevere, and all who participated in that early manifestation whereby the consecration of life was unto my Blessed Mother and to the mystery of the Christos unfolding the initiation of the white light through the sacred cup.

Let the cup, then, be extended. From my heart I take the cup of the Last Supper and I give you to drink.[19] So is the manifestation of that cup my gift of life this Eastertide. I give to you the elixir of the resurrection flame as I share with you my boundless joy in life begetting victory unto victory.

The love that we have known and shared, the love of the hundred forty and four thousand[20] and so many of the precious children of God, forms a link passing through time and space unto eternity and unto the very throne of Alpha and Omega. I am touched by your devotion and your service to my father Joseph, to my mother Mary, and to all of the saints who have gone before.

LIFT UP THE LIGHT OF THE RESURRECTION WITHIN YOU

I bless you with the joy of the white lilies abroad in the land. I bless you with the joy of the cosmic cross of white fire. I take you by the hand and I lead you into paths of righteousness for the sake of the I AM THAT I AM and its manifest presence in the Christ within you.[21]

O souls of my heart, souls of my heart, hear my Call! Hear my Call and enter into new life and the acceleration of love. For our outpouring of the resurrection flame in this hour is to counteract the darkness of the Dark Cycle moving onward, then, into the return of the misqualified energies under the hierarchy of Sagittarius.

Beware, then, the momentums of anti-victory. Beware, then, of that which would turn against the light and the lightbearer. All of this must be swallowed up in the essence of your own resurrection. And if you lift up the light of the resurrection within you by Christ, so you will draw into that mighty spiral that darkness which will be translated into light and thereby seize from the toilers their very weapons that they would use against the light. Seizing them, transmute them, and let the light go forth to consume their darkness—to check it, to challenge it, to bind them, and to put down the oppressors of my children in the earth.

O rising tide of resurrection's glory, rising tide of resurrection's glory, angels of the light, angels of the light and the ageless story of my victory, I come forth. I come forth in the name of God. And I sound the Word for the raising up of the rod, the rod of Jesse[22] within you whereby the resurrection spiral is become the manifest presence of your own Godhood, your own Real Self.

Lo, I AM come! Lo, my Word is true! Lo, I have spoken it unto you! Lo, I seal you in the fire of the Holy Spirit! Seek the Person of the Holy Ghost. Seek the LORD within and come into newness of life. This is my admonishment and my Easter joy.

Now, my children, come unto me that I may bless you and fill you with my light.[23]

By the hand of God, I seal you as of old. I seal you for the hour of your overcoming of the last vestiges of sin and the sense of sin. I seal you for the hour when the tempter and the toiler comes. I seal you for the hour of the moment of union.

In the name of the Father, in the name of the Son and the Holy Spirit, let the threefold flame expand. In the name of the Mother, let the glorious light of the Cosmic Christ appear in the Manchild.[24]

April 6, 1980
Camelot
Los Angeles County, California
ECP

CHAPTER 17

*It is not necessary that all of the people understand
either the mystery of the Word or the nature of Antichrist....
Once the exposure has come, once there is a cross section
of the people who denounce it and therefore choose rightly
that they will serve the living God—then the action
of the violet flame will erase it utterly!*

CHAPTER 17

"ALMOST FREE!"

The New Era of the Rising Son of Righteousness

Come, my beloved. Sit thou upon my right hand. For I would sup with thee in glory.

I AM thy Lord and thy Saviour. I have come to thy home of light nestled here in the heart of America. I have come to be with you to sing praise unto the Ancient of Days and all who are our mutual sponsors of light. I AM here because I AM at home in Bethany, in the house of light tended by holy women and by the very heart of my own beloved Mother.

I AM with you for the celebration of the victorious light now manifest in the heart of the messenger—and from that heart into thy heart and into all America. I come to bear witness unto the resurrection of life here, now, within her, that you might know that a mighty work of the ages has been performed by Saint Germain and others of the ascended hosts who have kindled a more than ordinary light that the prophecy might be fulfilled of a Woman who stands in the land holding on high the torch of freedom and bearing in her heart the gift of God that is the Manchild.

I come, then, to rebuke those upon the face of the earth who do not desire to see the day of her coming in my name, preaching my Word and my light, vesting others with that healing light.

I rebuke the proud spirits who have hated our light from the beginning, who have desired not to see the victory of each and every saint. With this miracle of light proclaimed to you by Saint Germain,[1] there is come the end of an era of Serpent's power and the beginning of the new era of the rising Sun of righteousness[2] in all of my children.

You look with joy and with deliberation upon the victory, which is even a surprise unto those who are called to bear Victory's flame. Yet I confirm and I witness that it is always so—that when one son or daughter of God is raised up, there is the raising up of many nations.

THE PILLAR OF FIRE THAT IS THE LIVING TRUTH— THE VORTEX OF ASCENSION'S FLAME

The ascended hosts assemble, then, to give glory to God and to acknowledge that the Highest is in manifest form. And therefore opportunity—in a very physical sense—within these octaves *is* come because beloved Saint Germain has secured from Alpha and Omega this dispensation. And I affirm it to you because of the blasphemous ones who will deny it! Therefore I affirm it again. And by my Word that is truth I allow you to share in this most intimate cup of our communion—that truly this victory is won that earth and her evolutions might be spared a long night of terror.

Thus let those who have shared in the cup of sorrow as well as the cup of joy also be vindicated. For there is a need for hearts who have defended our name in the face of most intense adversity to know that by this grace that has come through my heart to the messenger, all who are truly tied in love to her are also brought to Victory's crown—themselves the laurel wreath and the very components of this community that is the mystical body of myself. Thus I infuse you with my body and with my blood as light's essence intensifying!

Wherefore judge not, lest ye be judged.[3] Wherefore *judge righteous judgment*[4] and discern the pillar of fire that is the living truth that truly is the vortex of ascension's flame, of which you may be a part if you do not defame that flame that I have determined to place where this messenger stands, truly anchored in soul and heart and body.

Thus, beloved ones, a new era of light dawns and with it a new era of persecution as the fallen ones make mockery of the truth of this flaming Word that I AM. Thus *let the record stand* as hierarchy has affirmed it that truly here is the balance of 100 percent of karma of this lifestream that thereby the full cross of planetary karma might be borne through devoted, loving, and obedient chelas. For this is the karma that may be taken—that which is of the disciples of my heart who love and continue to love and to believe on the one that I have sent.[5]

We will see the vindication of Magda through this ministry and all of the defamation of the very name of that beloved one whom you have known and loved as Aimee Semple McPherson. Truly there will be the vindication of Mary, embodied as Mary Baker Eddy, and every soul of my heart whom I have sent forth, each and every saint who has wrought the miracles of healing, of resurrection, and of life.

Thus the liberty that is manifest must be turned into the very forcefields where my children are captive to every form of malpractice and Satanism. I therefore direct this ray of liberty immediately into the cause and core of the rising rate of murder in this City of the Angels. And I expose to you that which has not been understood by those in embodiment who serve on the police force of this city and as guardians of life in America.

It is clear that the ministry of the two witnesses has set itself toward the exposure and the binding and the casting out of Serpent and his seed who are called "the Liar," who have spawned the lie from the beginning. This is one branch of the false hierarchy and of its sinister force implemented by all others.

THE FUSION OF YOUR SOUL WITH YOUR MIGHTY I AM PRESENCE IS THAT WHICH IS OPPOSED BY THE FALLEN ONES

Let us turn our attention, then, to those members of the false hierarchy that come under the name of Satan. And they are called Satanists because they embody the principle of murder and the murderous intent. It is, my beloved, their intent to murder all those who are the offspring of God, to murder Truth in its inception, and, above all, to murder the Mother and Child.

The philosophy of Satanism has been spawned in America in the tearing down of woman. Everywhere where the noble archetype of womanhood is torn down, there is the practice of Satanism, there are the astral hordes as legions of Satan. Though he himself be behind bars on Sirius,[6] yet, I tell you, those who are his sympathizers, those who yet have the sense of injustice that life has not given to Satan himself the fullness of the cup of justice—these are abroad in the land defending this Murderer and his murderous intent among the children of the light.

Let it be realized, then, that wherever there is the tearing down of the feminine principle of the Godhead as the soul of every lifestream, as the Mother of the World, as Mary, my own Mother—there you will find this murderous intent. Wherever the light of the Virgin is greatest, there will the fallen ones assail.

This City of the Angels was dedicated to my Mother. It is the city of Mother Mary, the Queen of the Angels. Her very name is enshrined in the ethers. Her very image is breathed by all of elemental life. This is the city of my Mother, my Queen, and the Blessed One of Promise. Therefore for the redemption of her flame I have sent the messenger and all of you to camp within its walls, here within this forcefield, that you might raise up the Mother light. And therefore it is in this city of the New Jerusalem[7] that I have bidden you to tarry!

I bade you come and you have come—and here you will tarry

until you be endued with power from on high.[8] And that power from on high is the power of the blessed Father and the Son and the Holy Spirit that meets the bride of the Trinity midair. And therefore this city where my own beloved Magda preached is the city where souls can rise on the great pillar of resurrection flame established here millennia ago.

The rising up of souls in this city to meet the Great God Presence and the Great God flame is the miraculous manifestation of the Father and the Son and the Holy Spirit. This fusion, then, of your soul with your mighty I AM Presence is that which is opposed by the fallen ones. And they have the deliberate intent, the murderous intent, to stop the rising of souls before they can enter into the white-fire core of the light of the ages.

Beloved hearts, therefore with the intensification of the light is the intensification of the fallen ones who are the opponents of the Mother. Thus Satan has vowed his vow against my own beloved Mother Mary, against Magda, against this messenger and the two witnesses, and each and every one of you and your children and your children's children, that they should not receive the impetus of freedom from the heart of Saint Germain and of the resurrection flame from my own heart.

Therefore this day as you have tarried in the sanctuary of the Holy Grail, keeping the vigil in the very city where the hordes of darkness seek to press in against the light, my angels have been abuilding with Saint Germain's a mighty pillar-action of the braiding of the light of the resurrection flame, the violet flame, and the ruby ray. And this pillar of fire is specifically for the raising up of souls of light on its very coils that you might experience dominion —that dominion that comes because the soul is fused with the mighty I AM Presence!

Now lean upon the arm of the LORD and lean upon the breast of the Mother and realize that it is this fusion that we have desired to see take place in the physical octave. And that is why it became necessary for the mandate of light to come forth through Saint Germain and my own heart for the removal of the last vestiges of karma of the messenger that one might stand in this fusion in the physical octave.

When that karma is balanced, beloved ones, there is no longer any thing that stands between the soul and the Holy of Holies. The veil is rent in twain.[9] The soul and the I AM Presence are fused as one. Thus those who are the fallen ones who have the murderous intent may direct all of their venom, their momentum of hate and hate creation, against that light that now becomes not only symbolical but actual as the point of glory and victory for each and every one of you.

IN THE RAISING UP OF THE LIGHT, THERE IS ANTI-LIGHT

We have no favorite sons or daughters. We raise up the single lifestream that all might be raised. Therefore "God is no respecter of persons."[10] And those who hear my word must understand this word by the Holy Spirit and not by the outer questioning mind. For this *is* the mystery of the Word incarnate within you! This mystery must be displayed and portrayed.

Understand, then, that when the resurrection flame is nigh, it raises up darkness and light that all might come to the surface. And therefore the resurrection flame is manifest to bring to the very surface of men's minds the point/counterpoint of the Law, the Christ/the Antichrist, that all might see the choices of life and by the action of the ruby ray know that which is cosmic justice. For the ruby ray and the intensity of love imparts the power of discernment whereby discernment of true justice is understood.

It is justice that there might be opportunity for the raising up of not one son of God but many sons of God in this hour. *This,* my beloved, is cosmic justice!

Therefore in the raising up of the light, there is anti-light.

The ruby ray gives you the power of discrimination. And the violet flame is for the instantaneous alchemy of consuming that error when that error is *seen* as error—when it is exposed and when men make choices to cast it out into the everlasting sacred fire!

Understand, then, that that violet flame does not act to consume the cause and core of the Liar and the lie or the Murderer and his murderous intent until some among the people can *see* the truth and *claim* the truth and therefore know that by conscious deliberation—"Come now, let us reason together, saith the LORD"[11]—they have arrived at the principle of Truth whereby all error is vanquished!

It is not necessary that all of the people understand either the mystery of the Word or the nature of Antichrist. But it is necessary that the remnant encamped within this city of light *see* and *know* and *accept* the truth that is Truth and call for the judgment of the error that is error and that is embodied among the satanic councils and those who are the seed of the wicked. Once the exposure has come, once there is a cross section of the people who denounce it and therefore choose rightly that they will serve the living God—then the action of the violet flame will erase it utterly!

For there must be initiation in the community. *There must be the telling of the Word!* There must be a foundation for right choice in the future when this class, this graduating class in the resurrection flame, are no longer in physical embodiment and others must come to the fore and pass similar tests and the temptations of the fallen ones.

Beloved hearts of light, therefore understand that now is the hour when you can turn your attention—by the love and the initiation of the Lord Sanat Kumara—to the Satanists and their murderous intent not only in the City of the Angels but in every city upon earth. For truly, bloodshed is the sign of that Fallen One who relinquished his individual responsibility to outpicture the fullness of the Godhead through that universal Christ who I AM.

Realize, beloved one, that this moment of irresponsibility is the moment when the Antichrist is born. Therefore murder is the ultimate act of irresponsibility, the failure to support life in all of its manifestations from the least unto the greatest—from the child aborning in the womb unto the man who has the right to walk down the streets of the cities of this earth unto the woman who has a right to be free to be with her children, buoyed up in the light, and to roam this earth because it is our LORD's and the fullness thereof.[12]

Beloved hearts, therefore let this defense of life *be* the mark of true justice and its cosmic sense! Let the sense of justice begin with the defense of life where you are. I say, Cast out the Satanists from this temple of the living Word! Cast them out of America! Cast them out of the hearts of my people! Cast down the carnal mind that would enthrone itself in place of the living Christ!

By the Holy Spirit I come and I show to you that, even as there has been for a number of years the momentum of the buildup of light that has culminated in this vortex of victory in the heart of the messenger, even so there has been the raising of the hand of the fallen ones in defiance of that light! And therefore millions have suffered by the wanton murder of these satanic hordes, sometimes embodied and sometimes moving through those who have not claimed their own right to the threefold flame of life.

Yes, the right to life is the right to have a threefold flame and to have that flame expand through the path of discipleship. This is the right to life that we defend! We do not defend that life which is turned into death by the fallen ones and then made the foundation of demands for justice here and justice there in defense of those who are the spoilers of my people and of the nations.

DOUBT THAT ASSAILS COMES IN THE VERY NIGHT BEFORE YOUR VICTORY

Let mercy abound in your heart. Understand the momentum of doubt that assails every one of you who would be fused to me in the Piscean dispensation whereby I impart to you the flame of my own God-mastery.

You have heard a number of dictations on this very substance. Beloved hearts, it is pitted against your God flame and against your soul. It cannot touch you once you have entered into the fusion with your own Christ Self that must precede the fusion of your soul with your mighty I AM Presence. Therefore, doubt that assails comes in the very night before your victory, the very night before your initiation.

Did not doubt assail me in the Garden of Gethsemane?[13] Did not all the hordes of the planetary momentum of death assail me as I myself would face the hour of apparent death? Beloved hearts of light, they did. And I will tell you that our Father has provided the solution to this entire momentum of death and doubt and fear. It is the love, the very love of the will of God.

For when you love God's will so very much that you will give your life for it and you will lay down your life for it, the will of God appears to you as the very Person of our Father. And therefore the Christ of your heart cries out, "Abba! Father!"[14] and the crying out unto the Father as the very personification of the will of God results in this fusion of the Son of God with the mighty I AM Presence. And therefore that Son may go forth on the morrow and subject himself to the fallen ones and to the crucifixion that it might be proclaimed that the cosmic cross of white fire is truly the mark of the victory of the Son of God and is truly the proof that life *is* the victor over hell and death!

Realize then that the more you are assailed by doubt, the more you are rubbing noses with serpents and Satanists. For they press their faces of mockery against the windowpanes of the soul and thereby their distorted and grotesque features appear in the night, pretenders to some reality of angelic heights. They are nothing but harbingers of doom and failure and the failure syndrome. And you must be at the invincible point of the cosmic sword, at the very edge where life descends. And in a clap of thunder and lightning that life itself, because of your affirmation of the will of God, *does* strike the deathblow unto these hordes that assail you and your permanent identity!

I have seen the fallen ones send their "destroyer"—their imitator of the Holy Spirit—into the very face of the Mother. I have seen all of these tests and the temptations of Satan himself. Beloved hearts, I have watched and I have upheld the immaculate conception of her victory although many of the Brotherhood have not been allowed to intercede, for each son of God must stand alone. There has been a ring of lightbearers on earth and in heaven understanding the nature of this victory and all that it would portend who have held a circle of light—though at times a distant circle—yet a circle of light, almost as observers to the Mother in the ring with Satan.

THE LEVER OF DEVOTION AND THE LEVER OF DECISION ARE YOUR OWN!

Beloved hearts, each and every one of you must *defeat the Adversary!* I've said it long ago and I say it again, as my Father has taught me, that even if I would I could not descend and give to you your victory. Nevertheless, every grace and mercy that is available from on high is given, even by the hand of angel ministrants.

You must realize that my heart has long been one with the hearts of the messengers. I know their hearts. I know how they, too, could —and would if they could by cosmic law—impart to you this mantle of victory as your own. But, beloved ones, your weaving of the mantle of victory is your own opportunity to attain integration of identity with God.

Therefore realize that by example and by the pillar of fire in the midst, you can win. But the lever of devotion and the lever of decision are your own! I say it again that you might remember with ringing in your ears: *The lever of devotion, the lever of decision are your own!*

Realize what this means! *You* determine! *You* decide! *You* devote your soul unto the Great God flame! And this lever becomes the means whereby there is the opening of the valve and the light descends and you are fused unto the One Light for your victory. Therefore only by free will and not by vicarious atonement may you utter: Not my will but thine be done! Father, not my will but thine be done.[15]

By love and by enlightenment you utter this prayer because you know in your heart of hearts the consequences of this edict. There are consequences. And when you surrender, the Law acts. Therefore do not withdraw that which you surrender. Do not surrender by rote, but know that God in you is the surrendering light and that it is an act of pure love for me.

Surrender is an act of pure love for me. I say this that you might remember that as you surrender I am able to come down from the cross and walk with you on the path of the resurrection and the life.

Thus, my beloved, when the hour of your Gethsemane is come, you may take heart that decisions made by the two witnesses—even the day-to-day decisions of life—have been made in that Gethsemane. And because these decisions have been made for the will of God and only for that will, there is the manifest victory. And yet even in this very hour when that resurrection becomes a mighty fiat of life—a gift bestowed and a mantle—yet it is the prayer of this messenger, "Let me be crucified again and again and again that more might be saved and there might be the shedding of blood for remission of sins."[16]

There are those in the outer fringes of this activity who point the accusing finger as they did—the very ones who accused Magdalene.[17] Beloved hearts, they point the finger at the messengers and they say, "How could all of this befall the messenger if she truly represents the Great White Brotherhood? Where are those who should stand to protect her now?"

Beloved hearts, when the Son of God volunteers to be crucified and knows what this means and knows that the earth is truly raised by the very process of the crucifixion, by free will it is given again. Therefore there come to the surface the momentums of hate and hate creation that instantaneously produce the judgment of those who then manifest these physically. And by this crucifixion there rises in the earth body souls of light who are magnetized by the very heart that is opened in the process. And these may drink the blood and eat the flesh of the living Son of God and inherit the light of Alpha and Omega.[18] And by this very rope of light, such as the one established this day by the angels—the ruby ray, the resurrection flame, and the violet flame—these souls mount up and they, too, may walk the Path. And therefore, beloved ones, the choice is made.

I made the choice. The saints have made the choice. And the messenger makes the choice again in the name of all of us who are ascended who can no longer enter the flesh and be crucified. Therefore we do enter and we do experience the very crucifixion again and again that the earth might be raised up in this sacred fire.

There are two choices, then: the choice to move on in personal popularity at this level of attainment that she bears or to move on carrying the cross of Christ and him crucified.

Realize that your messenger is a pragmatist, as you would say, that she has seen the Great Law and the geometry thereof and knows very simply that the shortest distance between two points— point A and B (point A, where mankind are now today; point B, in the very vortex of salvation)—is by the path of the crucifixion.

And therefore let them speak what they will speak! Let them say what they will say. But I stand where the messenger stands. And those who have believed this have received my healing through my hands superimposed upon her hands. And those who have believed not and loved not have not had within their own hearts an anchoring point for the current of our healing light—the light of Magda and Mary and Lanello. Therefore let those who believe be rewarded by their own state of consciousness. For the Law is exact, as you have heard it said, and exacting. It exacts the price— the price that must be paid for each one's victory.

A soul of light who is a believer has asked, "What did the Mother do that such a victory should manifest across America in these elections?" Well, I would like to answer that one Keeper of the Flame who himself was elected to office by this flame:

What did the Mother do but lay down her life for this nation with Lanello, but submit to the crucifixion and those choices in life —public, private, planetary, and personal—that must be taken if the soul is to soar and be free. Having made those right choices, having planted feet firmly on the Rock of Christ, Saint Germain could work his work of light in this year and thereby through you hold the balance. What did the messenger do but love and love and love every one of you—and even the betrayers and all upon earth. And the love flows steadfastly because it is the love of my heart.

I SPEAK TO YOU TRUTH

I AM Jesus the Christ. I speak to you Truth. Let Truth, as the vibration of my Presence, vindicate now every son of liberty, every child of the light, every Keeper of the Flame! And let the world know that because sacrifice is understood and upheld and given freely, lo, I AM in your midst and I proclaim the light of love in one who is almost free—almost free but not yet because she has chosen not to be free but to be bound by the same cords of bondage that bind the captives, nation by nation, and to be bound until all are free. And therefore let the fallen ones who bind my children in the Soviet Union and across the earth, even in the ghettos of America, know that your Mother is similarly bound by cords of love to be here in the earth for this mighty work of the ages.

Let us, then, move on with the divine plan released from the heart of the God Star, Sirius. Let us be joyous. Let us be one. Let us sup together in communion. For I desire to sup with you in the Royal Teton Retreat, for I desire that you should know how much I have loved you.

My beloved, come into our heart that is one heart. And if you come by free will with your eyes opened by the flame of opportunity and the enlightenment that it has brought, then in entering our heart the doubt will be screened out and the records of death, and you may truly share in that blazing sun of glory, even the heart of hearts of the Mother, of the Christed One, of the Buddha, of the Holy Spirit, and of the Father manifest in your own mighty I AM Presence.

It is lawful and truly opportune for you to meditate upon the heart that is sacred, that is my heart in the heart of the messenger. For by this meditation, there is purification of your own heart and the oneness that you seek in the Guru-chela relationship with Sanat Kumara.

This heart available to you, beating physically in this octave, is closer to you in frequency than the heart even of the ascended masters. It is an open door, if you will—a passageway clear and true to the Great God flame of your own God Presence, to my own, and to every ascended master. This is why the messenger tarries. And this is the law of consecrated being extending through the octaves of life.

Life begets life and only life where I AM! And I AM here as the Word incarnate. And I AM *here!*—ready for the arcing of that love to leap that you might also accelerate in the resurrection flame and experience the same balancing of karma that you are called upon to balance following in the footsteps of the Guru who is Mother.

I seal you in the truth of life. And I ask that life itself shall be unto you living proof of my witness. Now, therefore, let the faithful the world around be sealed! Let them abound in love and be one! For we are one as we face all of those who would deny this victory because this victory is become the victory whereby death and hell are swallowed up[19] and the ascension is the reality for souls who reach the goalpost.

Forevermore I AM the bread of life.[20] I call you to sup with me in glory. And I rejoice that each and every one of you, through the white robes of your messenger, can say: "I AM also that soul that is almost free!"

November 9, 1980
Camelot
Los Angeles County, California
ECP

CHAPTER 18

*Your path toward the Immaculate Heart is one
of stewardship of God's most sacred gifts where virtues
and graces, not only extolled, must expand and expand
until they become a million faces of starry bands,
angelic hosts who cannot resist surrounding you.*

CHAPTER 18

THE SACRED WALK TO THE IMMACULATE HEART OF MARY

Children of the light, blessed sons and daughters of the Most High, I assemble with you and with angels of our hosts who have come in this hour from far-off worlds for the celebration of that mighty flame of God-gratitude.

By this flame, my beloved, we who are the servants of God amplify the glory of the Word, amplify in you that which is our blood and our very own body. By the flame of gratitude is the crystallization of the God flame received in flesh, and the Word is there incarnate.

O rejoice and be glad, Israel—light in the heart of America! For I stand with you and I AM the everlasting Son of God come for the salvation of all people. Therefore let them come! For I open the highways of our God that they might come into that light of abundance, into the very heart of my Mother Mary and the heart of our messenger, even into your own hearts.

I AM opening up the passageways for lightbearers. And legions of seraphim accompanied by fiery salamanders go forth from their vigil here at Camelot to the four corners of the earth that the children of the light might walk the sacred walk to the Immaculate Heart of Mary.

Indeed this is a sacred walk. And all pilgrims of the Spirit who come into the fullness of the joy of the Trinity, when they first acknowledge the Mother light and bend the knee and confess that she is Mother, that out of Mary is the issue of life—there and then they begin the sacred walk to her Immaculate Heart. Won't you be seated as I tell you of this walk.

Pilgrims on distant shores breathing the air of freedom, the fresh winds blowing from the West, called by the Mother to the promised land, my own Blessed Mother, the very heart of Glastonbury and Camelot of old—her heart, her light yet a beacon of hope in England —yet she, implanting her rod and the light of her Cosmic Christ conception, did magnetize the pilgrims of the Holy Spirit to the New World.

All those anointed by that Spirit and imbued with the light of the sacred seed came to the New World, hearing the call of that Woman clothed with the Sun.[1] Indeed some came intending to be a barrier in the way of light, but they could not long enslave my children. Though the fallen ones would come, they would be there only as instruments of satanic lore to sharpen the minds and hearts of my children.

Thus the pilgrims began their sacred walk to the Immaculate Heart of Mary. And this city named after the Queen of the Angels, my Blessed Mother, became the resting place and the ultimate goal of many who followed the golden flame of her heart, even the flame of the abundant life. And therefore the impetus for this sacred walk to continue and to carry the souls of light to the Western shore was by that very promise that I gave unto all: I AM come that ye might have life and that more abundantly.[2]

GOD-GRATITUDE IS THE ABUNDANT LIFE

God-gratitude is the abundant life—the joy of gratitude that I AM born of the Cosmic Virgin. God is my Mother! God is my Father! I AM walking back to the Immaculate Heart of Alpha and Omega.

Lo, I bow before the flame of the Virgin Mary. For, lo, she is the bride of the Holy Spirit. Lo, she is the Mother of all life. Therefore in her I perceive and I AM one with the issue of Christ and I accept my inheritance with him.

Learn of me through my Mother, O blessed hearts. Learn of me through my Father, Saint Germain. Learn through Magda and Portia and Raphael—twin flames of our Trinity—of the wholeness of God and of this sacred walk.

Walking toward the Immaculate Heart is walking toward the Central Sun of life. As you approach, that fervent heat of God's devotion unto your soul begins to melt that pride and that ambition in lesser goal. Beloved hearts, when you aim for the Sun of the Mother you are walking the path of initiation under Omega, taught by Mother Mary, administered by her messenger, and truly known of your own soul through the sacred fount of life and the blessed Mediator, your own Christ Self.

Therefore I come to express gratitude. I come with legions of angels singing paeans of thanksgiving unto the Cosmic Virgin for the sacred walk and for the goal established of the Immaculate Heart. All the while as you walk toward that heart, my beloved, understand that the heart of the Mother beholds you immaculately. And in that very definite eye, that all-seeing eye of Mother, there is the penetration of crystal—emerald light, tempered by ruby, accelerated by the diamond jewel of her heart.

Realize then that when you walk straight to the heart of the starry body who is Mother there is divested from you all that is unreal. This requires initiation and sometimes burdens of life, testings of the soul, exercising to see how much you can do without and then again how much of the abundant life entrusted to your care you may faithfully administer on behalf of the children of the light and the community of the Holy Spirit.

Whether in seeming poverty—which may be the mere absence of material possessions in the riches of the Spirit—or in the abundant life complete in heaven and on earth, your path toward the Immaculate Heart is one of stewardship of God's most sacred gifts where virtues and graces, not only extolled, must expand and expand until they become a million faces of starry bands, angelic hosts who cannot resist surrounding you and rounding you with daisies of the field and chains of glory and crowns, as diadems of flowers upon your head mark the place and the light of the buddhic encounter.

Yes, encounter the Buddha you shall as you walk the sacred walk to the Immaculate Heart. For Mary is the Mother of Gautama. Mary is the Mother of all life and would teach you even to be the handmaid of the Lord of the World.[3]

A FORTIFICATION OF THE MYSTICAL BODY OF GOD

Realize then that through her Mother heart you will indeed encounter the legions of light and ascended masters and some saints of our inner bands whom you have known in other years and cycles. Some of these saints you have yet to interact with, for there remains a debt of karma—perhaps in your heart disdain for one who has been a sinner or a humble servant who now enjoys the grace of our inner retreats.

In this hour of thanksgiving, then, let us bow our heads and confess—confess all sin and misuse of the light of God's holy will. Let there be that mercy from God which precedes the full manifestation of justice. Let there be that mercy as the wine of forgiveness, for out of the law of forgiveness there is the rapprochement of yourself with every saint in heaven.

Beloved hearts, my legions have come and the legions of the Immaculate Heart of Mary here in this place to assist you now in consuming all that separates you from the saints in heaven—the nameless ones, your dearest friends and brothers and sisters on the Path. We desire that there should be a fortification of the mystical body of God. For as we contemplate Armageddon and the promised coming of the dragon who does make war with the Woman and her seed,[4] we contemplate the unity of the forces of Sanat Kumara and of their victory from the beginning—the mounting victory, the accelerating victory which is indeed our victory of love.

It is a rolling sacred fire. It is legions without number manifesting the Word, intoning the sacred AUM, meeting then the Adversary in perfect peace and perfect love.

PREPARE TO DELIVER THE MOMENTUM OF LIGHT THAT WILL SWALLOW UP THE DARKNESS

Beloved hearts, my revelation to John[5] was not given to frighten any or to place an aura of gloom or doom around the blessed earth but only to give you a prior reading of akasha of the intent of the murderous ones, of the plots and strategies of the Liar and his lie. Realize, then, that with the foreknowledge of the strategy of the fallen ones and the reading of the stars and the certain knowledge of the hour and the day of their coming you can mount up with light, with eagles,[6] with the Holy Kumaras—understanding that all revelation and prophecy of this nature is that you might be prepared to deliver the momentum of light that will ultimately swallow up the darkness and make this blessed earth safe for the little children.

Do we not see the dragon manifesting in the momentum of planetary darkness invading our youth through the subculture of drugs and rock and the opening of the bottomless pit? Hearts of light, these things are prophesied and they must be dealt with. Therefore I beseech Archangel Michael to assemble legions, many more legions of light to fight for the life of our youth.

I encourage you to understand the manipulation of the economy of the nations—this also foretold. And let those, then, who have been unwise in the investment of their supply be humble this day and bow before the altar of my heart, calling upon the law of forgiveness and asking to be purged of all that is impure in ambition and desire and pride—self-pride in one's ability to multiply the gifts and graces and supply of God.

Dear hearts, you wonder why your human investments go awry. Realize that it is because you ask amiss and receive not. You expect that your decrees, simply because you give them, are going to solve all of your problems and make things right.

You have heard me say, "Can a leopard change his spots?" Merely because you do something in the name of good does not make it good.

Self-righteousness may not prevail in the company of saints. Therefore let the wise ones first trust in God, first call upon the LORD to multiply the light of the heart and manifest as the abundant life.

Let individuals understand that there is a subtlety in the statement, "I will now go out and multiply my supply for God. I will now go out and do this thing for the LORD." Precious hearts, do you not hear the statement whereby you elevate yourself to the position of doer and consider that now you will become famous in the courts of heaven because you have done something for God? Namely you have become the instrument where God might become wealthy upon earth.

Precious hearts, consider the subtle yet blasphemous nature of this line of thinking. Let it be rooted out of the heart and soul. Your prayer ought rather to be

> *Father, forgive me. I call upon thy law of forgiveness for all misuses of the abundant life. Let thy mercy which endureth forever come now into my temple. And out of the heart of mercy, O God, for thy grace unto thy children do thou now enter my temple and be the multiplier of the bread of life.[7] Let me be merely the instrument and thou, O God, the welcome guest and indeed the occupier of my temple. I ask, O God, to be the instrument of thy life. Come now and perform thy perfect work through me.*

Precious hearts, the fallen ones play a most dangerous game with the children of the light. Do not be lured or tempted by any from within or without this community who present to you their schemes which are schemes for power in the name of good, schemes of ambition in the name of good.

Realize that the money beast that stalks the earth and the vibration of greed itself and the ambitions to that power of this world are not entirely rooted out of individuals, especially those who have not conquered the desire body or the carnal mind. The tentacles of the money beast are everywhere upon the planetary body. And the cult of success without God has even lured seekers away from the pure and perfect service and the givingness of self as well as supply upon the altar of God.

INVEST IN THE LORD AND IN HIS HOUSE AND IN THE PUBLISHING OF HIS WORD

Here upon the altar let us multiply the gifts of the harvest, the fruits of Thanksgiving! Let God be the sacred business of life. Let the altar be the place prepared for those gifts. Let us invest in the Lord and in his house and in the publishing of his Word. And let those who have been burned by the money beast be humble this day.

Be glad, therefore, that when this fire of the very pits of hell has come upon you that it has not destroyed the soul but only taken from you what you did not have the God-control to keep by sound reason, wise consideration, and selflessness in the plan.

I come, then, for the perfecting of the heart in the way of service for the mastery of the fifth ray. And professionalism in service is indeed a part of the sacred walk to the Immaculate Heart of Mary. And the sacred labor of the hand must be trusted far more than the path of usury and the desire for those grandiose schemes whereby it is as though you were gamblers in a casino, risking at great odds with very little knowledge of what you are about.

Let us then draw nigh unto the Lord and let us see that it is the subtlety of the discarnates and of the astral hordes as they attempt to pry an opening into the citadel of freedom that we must watch out for. Become then wise as serpents but harmless as doves[8] and keep out of the way of harm as there passes over the earth now in this hour, through the vials of the archangels,[9] the returning karma that is intended to affect not only economic conditions but conditions of the body temple through every form of plague and darkness.

The plague of locusts[10] is the plague of the returning momentum of the fear nestled in the subconscious of individuals. This, then, is the hour for immense imploring of the LORD GOD, for application to the holy angels. For it is the holy angels who keep the way of the Tree of Life[11] at Camelot and in your heart and in your respective centers.

There are those who are bent on maligning this activity with absolute lies concerning its position in doctrine, both religious and political. There are others determined upon destroying this messenger and the precious Guru-chela relationship.

THE FORTIFICATION OF COMMUNITY AS HOLY CHURCH FOR THE VICTORY OF LIGHT IN ALL AGES TO COME

I have come this day with my waiting bride, beloved Magda. We come to place our flame of intense love within your hearts. Have you not felt our presence in your midst? We are determined to defend the Church Universal and Triumphant even as you are determined to defend it. We are determined to warn and to instruct you, to assemble you together that you might understand the wiles of Serpent[12] and the attempt of Satan who is yet behind bars[13] to implement his seed on earth in this momentum of destructivity.

I tell you, this, too, shall pass away. And they shall not be able to pass over the sacred line, the hallowed forcefield of our love. Therefore our love as our twin causal bodies becomes now a forcefield in every true heart and devotee, in every teaching center and place of worship where there is harmony, in every home where there is a room or a closet set aside for the descent of light.

Let the whirling vortices, multiplied over and over again, of our star-fire bodies be for the sealing of the Holy Church in wholeness. Beloved hearts, this is the hour when the fortification of community as Holy Church will tell for the victory of light in all ages to come.

You are blessed cells in the body of God, maintaining individuality by your individual perspectives of his mind. Can you visualize a vast mind of God as a flaming sphere of light? Can you visualize yourselves all one within that sphere?

You are all of God. God is all of you. Billions of cells of consciousness compose the mind of God, each cell interacting by the interchange of the cosmic fluid with every other cell.

Realize then that your individuality in the mind of God is according to your positioning, your relative positioning one to the other. Thus you are much alike—fed on the same milk of the Mother's breast and the meat of the Word. You are much alike—nourished by the violet flame, loved by angelic hosts. Therefore your faces radiate the impulse of the very same love of God. For God shines upon you, and that shining is the note of oneness.

Realize then how you can maintain identity and yet be one person in God. It is a sacred mystery that I would impart to you, for this realization of oneness in and as the mind of God gives to you the strength of one-pointedness to act in concerted vibration on a planetary scale to challenge these fallen ones and an irresponsible press willing to publish any rumor or gossip without even the courtesy of a phone call to verify that which is put in print to fan the fires of division, prejudice, and hatred for Saint Germain midst the very body of God.

STALWART SOULS THE WORLD AROUND HAVE MET EVERY CRISIS

So much for that, beloved hearts. All of these things become the blessed challenge to strengthen you, to cause you to desire God more, to cause you to go to his heart and implore him for more light and grace, causing you to be grateful for the love that you share and your oneness and for miracles wrought by the legions of light in answer to your call as you face each and every challenge with victory.

Do you realize, beloved hearts, how many major and minor challenges you have faced together and you have endured and survived as one—and the movement marches on with Archangel Michael in the lead? Do you realize, beloved hearts, that we today offer praise and thanksgiving that you have held this ground, this holy ground for God? For we bow before the light within you and we say, to you belongs the tribute as instruments of God for the saving of Camelot in the physical dimension, at the mental level, at the level of the astral plane, and even in the etheric levels where the fallen ones seek to rise as the spiritually wicked in high places.[14]

Beloved hearts, there have been many challenges and threatenings and dire forebodings, but this day we rejoice that stalwart souls the world around have met every crisis. Therefore with the cross and with the crown we come. We reinforce the cosmic cross of white fire truly as the centerpiece of this Thanksgiving Day. For what could be more appropriate upon each table than the cosmic cross of white fire blazing—there the Son of God affixed. And behold the face of Mother and Child and of every child of the Woman in turn taking turns to be with me and with God upon that cross.

I bless you for your prayers for all who are in bonds. Truly we have heard the call. And though you have tarried and postponed your dinner in their behalf, we say, blessed are you who have preferred to be one in this service. And thereby we have sent our Christmas angels to prepare the consciousness of every lightbearer with this joy, this joyous gratitude that in each year anticipates the birth of the Divine Manchild as the light of winter solstice is not misqualified but requalified with light.

Therefore I stand. Therefore I challenge the satanic rite and cult that would misuse the sacred fires of the Christ Mass. Therefore let them be bound in advance for their contemplated evil against the servants of the light.

Therefore I stand and we are one. And we are determined that the light of this Christ Mass shall indeed descend and shall be unto earth a pillar of fire of judgment and of the opening of the way for every child of God to be reborn in and after the image of the universal Christ that I AM.

Blessed hearts, each year in anticipation of the great light of winter solstice realize that there are those who for aeons have celebrated this by satanic rite to misqualify the light of Father and Mother and Son and Holy Spirit in the body of earth's children. Let us begin this day in anticipation of that holy feast of the Christ Mass. Let us serve together as one, determined and intensifying the light to consume the atrocities of murder and war and the abuse of the holy innocents.

Blessed hearts, O my hearts of light, I take all of you into my heart in this hour. I impress upon you the true image of the Christed One that I AM. I impress within you and within every living cell the image of your mighty I AM Presence and of the heart of the Central Sun. I long for you to know me as I AM, to see me as I AM, and to be with me in glory. I have longed for you to be perfected in my heart for thousands of years.

THE CONSUMING OF THE DARKNESS OF THE DARK CYCLE

Now, then, the requirement of the Law before the end shall come is this consuming of the Darkness of the Dark Cycle and most intense layers of misqualified energy:

Let us keep our eye on the Middle East and let us keep our eye on the God Star. Let us be alert to intrusions of unidentified flying objects. Let us be alert to extraterrestrial visitants who would inject into this earth the manipulation and subjugation of the minds of the people. Let us be alert to those currents, subtle and yet penetrating, that move even now in the economy and the government of this nation in an attempt to thwart the divine plan of El Morya, Saint Germain, and the Great Divine Director for this nation.

Let us beware of the attempt of the fallen ones to overthrow the victories of the lightbearers. Let us not be dismayed either by the intensity of their misuse of the sacred fire or by the subtlety of their wiles. Let us be alert to the fact that we stand in the presence of the disintegrating personality. Let us realize that there is a disintegration factor in many of the fallen ones that causes them to manifest a final insanity, an irresponsibility, and a pressing out upon the earth of a stored hatred.

Realize then the erratic nature of these fallen ones and therefore the dangers of nuclear weapons in arsenals and the use of nuclear energy by those who do not have the God-control to maintain the necessary protection unto the people. Realize then that the safety and the security of America and this community is our concern on this Thanksgiving.

The gratitude of this people must count in place of an astuteness on the part of its leaders in protecting the population from germ warfare and from the outcropping of nuclear fallout and various conditions in the society such as new forms of viruses and disease that enter unexpectedly. Beloved hearts, the absence of the protection of this people from impurities and toxins in food and water —all of this put together renders many hopelessly unalert and unable to respond even when we cry out with loudness and intensity.

Beloved hearts, there must be a protection of this people from the influence of the very vibrations that pass through the television sets, mesmerizing and hypnotizing the people to believe whatever comes through that form of communication. Thus the lulling to sleep of America even in the midst of the victories of the lightbearers is also a dangerous condition. Let us keep our eye upon this mighty people! Let us pray for them daily.

I take my sacred walk to the heart of Immaculata, Omega, heart of Mother—to the Central Sun each day. And there I pray for earth and her evolutions and for other systems of worlds for whom I hold the image of the universal Christ.

I will take you in my heart with me each day to the Central Sun that your voice might count with my own. This has been my desire and I ask you to request it each day:

O Jesus, take me in your heart to the heart of God that I might pray with you for earth and the systems of worlds.

I will take you, beloved, I will take you in my heart and thereby a measure of grace and the balancing of karma may come to you. I will take you because I love you, because I am grateful for your service, because I appreciate your devotion and all that you have done that my true message is now spread abroad upon earth. And many of my children who would not have made progress spiritually on the Path without this message are now able to move forward swiftly to balance karma, to change garments, to be transfigured by the light of the "seamless" deathless solar body.

THE KNOWLEDGE OF THE VIOLET FLAME AND THE MIGHTY I AM PRESENCE IS THE MOST PRECIOUS AND PRICELESS GIFT OF ALL

Dear hearts, when the knowledge of the violet flame and the mighty I AM Presence is given it is the most precious and priceless gift of all. When you give that gift you are giving a gift in my name. The gift of the wise men at my birth was the gift of their love to assist me in imparting the sacred mysteries, in depositing those mysteries in the hearts of my disciples where they would be sealed to germinate for a thousand years and more until the coming of Saint Germain.

O blessed ones, I long to intensify my light in the earth. I long to be in your heart as you are in mine to roll back all of this hatred of my Father, Saint Germain. I long to do more; and yet I do not press or overpress myself in you, for I know that the more light that I give to you, the more you must bear and carry of that darkness. Therefore my angels guard and protect and nourish you.

We are grateful when you offer yourselves to carry more. And therefore I respond this Thanksgiving with more light to you who offer to bear the burdens of the earth, for this is indeed our assignment to the messenger and the chelas in this hour. And we are gratified that already this accelerating momentum has resulted in a lifting of burdens even as necessary cataclysm or catastrophe has also occurred as karma itself must be respected as the irrevocable law of divine grace. Thus the shortening of the days for the elect has occurred.[15]

And let all be blessed through the experience of the fire, for those whose works must be tried have been tried.[16] And those who thought that they needed their possessions to enjoy life have learned of me and my way and now they are impelled to take another step on the walk toward the Immaculate Heart of Mary.

Therefore we are grateful. We are grateful for Maitreya, the Great Initiator, who has seen fit to initiate souls in the New Jerusalem, in the City of the Angels.

Each and every one who is of the light who has passed through this experience has also had a balancing of karma and an opportunity to enter into the state of grace by finding the very core of light of the flame of gratitude by finding a single reason to be grateful even for loss of possessions or transient life itself. Indeed how blessed are they who are able to sing praise unto the LORD in the presence of adversity, for thereby is their love proven. Therefore listen, little children, and be grateful not merely when God gives to you favors but when you are also spanked and when your tree of life is pruned for a greater flowering and fruit.

All those, then, who passed through the testing of fire who are not of the light, who cursed God and took his name in vain, all those who gave not the glory for the abundant life that they enjoyed, those who retain anger and arrogance before the Almighty in the face of destruction and seeming desertion—they then find that their sins are multiplied unto them that they do not use the experience wisely to balance karma or to accelerate their own individual wisdom.

I pray for them that they might swiftly bend the knee and confess that the Lord is more important to them than all these things. May the lessons of Job, our own beloved, also be learned.[17]

Swiftly, swiftly do the seasons pass and the cycles roll. And each man in his own hour must be confronted by cosmic justice. Thus the Lord has sent the mighty feminine incarnation of cosmic justice in answer to the calls of life on earth.[18]

Our Thanksgiving prayer is that justice might increase wisdom and love. Let there be justice in this land this day—this is my prayer! Let justice return to each one the harvest of his sowings. Therefore I send light! I send light that you might reap the reward of your sowings, my beloved, by way of joy, by way of cosmic instruction, by way of lessons that must be learned.

Therefore I rejoice at the sendings of our God that the evildoers may be stopped in their evil ways by the return to them of the energy veil, even the black smoke of misqualified sacred fire breath that they have breathed out upon the children of the light. So let it be returned that they might look and examine and then choose whom they will serve.[19]

O blessed, blessed light, come into this temple! Come into the souls of my children! And let us see how, by the light of gratitude, the Eternal Christ will be born in this year and you, my children, will know him alive forevermore, alive forevermore in your very temple!

I would enter! O bid me welcome and I shall come.

November 27, 1980
Camelot
Los Angeles County, California
ECP

CHAPTER 19

Know that the standard is raised and the ensign of my people is raised up.... The sword is the sign of the teaching of the science of the Word. And it shall be a sign to all nations that there is a way out and that way is by Christ within you, by Immanuel born.

CHAPTER 19

THE HOUR OF THE SWORD IS COME

I come not to send peace but a sword. It is the sword of my Father and I bear it in the name of my Mother.

I AM come into the very heart of earth in this celebration of my birth. And I let the sword of the Cosmic Christ, even beloved Maitreya, descend.

I come not to send peace but a sword![1] Therefore know that those who give lip service to my name while denying my coming in the hearts of these little ones shall know the meaning of the sword in this hour, in this year, and in this decade.

How well I remember the misuse of the altar and the temple of my Father. They made it a den of thieves.[2] Thus in this hour I come to overturn the tables of the moneychangers in the halls of science and of religion and in the very hearth and home where the little child is aborted.

I, Jesus, come again with my Christmas message and I deliver unto you this mandate of Almighty God: *The karma will fall upon this nation, surely as I stand, unless this people shall rise up and take command of the ungodly slaughter of the holy innocents.*

I have spoken in his name. I have dwelt in his tabernacle. I have slept at the feet of the Almighty, and I have awakened to give praise unto my God—I have entered the nirvanic light into the eternal rest, and I have come forth for the mighty action. And I touch every heart—those who call themselves followers of me and those who do not. For the hour of the sword is come.

Therefore, my beloved, do not take lightly my word in this hour. For I tell you: This is the line. *Thus far and no farther!* The fallen ones shall not mock life or its essence or its purity or its precious element of love.

My beloved, the sacred law is written in your hearts. Why will you not obey it with that pure God-intent instead of manifesting as the twig that is bent out of the way of righteousness?

This is an hour when you will see sacred fire descend. And you will see the manifestation of plague, and you will see the manifestation of war, and you will see the manifestation of the Death Rider[3] and the opening up of the bowels of the earth and the very spirits of hell coming forth.[4]

Beloved hearts, unless this planetary body be purged of unrighteousness, where shall the righteous appear? Unless those false pastors[5] of my people be exposed through the Coming Revolution in Higher Consciousness,[6] unless the light of Almighty God descend to tear from the fallen ones their masks and their masquerades, where shall the Christed ones and the Buddha appear?

I AM not here with sweet words. For you can imagine them yourselves in your heart. You have heard them spoken without spirit and without love. And you have accepted the mechanization man for your leaders—even for your spiritual leaders. You have allowed them to bring into the temple of my Father their rock music, their drugs, and their perversion of the sacred fire, their consorting with demons in the name of the Holy Spirit.

I AM standing at every pulpit, at every altar of my churches throughout the earth. And some are even empty on this Christmas morn while they revel in their merriment! Do they think that God will forever wink? Beloved hearts, in the twinkling of an eye they shall be no more.

Have they not read what is in store? Do they think the prophets are old-fashioned? Do they think that somehow the Holy Spirit that spoke long ago is in a state of decay, is no longer relevant to the hour?

They have put out those with the Holy Spirit from my temple. And they have allowed those who are the agnostics and the doubters and the nonbelievers to enter the pulpits and to denounce my God flame where I AM.

Lo, I AM come into this land! They have called me by their lips. Now I come for the purging of their hearts! And they have not known the meaning of the sword. Therefore, I say, let it go forth!

Angels of light are relieved that ultimately there can be the separating out of Light from Darkness and the binding and the judgment—no more, then, to strive with flesh,[7] no more, then, to indulge those who flaunt the Law and continue to flaunt it.

Those who have the most precious teachings of all, those who have had the way made plain through my brothers and sisters in the ascended octaves, ought the more to consider themselves at the hand of the Lord's mercy for their own disobedience, their own ignorance, their own setting aside of the highest teachings while they have gone here and there in the marts of entertainment or the cult of success.

Let all who call themselves Keepers of the Flame realize that even the Death Angel will not bypass those who have abused the violet flame, who have continued to flaunt the Law and then to invoke forgiveness as though somehow they were dealing in a fantasyland and a fairy world where we are not really real.

Well, beloved hearts, either we are real or we are not! And it is very simple. I AM here, I AM real. El Morya is real. The Great Divine Director is real. And we have not come to steal a single identity but to reinforce life!

Indeed the meaning of my birth is the availability of Personhood in God, of the descent of Christ. Let all other gifts be set aside and let them pursue the highest gift. For it is the pearl of great price,[8] even the Great Causal Body of Almighty God. And it is offered to you as the hand of God even offers to you a world, saying: "Take dominion over the earth! Take dominion over life! I give it unto thee." Therefore let us take dominion over these fallen ones who are murdering our children.

Beloved hearts, I AM here with a fervor of my life and I pour it into your waiting vessels and I say: I wait no longer. *You* can wait no longer! It is the hour for the overturning of the tables of these fallen ones and it is the hour when you have the full reinforcement of the archangels.

Will I remain silent when a world reeks with hollow mockery and does nothing that could be done very simply to release those hostages in Iran? As they cry out to me, I cry out to the people: Do you not see how your leaders have betrayed you, how they fear their own exposure and therefore do not act in concerted alliance?

I rebuke the leaders of NATO! I rebuke the president of France and the heads of state of Germany and those nations who have refused to do exactly what ought to be done!—to cut off Iran from all commodities and supplies, to take intense action against these fallen ones. How can you dally? How can you be divisive? How can you not act in support and in the cosmic honor flame of the United States of America whose lifeblood delivered you from the toilers and the spoilers in World War II and beyond?[9]

Blessed hearts of light, this is a gross selfishness that is manifest. And these leaders are the fallen ones and I declare their judgment. And I say in God's name I AM THAT I AM: *They shall not pass!*

Those who have refused to act against the Soviet Union in Afghanistan by denying to that nation more wheat, more technology, more of anything and everything they want—I say: *They shall not pass!* They are judged! And the blood of those who have been lost in Afghanistan is required of them in this hour. And *they shall not pass!* And I send the sword of my Father. Watch and pray.

Do you understand that the very presence of Soviet troops aligned on the border of Poland is enough to cause all nations of the earth to cut off the Soviet Union? That is a threat, as surely as the threat to Cuba.

Where is the spine? Where is the Kundalini? I will tell you. It is lying in a bed of wickedness! It is spent upon surfeiting in pleasure.

And these fallen ones, I say, their day is done!—they and their house. Let the children of the light cry out with a mighty shout! Let them invoke the judgment of God, for the hour of that judgment is come. *They shall not pass!*

And the Lord God Almighty will not allow it—will not allow the encroachment upon our light, our activity, our messenger, and our chelas of the mockery of the Word, the mockery of the testimony of the Lamb. Therefore I AM come. And my Electronic Presence contains the momentum—the momentum of the entire Spirit of the Great White Brotherhood.

I represent the hosts of the Lord. I come as the Prince of Peace, and my sword shall ultimately ring with peace throughout the earth. And there shall be peace. And that peace shall be a resolution and not a covering over and not a hiding of sin or a misuse of the light —not in Ghana, not in any area of this activity.

We will come, we will expose, and we will reveal that the foundation of service of life on earth is the flame of purity and of individual Christhood. And this is the Rock upon which we build. And we reject those stones who have not allowed themselves to pass through the furnace of the Lord God Almighty for the purging of those elements of Antichrist. You cannot slip into the temple and allow yourself to become a part of its building when you have not passed through the fires of initiation.

There are none who are counted my own save those who will enter by the door of the personal crucifixion. There is no way that you can come around or under or over the Law. You must pass through the very gate of the nexus of the living Christ.

This is my message and *I will not have it flaunted!* I am undaunted in the will of God in this hour and I move with the fury of the intense white-fire purity of the wrath of the Almighty.

THE RODS AND CONES OF THE ALMIGHTY

And therefore I descend and I bring the message of the coming of The Lord Our Righteousness[10] and the overturning of the false pastors and those who have perverted the way of the true shepherds. Let the hirelings be judged![11] Let there come the hour of the mighty rods, the rods and cones of the Almighty.

Beloved hearts, there are instruments of power which the Lords of Karma and the ascended hosts may insert into planetary bodies and worlds when the moment and the hour for the intense release of the judgment is come, I tell you, by the hand of Elohim. In this Christ Mass, as I speak, Elohim of God insert into the earth those rods and cones that are for the stripping of the fallen ones of their misused light—for the judgment, for the acceleration of light unto the righteous, and for the bringing in of the great golden age.

Beloved hearts of light, you have seen the signal of the passing of an era. You have seen the signal of the coming of the judgment of the fallen ones who have opened up the very pits of hell with their rock music. Let them be dismayed. Let them have their sympathy. Let them cry in their beer. I tell you, they will weep. And there will be weeping and gnashing of teeth! For it is the sign of the judgment of serpents.[12]

Do you think that the Lord God will stand by and allow the Satanists to take over this planetary body in their murderous intents, in their blood rites and rituals, in their misuse of life as it is my life in the holy child? I tell you, *Nay!*

God is alive and well on planet Earth. And the future of Earth is in his hands. Contrary to all appearances, the light is ongoing. The light is in his stars appearing within you.

Therefore I demand response! I demand a leaping into the

sacred fire as you would leap into a mighty waterfall of cooling light descending! I ask that you leap into the very sacred fire, that you assimilate it, that your word become the very flow of this infinite light to earth, and that therefore there come an era of God-justice and a turning back of crime.

Beloved hearts of light, when my legions in embodiment, serving as best they can, spend hours and days and nights pursuing those who have murdered, only to turn them over to the courts and find that they are released once again on society to murder again—what do you think? It is discouragement, it is hopelessness, and it is the beginning of the crumbling of society itself when that law and that order is not kept.

This people have allowed drugs to enter their marts. They have defended their freedom to have all manner of license and misuse of the sacred fire and the perversion of the life force—defending homosexuality, defending lesbianism as though it were of God, and attempting to lead the children of the light into these activities.

Is it any wonder there is murder and crime in the streets and insanity? It is the abuse of the Mother flame. And *they shall not pass!* And all who remain silent and all who are led in these directions— they will pay the price and they will be swept aside with the coming of the wave and with the coming of the sword.

Do you not think that I cry out? I indeed am crucified anew when I see the killing, the slaughter, and the murder of my own in senseless manifestations of war. In the very midst of the prophecy of Isaiah for the birth of the Child—there was war, there was bloodshed, there was the threat of the enemy of light. Has there ever been another condition?

BE THE INSTRUMENT OF THE SEPARATION OF THE TARES AND THE WHEAT

As my Mother has told you, study well the conditions and circumstances of the war of the Nephilim[13] and their councils.

For, beloved ones, there are more among you that have known death by Herod's sword than I would care to enumerate.

Beloved hearts, if you have paid the ultimate price embodiment after embodiment, I tell you—and it is so—you are entitled in this hour to know the protection of the Great White Brotherhood and to realize that you have given that sacrifice and you are come again to live under our protection.

We cannot give it if you do not invoke it. We cannot descend unless you speak our name. But the karma is there, the good karma, to rejoice in that grace which is due your lifestream whereby you can know God face-to-face, enter the arena of life, and be the instrument of the separation of the tares and the wheat.[14]

Legions of light are on the march.[15] And when you see the infamy against elemental life, when you see a single soul risk his life for the freeing of 600 porpoises caught and ready to be slaughtered[16]—is there not one among you who will risk his life for the freeing of those children about to be aborted as soon as they come forth from the womb?

Beloved hearts, elemental life cry out as they are aborted. Children of the Sun cry out—and I demand that you give answer! And I demand that those who are the insane fallen ones, who appear to be the leaders of this planet, give their accounting in this hour!

You will watch and you will see as my Word is released, for it is the certain Word of the entire Spirit of the Great White Brotherhood reflecting the very altar of Almighty God. For emissaries of earth and saints of the inner church have appealed before his very throne in my name. You have seen demonstrations upon earth. I tell you, the saints robed in white have demonstrated in this hour for* the utter desecration of this Christ Mass throughout the earth.

Where, oh, where is Christ born in this hour? Let him be born within you! For unless he be born, there is no life in earth, there is no manifestation of Sanat Kumara.

**for:* for the reason that; because (*Merriam-Webster's Collegiate Dictionary,* eleventh edition)

Let there be the binding of the fallen ones. Let there be the binding of the seed of Satan, for the prophecy is written. You need only read and run with the many, many promises of victory.

PROFOUND PEACE COMES WITH YOUR ALIGNMENT WITH GOD

I AM Jesus. I come to nourish the children of my heart. I come with the strength of cosmic love. Fear not, little flock, I carry you in my arm, I enfold you in the light of my mantle, I carry you beyond harm, I carry you far, far beyond the alarm of the fallen ones.

Precious hearts, can you know how—simultaneously—the peace, the profound peace that comes with your alignment with God and your obedience to his will, can be established in you, even as all these things must also come to pass? Beloved, in my Father's house are many mansions: if it were not so, I would have told you.[17] I seal you now in the mansion of my own causal body that you might dwell there—dwell there safely while in the very midst of the battle. Beloved hearts, fear not.

Some of you postpone the choice of your own reckoning with Truth and with Reality. The battle is upon us. There is no thought yea or nay. All will take up the sword [of the sacred Word]. All will fight.* All will prepare themselves as God has given you potential and mind and heart and resources.

So I say, You *will* prepare! You *will* enter into the divine calling!

Let the seed of light descend. Let the divine potential be welcomed. And cast aside all resistance to the inner God-man.

When you enter the war and you see souls literally being destroyed, when you see body temples desecrated, when you see the flow of the abundant life in this nation hoarded, misused, manipulated for profit, for filthy lucre, by multinationalists, by those who have no God in them—will you turn your back and go away with your loved ones and say, "Let us enjoy another lifetime. Let us not look"? I say, you will not!

---
*to put forth a determined effort

You will assail them* and their bastions on Wall Street! You will tackle the international bankers! You will turn over the tables of these moneychangers! For if you do not, beloved hearts, then the golden age will not come.

Look at those who have been selected. Do you think that they have the elevation of Christ within them, serving in the cabinet and as department heads and in agencies? They have, beloved hearts, at best, human experience. But it requires more than human experience. It requires the all-power of heaven and earth.[18] And therefore, I give it unto my messenger.

Let them say what they will! I give it. I deposit it in her heart. And I say to you: I have raised her up and I have raised you up to be with me a mighty people! We are determined that this body of light shall serve as the anchor point for the armies of Sanat Kumara.

THE HOUR IS COME

Let us be up and doing! Let us not allow them to taunt, mock, blackmail, abuse, and make folly of this nation. Let those within it who do not honor the cosmic honor flame understand that the hour is come—the hour is come and the descent of the sword into the marts of pornography, into the very focuses of prostitution and the misuse of the sacred fire in motion pictures illustrating that misuse throughout this city and every nation.

The judgment descends. They are overturned. And the armies of fiery salamanders, sylphs, gnomes, and undines are ready. And they follow with Archangel Michael, and they don their helmets and their blue-flame swords. And, beloved hearts of light, you can scarcely tell them from blue-flame angels for they have so identified with this cosmic purpose of the deliverance of the Divine Woman and the Manchild.[19] You would rejoice to see them! And therefore I open the veil that you might see these elementals as they troop in mighty formation with the legions of the seven archangels.

---

*to confront principalities of spiritual darkness with the sacred Word

The Christed ones are here! The hosts of the Lords[20] are here! And they will not allow this infamy to pass. They will not allow this desecration of my Father's house and his kingdom to pass. Therefore let us see how the children of the light and the sons of God will respond, for you must give that mighty thrust and that call.

Beloved ones, I challenge you with the full fire of my Sacred Heart to speak the Call into the face of every injustice as you have never done before, and watch how God will show you the outcome of your invocation. And you will see them go down, even as the light of God that never fails can arrest a plague of locusts upon an entire nation.

So the God of Israel is in the midst of his people! That God is upon us. Let them rise up! For opportunity is at hand as the sword that I bear, as the sword that I wield, as the sword that goeth forth out of my heart, out of my mouth. It is the flaming sword! It is the sword of the Faithful and True![21] Thus you will see that mighty sword, as thoughtform, going out of the mouth of Gautama Buddha, of Sanat Kumara, of Lord Maitreya.

Truly the hour of the judgment is come. Truly those who have wearied in this message of the judgment may not weary much longer, for they themselves will know the meaning of it. Therefore set thy house in order, my beloved. Let each and every one be a part of angelic bands and when weighed in the great scale of life not be found wanting.

Let us rejoice! For our rejoicing is in the deeper mysteries of God. Most would not hear my message. They prefer to dwell upon an event that took place 2,000 years ago. We live in the present, not in the past. We live in the moment. We live in the light of God. We live in the eternal and progressive revelation of the Holy Spirit.

Lo, I AM the fullness of that Spirit unto ye all and unto my people everywhere! And by the fire of the Holy Spirit, I AM come to heal the brokenhearted. I AM come to heal and make whole those who are mine and of my very soul, born with me in the Beginning of the Word.

I search them out. I send out the line of my heart. And every one of mine own is touched in this hour. And I reinforce that love, oh, the love of the Father and the Son, as we come to dwell in each little one—those who keep our Word, those who love, those who understand that my commandments are the very bastions of identity.

O love that will not let me go, O love that would bestow upon mine own that nectar of the Spirit, O precious child—for one precious child born into the midst of community, I tell you, the entire Spirit of the Great White Brotherhood would gladly lay down its life.

The Brotherhood is nigh. The Brotherhood is determined that these little ones shall not be desecrated, shall not be decimated or know the discouragement of the apostates, the atheists, the rebels against my Father.

They hated without cause.[22] And they continue to hate without cause. And their anger against the Mother is even greater than their anger against the Father. For it is Mother who is in the Matter cosmos, who is in the very earth—exacting the requirements of the Law as Guru, exacting the judgment, demanding proof and testimony of their use or misuse of the sacred fire.

It is Mother who exposes. Therefore behold the hatred of the Virgin Mary. I strip it! I expose it! I uncover the ugly recesses of the subconscious! And I call to the Elohim Astrea and legions of light: Bind these interlopers! Bind the invaders of the temple of all mankind! Bind the hordes of war and demons and death! Bind them in my name! For I AM Jesus. And in that name shall all evolutions of earth know the fullness of the light of the eternal salvation and of the second death.

Beloved hearts, it is the hour. And therefore let none mistake, let none think that somehow the light of our prophecy has gone out and that we are not speaking the effective Word. Beloved hearts, this Word pushes out. This Word is saturating your very bodies to the core. This light is the light which composes your atoms, the very stuff of which you are made. It is the substance of life.

And as this light that I give you now is assimilated in your bodies, there is an accentuation of light. There is a forcing out of the pores of being of those subliminal rebellions against the Spirit. And as this occurs in your temples with some uncomfortability, know that for the fallen ones it is not a simple uncomfortability. It is the very annihilation of their seat of mockery and scorn and condemnation. And therefore there is upheaval. There is overturning. And there is earthquake in the earth.

In this hour, my beloved, there is a mighty action of Virgo and Pelleur. And that very readjustment in the etheric plane has reverberations in the mental belt, in the emotional body, and in the physical body. For I will not leave this earth as I have found it! I will not leave it. And I will not leave you comfortless.[23]

And my comfort in this hour is the mighty sword. And as I hold it before you, my beloved hearts, you know that the standard is raised and the ensign of my people is raised up.[24] And the sword is the sign of the teaching of the science of the Word. And it shall be a sign to all nations that there is a way out and that way is by Christ within you, by Immanuel born.[25]

And there are some who deny him in toto. They deny his Spirit, his flame, his joy, his birth. They do not want him in their temple. And I tell you, even these very ones are forced to receive him. For they are born into the families of the fallen ones—even the children of the light, even a son of God—to confound them, to rise up and to raise the sword and to cleave the Real from the unreal in the generations of mankind upon this earth.

Thus, beloved hearts, where they have denied him within their own temple, their own karma has dictated that they labor and travail to give birth to him—only to see that little one arise with the hand, the right hand of authority. And the light shall descend and they shall mourn and there shall be mourning of the tribes of the earth for the coming of the Christed ones. For they shall not be stopped. They shall not be stopped, beloved hearts.

Our ways are not the ways of the fallen ones. Ours are the ways of infinite power. And even the power of God is justified, even as wisdom is justified in her children. Therefore let the children of the Mother rise and defend true wisdom. Let them seize now the holy light and the torch of the Goddess of Liberty! Let them seize the true wisdom of the ancient texts and of the light of Sanat Kumara. And let all of Israel and Judah know the real inheritance of my people and the real teaching of Immanuel who is come.

Beloved hearts, ignorance shall no longer remain. I set a torch to it. And it begins to burn.

Watch, then, the burning of the layers of ignorance. Watch the burning of that trash literature that ought never to be precipitated in Matter. Watch the judgment of Oromasis and Diana and the fiery salamanders. For this is the hour of the victory of our God and this is the hour of his vengeance. Therefore in these final months of this cycle of the Dark Cycle,[26] you will see what is the meaning of the vengeance of our God.

Hold fast what thou hast received! Hold fast unto the light and do not forget my Word! Do not forget my release. For I am giving you the light in this hour to meet the Adversary for an entire year!

Therefore tarry in the temple and know that on this day—I AM Jesus, I AM your Lord and your Saviour, subject unto the LORD God Almighty even as ye are all subject unto him. And I have come to see to it that your lamps are filled with oil[27] and that you invoke the light that will also see to it that the physical oil of this nation is protected and that the energy of Almighty God flows freely unto this people.

I AM come, therefore, giving you increments of light for your chakras. See that those candles do not go out. See that you do not squander this light in any form of unrighteousness, any form of riotous living—should you be so tempted. Beloved hearts, you will need every erg of energy that I am transferring to you that I have gained as grant from my Father, from Alpha and Omega in the Great

Central Sun, from the supreme mighty I AM Presence of all life.

I have secured it. I give it to you. And until the hour of my return in the Spirit of the Christ Mass in 1981, I expect that you will respond in my name to the Adversary, that you will have the courage to speak out and know that as you speak out and rebuke and chastise and even bring the mighty sword of the Word to bear upon these fallen ones, that you will always have the reinforcement of my Electronic Presence, you will always have access to sufficient light and power of heaven and earth to defeat, to roll back, and to silence their blasphemy against the living Word.

Therefore use it wisely. For the hours of intensity of the battle always appear in the month before winter solstice, and that is the hour when you require the last morsels of light held in the very flasks of your own inner laboratory of the soul. Therefore that which is received in solstice is for every day of the coming year. Treasure it. Use it. It is the most precious commodity of life.

We are intense in this hour because Sanat Kumara is intense. Therefore let us meditate upon the intensity of our God and let us not let the light of true prophecy go out in the land.

Where the Spirit of the prophet is, where the Spirit of the messenger is in the heart of the chela, there the entire mantle of the Great White Brotherhood is upon you. Where there is true inner alignment and not mere lip service, where there is the willingness to be divested of all filthiness and uncleanness, where there is the willingness for the exposure of the lie of self-deception—there the true Spirit of prophecy will flow!

Early seek counsel while I AM here. Early seek light while ye have the light. And do not be as the betrayers, sorting out a mechanical righteousness to this side and to that of an apparent (apparent to their eye) human consciousness in the messenger.

Beloved hearts, they have their day and they have their hour which is the hour of darkness.[28] Let them speak and let them be silenced by God. For by their expression of their own uncleanness they, too, manifest the acts, the decisions that result in their own judgment.

It is written that they will wax dull and therefore not be able to receive the truth lest they should repent and be saved. It is written that they will believe the lie and that their damnation will be just.[29] It is not just merely because they have believed the lie, but because they themselves are the fabric and the seed of the Liar. What they are is their judgment. What they do remains proof of what they are.

We come to bear witness to the light in your heart. You require that witness. The messenger requires that witness.

I AM the affirmation of the I AM Presence and the living Christ indwelling in ye all—all who submit unto that light in purest love. I AM the ever-present witness. I AM walking with you on the road to Emmaus,[30] which is the road to your own divine plan fulfilled on the path of initiation which I have walked.

I will not leave thee, my beloved. I will not leave thee in ignorance of what is coming upon the earth. I will not leave thee in a state of confusion or unknowing. I will not leave thee without the comfort of truth. And in this hour, truth is a sword. Thus be comforted in knowing. For when you know, you can act; and your actions will fulfill the requirements of the Law.

Make haste to the Inner Retreat.

I seal you and I seal my place in the cosmic cross of white fire. It is indeed a joyous Christ Mass on earth and in heaven in the heart of all who are of the mystical body of the eternal Christos.

In the name of my beloved Mother and my beloved Father, I salute you, child of my heart.

December 25, 1980
Camelot
Los Angeles County, California
ECP

NOTES*

FOREWORD
1. Gal. 1:12.
2. Rev. 1:1.
3. Luke 17:21.
4. Matt. 24.
5. John 14:12.

CHAPTER 1: "Except Ye Eat the Flesh of the Son of Man…"
1. John 10:30.
2. Rev. 3:8.
3. John 6:53–58.
4. Heb. 13:8.
5. Matt. 25:1–13.
6. John 10:10.
7. Matt. 21:12.
8. Matt. 13:24–30, 36–43.
9. Matt. 10:40.
10. Rev. 1–3.
11. Luke 21:19.
12. Isa. 52:10.

CHAPTER 2: Be the Saviour of One Life
1. Phil. 4:7.
2. I John 4:4.
3. John 16:33.
4. Lake Titicaca. The retreat of the God and Goddess Meru, Manus of the sixth root race, is located in the etheric plane over Lake Titicaca in the Andes. The ascended master Casimir Poseidon ruled an ancient civilization on the continent of South America during its rise to the

---
*N.B. Books listed here are published by Summit University Press unless otherwise noted.

heights of a golden age. In a dictation given October 5, 1975, Casimir Poseidon explained that this civilization declined because the people "did not give the glory unto the Lord for every accomplishment of science and culture," and it was eventually destroyed by cataclysm. Before this took place, he and a band of disciples "withdrew to North America to seal that light, to seal the scrolls of that culture in a place, the point of a pyramid now located in Colorado. And we anchored there the records of the ancient civilization."

5. See Luke 10:1.
6. See Rom. 10:13.
7. John 14:2.

CHAPTER 3: **Our Sacred Labor of Love in the New Jerusalem**

1. John 17:20–26.
2. Matt. 24:35; Mark 13:31; Luke 21:33; I Pet. 1:24, 25.
3. Mark 7:34.
4. Ps. 2:7; Acts 13:33; Heb. 1:5; 5:5.

CHAPTER 4: **The Messenger and the Living Church**

1. John 18:36.
2. Eph. 6:11.
3. Catherine of Siena (1347–1380) was a saint, mystic, Dominican tertiary, prolific author, and activist during the turbulent fourteenth century in Italy. She is known for her attempts to reform a corrupt Church and for convincing Pope Gregory XI to return the papacy to Rome, which occurred on January 17, 1377, after being in Avignon, France, for seventy years. When the "Great Schism" broke out between Pope Gregory's successor, Urban VI, and a rival pope (antipope) whom the cardinals elected in Avignon, Catherine devoted herself to restoring the papacy and the legitimate pope, which was accomplished after her death. Catherine gave her life at age thirty-three to save the Church and the papacy. Her greatest work is the *Dialogue,* a spiritual treatise in the form of conversations with God the Father dictated by Catherine to her secretaries during a five-day state of ecstasy. Nearly 400 of her letters to prelates, sovereigns, and her disciples have survived, as well as twenty-six of her prayers. Catherine was declared a Doctor of the Church in 1970.
4. *Her life as blessed Catherine.* The messenger Elizabeth Clare Prophet was previously embodied as Saint Catherine of Siena.
5. *I have placed upon her the burden to be my vicar.* On July 2, 1973, the ascended lady master Portia announced that Elizabeth Clare Prophet,

the Mother of the Flame, had been anointed as the Vicar of Christ in this age: "It has become necessary and it has been decided by the Knight Commander, by Jesus the Christ, and by the Darjeeling Council that the Great White Brotherhood should vest the authority of the Vicar of Christ and the head of the true Church, the Church Universal and Triumphant, in the Mother of the Flame. Although she has not desired to make this known to you or to tell you publicly of the visitation which she received a year ago from Jesus the Christ in which he anointed her as the Vicar of Christ, we have desired to make this announcement to this body this day." (1973 *Pearls of Wisdom*, vol. 16, no. 51)
6. Mark 14:58.
7. See Acts 2:20.
8. See Josh. 4:23.
9. Matt. 25:40.
10. Luke 10:19.

CHAPTER 5:   **The Sacred Fire Judgment of the Holy Spirit**

1. Exod. 13:21.
2. James 1:22.
3. Matt. 5:18.

CHAPTER 6:   **My Mission with Saint Germain**

1. See Ps. 118:19.
2. Matt. 18:14.
3. Matt. 7:15.
4. See Rev. 19:12.
5. The motion picture you have begun. Jesus is referring to the movie on the history of The Summit Lighthouse, which had been many years in the making. Now entitled *The Extraordinary Story of The Summit Lighthouse: 1958–2018,* it is an inspiring film that takes the viewer on a sacred journey with Mark and Elizabeth Prophet as they individually meet the master El Morya and embark on their special mission. It includes all dictations given at the founding of The Summit Lighthouse on August 7, 1958, and dictations from the thirty-third anniversary of The Summit Lighthouse on August 11, 1991. The album contains three DVDs and one MP3 audio CD; available at https://Store.SummitLighthouse.org.
6. Matt. 8:28–34; Mark 5:1–17; Luke 8:26–33.
7. See Rev. 19:20.
8. Animal magnetism is a magnetic forcefield surrounding all persons,

which is determined by the rate of vibration of their individual thoughts, feelings, and records of past lives, including those recorded in the electronic belt (the subconscious and unconscious mind). An individual's personal magnetism or magnetic personality is an intangible quality made up of the combination of many complex factors of the ego. For further teaching on the four types of animal magnetism (malicious, ignorant, sympathetic, and delicious), see Mark L. Prophet and Elizabeth Clare Prophet, *Paths of Light and Darkness,* pp. 174–78; available at https://Store.SummitLighthouse.org.
9. See Matt. 18:20; Mark 16:17; John 14:13; 16:23; Acts 4:10, 12; Phil. 2:10–12; Col. 3:17.
10. Gen. 32.
11. John 1:14.

CHAPTER 7:   Come to the Marriage Feast

1. Ps. 121:8.
2. Isa. 45:11.
3. Matt. 20:23.
4. Matt. 28:20.
5. John 6:39, 40, 44, 54.
6. Matt. 22:2–14.
7. John 2:6–11.
8. Matt. 22:4.
9. Ps. 23:5.
10. Matt. 22:5.
11. John 16:2.
12. Luke 23:34.
13. I John 2:23.
14. Rev. 10:7; 11:10, 18.
15. Matt. 25:29.
16. Luke 17:21.
17. Rom. 8:6.
18. Matt. 19:26.
19. Eph. 5:1.
20. James 1:17.
21. Dan. 12:5.
22. Rev. 21:9.
23. Matt. 22:13.
24. I Cor. 6:20.
25. Phil. 3:13, 14.
26. Matt. 22:14.

CHAPTER 8: As My Father Hath Sent Me, Even So Send I You

1. Rev. 1:10.
2. See John 14:26.
3. Matt. 13:13.
4. Matt. 16:23; Mark 8:33.
5. Acts 10:34; Rom. 2:11.
6. See Eph. 2:20.
7. See Luke 1:35.
8. Matt. 22:14.
9. Matt. 8:12; 13:42, 50; 25:30; Luke 13:28.
10. Eph. 6:12.
11. Matt. 21:12–13; Mark 11:15–17; Luke 19:45–46; John 2:13–16.
12. Isa. 9:7; Luke 1:33.
13. Matt. 16:18.
14. See Matt. 5:18.
15. See John 2:19–21.
16. Bishop Lefebvre. Marcel Lefebvre (1905–1991) was a French Roman Catholic archbishop who strongly objected to the changes and reforms of the Second Vatican Council (1962–1965), under the reign of Pope Paul VI (1963–1978), as well as to socialist and Marxist trends within the Catholic Church. Lefebvre believed that the reforms were "contributing to the destruction of the Church." Lefebvre was in favor of retaining the Traditional Latin Mass as opposed to the New Mass of Paul VI. Although excommunicated by Pope John Paul II in 1988, Lefebvre never relinquished his office as archbishop and continued to ordain priests according to the Traditional Latin Rite. Lefebvre was the author of many books, which are still available today.
17. Isa. 55:8.
18. Cardinal Mindszenty (1892–1975) was a Hungarian prelate of the Roman Catholic Church and was known for his uncompromising stance against fascism, the Hungarian Nazi movement, and the Communist regime in Hungary. Mindszenty was created a cardinal by Pope Pius XII in 1946. He opposed the secularization of Catholic Schools and the seizing of Church properties by the Communist regime. Mindszenty was arrested in 1948, accused of treason and conspiracy against the Communist Hungarian People's Republic, imprisoned, tortured, and eventually forced to confess. In 1956 Mindszenty was released and granted asylum in the United States Embassy in Budapest when the Russian Soviets invaded Hungary, and in 1971 he was permitted to leave Hungary to live in Vienna, Austria. Pope Paul VI requested that Mindszenty resign his titles and

rank in the Catholic Church, but Mindszenty never complied. In 1973, Pope Paul VI stripped Cardinal Mindszenty of all of his titles and he was forbidden to speak against the Communists. Cardinal Mindszenty died on May 6, 1975, at age 83. His *Memoirs* were published in 1974 and are still available. On February 4, 1975, Elizabeth Clare Prophet commented that Pope Paul VI did not have the courage to ever physically face Cardinal Mindszenty. She said, "The Pope, you see, in his state of compromise, cannot look into the bright light of this man's soul. You know why? Because he would be looking into the face of Jesus Christ." The messenger has also stated that Cardinal Mindszenty is an ascended master.

19. Jer. 23:1.
20. See Dan. 3:16–28.
21. Matt. 25:23.
22. Matt. 3:17; 17:5; Mark 1:11; 9:7; Luke 9:35; II Pet. 1:17.
23. Rom. 12:19.
24. See Matt. 11:10; Mark 1:2; Luke 1:17; 3:4; 7:27.
25. Matt. 10:22; 24:13; Mark 13:13.
26. Mark 16:15.
27. Matt. 10:40.
28. Ps. 118:26; Matt. 23:39; Mark 11:19; Luke 19:30.
29. Gen. 3:24.
30. John 14:23.
31. See Matt. 25:40.
32. Matt. 24:42, 44; 25:13; Luke 12:40.
33. Rev. 1:8; 22:13.
34. Heb. 13:2.
35. Luke 17:21.
36. Matt. 11:28.
37. Matt. 11:30.
38. "God tempers the wind to the shorn lamb" was originally a French proverb made popular in English by Laurence Sterne (1713–1768) from his novel *A Sentimental Journey* (1768).
39. See Rev. 6:9.
40. Matt. 28:20.

CHAPTER 9: They Shall Not Pass!

1. John 11:25.
2. Isa. 55:11.
3. Rev. 12:17.
4. Matt. 7:24–25; 16:18; I Cor. 10:4.

5. Rev. 15–17.
6. Luke 17:23.
7. Matt. 16:17; I Cor. 15:50.
8. I Pet. 3:4.
9. Luke 21:28.
10. Exod. 7:10.
11. See Djwal Kul and Kuthumi, *The Human Aura: How to Activate and Energize Your Aura and Chakras* (2015 ed.), Book 2, chapter 8; available at https://Store.SummitLighthouse.org.
12. Matt. 9:20–22.
13. I John 4:4.
14. Rev. 19:11.
15. Mark 5:9.
16. Dan. 5:27.
17. Rev. 12:6.
18. John 1:9.
19. Rev. 12:1.

CHAPTER 10: **The Communication of the Word**

1. Matt. 5:17.
2. Luke 1:46–55. Also see song 98, "The Magnificat," in Church Universal and Triumphant's *Book of Hymns and Songs;* available at https://Store.SummitLighthouse.org.
3. Ps. 70:4.
4. The two-by-two, door-to-door program was introduced at Summit University in 1976. Students went two by two, knocking on doors to introduce people to the teachings of the ascended masters, gave them flyers or a packet of information, and invited them to a lecture or conference. The program was designed to fulfill a required initiation on the Path based on Jesus' sending forth his disciples to preach (Matt. 10:5–14; Mark 6:7–13; Luke 9:1–6). The emphasis of this program was the heart-to-heart contact with each individual. On December 24, 1976, Elizabeth Clare Prophet explained: "The reason Jesus gave the initiation without purse, without scrip [sack or pouch] was for the initiation of the Holy Spirit and that white light, that fourth ray, the utter reliance upon the spirit within, without preparation, without knowing what you will say to deliver unto the people that message of salvation.... So the alchemy is between the flame in your heart, the flame in the people inside that house, and the flame of the ascended masters who accompany you." Mrs. Prophet also stated that the mantra of the two-by-two, door-to-door program is

"I AM the open door which no man can shut."
5. Jim Jones (1931–1978) was the leader and self-proclaimed prophet and messiah of a religious community in Guyana, South America, which he named Jonestown, originally located in San Francisco and named the People's Temple. As a result of accusations that Jones was diverting the income of community members for his own use, Jones and his followers immigrated to Guyana in 1977 and established his agricultural utopian community. The following year, U.S. Rep. Leo Ryan of California arrived in Jonestown with reporters and relatives of community members in order to investigate (unofficially) alleged financial and physical abuses. Jones ordered them assassinated, and Ryan and four others were murdered. On November 18, 1978, Jones ordered his followers to drink cyanide "punch." Over 900 of his followers were found dead when Guyanese troops arrived. Jones died of a gunshot wound to the head, possibly self-inflicted.
6. Rev. Moon (1920–2012) was the leader of the Unification Church, founded in South Korea in 1954. Moon moved his church to the United States and his movement became popular in the 1970s, although he received much criticism. Moon was eventually convicted and imprisoned for tax evasion. His church expanded in the 1990s, and in 1994 Moon founded the International Federation of World Peace. His followers proclaimed him the Messiah. Master Kuthumi writes of Moon as follows: "He is counted by us [to be] among the arch-deceivers of mankind.... You can read in Moon's Divine Principle the work of the Serpent himself.... In the step-by-step, computerized, mechanized carnal logic of the Serpent, he presents his condemnation and his judgment of the life and mission and teaching of Jesus Christ, John the Baptist, and others. He says that because they failed, the Lord of the Second Advent, the Messiah [Moon], must come to open the way to the kingdom of heaven." (1976 *Pearls of Wisdom*, vol. 19, no. 11)
7. Guru Nanak (1469–1539) was the founder of the Sikh religious movement dedicated to the message and worship of the One God. Sikhs are devoted to the practice of chanting the name of God. Sikhism (from the Sanskrit root meaning "disciple" or "learner") is the world's fifth largest organized religion.
8. See Rev. 2:9.
9. Matt. 26:1–5, 57; John 11:47–51; 18:12–14, 24, 28. Joseph ben Caiaphas (14 B.C.–A.D. 46) was the Jewish high priest and head of the Sanhedrin who engineered the trial and crucifixion of Jesus. Caiaphas held the office of high priest from A.D. 18 to A.D. 36.
10. See Luke 10:1.
11. Jesus may be referring to the 144 sons and daughters who were

chosen by Sanat Kumara to go to earth to prepare the way for the 144,000 souls who had volunteered to go with him to save the planet from darkness.
12. The Chapel of the Holy Grail was the main sanctuary at Camelot in Malibu, California, headquarters of The Summit Lighthouse and Church Universal and Triumphant from 1978 through 1986.
13. See II Kings 5:1–14.
14. See Ezek. 10:10.
15. "The New Colossus" is referring to the poem by Emma Lazarus located at the base of the Statue of Liberty.
16. John Wierlo (1919–2000), later known as Johnny Lovewisdom, was an American-Finnish author of books on religion, spirituality, diet, health, clairvoyance, and "ascensional science," and was named the "hermit-saint of the Andes." Lovewisdom believed himself to be the reincarnation of Ananda (disciple of Gautama Buddha), Milarepa, and John the Baptist, and to be the official successor to Kuthumi Lal Singh. He founded the International University of Natural Living at Vilcabamba, Ecuador, in 1962, where he promoted a strict fruitarian diet. His two-volume autobiography is entitled *Maitreya: The New Age World Teacher*. Many of his books sold millions of copies and are still available today.
17. The retreat of the God and Goddess Meru, known as the Temple of Illumination, is located over Lake Titicaca, high in the Andes Mountains on the Peru-Bolivia border. Jesus, the Blessed Mother, and many saints have studied in this retreat. The center of the retreat is directly over the remains of an ancient temple on an island in this lake called the Island of the Sun. For a description of this retreat, see *The Masters and Their Retreats*, by Mark L. Prophet and Elizabeth Clare Prophet, pp. 478–80; available at https://Store.SummitLighthouse.org.
18. See note 5 on Jim Jones.
19. The term *stump* means to travel over a region making political speeches and to promote a cause. On November 1, 1977, the messenger Elizabeth Clare Prophet was called by El Morya to stump the cities of America, preaching the basic message of the I AM Presence, the violet flame, and the science of the spoken Word. After traveling to Ghana, Liberia, and England, the messenger began stumping in the U.S. in the winter and fall of 1978, concluding on November 14, 1978, having traveled to twenty-seven cities.
20. Rev. 3:16.
21. Matt. 16:23; Mark 8:33.
22. See Matt. 19:28.
23. Rev. 12:1.

24. Decree 0.05, "I AM Alert, Awake, Awake!" in *Prayers, Meditations and Dynamic Decrees for Personal and World Transformation;* available at https://Store.SummitLighthouse.org.
25. Rev. 19:7. Jesus may be stating that Francis and Clare (who are not twin flames) held the focus for the twin flames Jesus and Magda during Francis' and Clare's mission in the Franciscan Order.

CHAPTER 11: **Dedicate Yourself to the Issue of Abortion, for upon This Issue Hang All Others**

1. John 10:30.
2. Matt. 18:5, 6.
3. In a letter dated April 26, 1951, before the founding of The Summit Lighthouse, Mark L. Prophet announced to his chelas the formation of the Order of the Holy Child—a sacred order for legislators, rulers, directors of culture and citizens who would promise to be "ever-mindful of the little child of the future." Now as the ascended master Lanello, Mark Prophet continues to sponsor this holy order for the defense and protection of the little child. For more on the Order of the Holy Child and how to become a member, go to www.HolyOrders.org.
4. The Order of the Sons and Daughters of Dominion was founded by Mother Mary in 1972 for those who would elect to master energy-in-motion, or the emotions. It was a spiritual order of men and women who were pledged to the service of the Mother through their vows to take dominion over the elements, the astral plane and lunar energies, and to gain self-mastery in the planes of Matter through the example of Jesus Christ. This holy order has been inactive since the 1980s.
5. *The Feast of Saint Stephen* was a four-day conference held at Camelot a few days after this dictation was delivered.
6. Handbook on abortion. The handbook *Life Begets Life* is no longer available. However, in 1991 the messenger Elizabeth Clare Prophet conducted the seminar "Life Begets Life," parts of which are published as "The Continuity of the Soul," available on DVD, and "The Dilemma of Life on Earth," on three MP3 discs. See also Dr. Neroli Duffy, *Wanting to Be Born: The Cry of the Soul,* based on the teachings of Elizabeth Clare Prophet. All are available at https://Store.Summit Lighthouse.org.
7. Matt. 24:22; Mark 13:20.
8. Montessori International was a private school founded by Mark and Elizabeth Prophet in 1970 for children from preschool through the twelfth grade. The curriculum was based on the educational principles set forth by Dr. Maria Montessori and the ascended masters.

9. Matt. 13:24–30.
10. Matt. 10:6.
11. Zero Population Growth (ZPG) is a theory of demographic balance in which the number of people in a specific population is maintained at a consistent level by allowing only the amount of live births that are necessary to replace the existing population. The organization Population Connection promotes ZPG, striving to ensure that every woman "who wants to delay or end her childbearing" is able to do so, and working "directly with Congress and the White House to inform family planning policy and funding levels."
12. Before this dictation, the messenger read and gave teachings from the Book of Isaiah, particularly chapters 44 and 45 as well as 9:2, 3 and 55:11.

CHAPTER 12: The Symphony of the Resurrection Flame

1. Joseph, the father of Jesus and husband of Mary, was a previous embodiment of Saint Germain, the God of Freedom for the New Age. Francis Bacon (another embodiment of Saint Germain) wrote the utopian novel *New Atlantis*.
2. Luke 20:9–18.
3. Rev. 3:11.
4. Samuel (early 11th century B.C.), prophet and judge in Israel, was a previous embodiment of Saint Germain.
5. See Mark 9:1.
6. John 14:18.
7. Jesus is referring to the content and teaching given in the Book of Revelation. Although the four cosmic forces are not mentioned by name in Revelation, they have been equated by the ascended masters with the offices of the Lion, the Calf, the Man, and the Eagle, also known as the four beasts. (Rev. 4:7–8) These offices are held by Lord Maitreya, Gautama Buddha, Jesus Christ, and Sanat Kumara, respectively. For extensive teaching, see the index under "Four Cosmic Forces," in Mark L. Prophet and Elizabeth Clare Prophet, *The Opening of the Seventh Seal: Sanat Kumara on the Path of the Ruby Ray;* available at https://Store.SummitLighthouse.org.
8. See Rev. 22:1.
9. Our coming through our witness. The messenger Elizabeth Clare Prophet traveled to Ghana, Africa, from September 12–19, 1976, and in January of 1978, on a mission for the masters where she delivered many lectures, dictations, and admonitions to the people and government of Ghana.

10. The crumbling of the temple wall. Jesus is alluding to the destruction of the temple in Jerusalem by the Romans in A.D. 70. See Matt. 24:1–2; Mark 13:1–2.
11. The two angels. Jesus is referring to the scenario of his resurrection, where he appears to Mary Magdalene. John 20:11–12 reads: "But Mary stood without at the sepulchre weeping: and as she wept, she stooped down, and looked into the sepulchre, and seeth two angels in white sitting, the one at the head, and the other at the feet, where the body of Jesus had lain."
12. The retreat of the resurrection flame is called The Resurrection Temple, which is a focus of the resurrection flame and the retreat of Jesus and Mary in the etheric realm over the Holy Land. Angels of the resurrection flame serve there, and Uriel and Aurora and Gabriel and Hope frequent the retreat in order to expand the flame of the resurrection on behalf of mankind. For a description of this retreat, see *The Masters and Their Retreats*, pp. 456–58; available at https://Store.SummitLighthouse.org.
13. Matt. 25:40.
14. Matt. 7:9.
15. Matt. 28:20.

CHAPTER 13: Take My Cup, and Drink Ye All of It

1. Saint Germain inaugurated Mission Amethyst Jewel in a dictation given on November 19, 1978, for the guarding of the flame of freedom "from Alaska to the very tip of South America." Saint Germain requested that the messenger appoint and anoint sons and daughters of God to go forth from Camelot two by two into the nations. In a lecture given on April 14, 1979, the messenger explained that "Mission Amethyst Jewel is based upon the principle of the violet flame burning within the heart of the chela. The chela is the jewel, and as chelas place themselves together as atoms that become molecules that form outer centers, the Mission Amethyst Jewel becomes crystallized.... So Amethyst Jewel, then, is Saint Germain's commitment to send chelas to the nations of the earth, beginning with the most important cities.... The requirement for a nucleus of lightbearers in any city is two or three."
2. Jesus may be explaining that the mysteries of the Holy Grail are for the children of the light rather than for the fallen ones. On February 17, 1979, Elizabeth Clare Prophet said: "Jesus never gave his body and his blood to Satan, to Lucifer, to Beelzebub or any of the fallen angels who denied the Word, nor will he give it to those of them who

remain in embodiment today. And so in this hour, as it has ever been, the mysteries of the Holy Grail are given to the children of the light. The words that I speak may be respoken by others, but the energy of God is never conveyed with those words to the fallen ones. They may read [them], they may intellectually be able to explain the mysteries, but they can never in all eternity sit and sup at the Lord's table."
3. Elizabeth Clare Prophet explains that at summer solstice the earth receives its third increment of light for the energizing and mastery of the desire body. This light is also for the mastery of the flow of emotion, or energy-in-motion. Transmuting the emotional energies of the planet is one of the purposes of the July conference every year, as well as to anchor the flame of the Mother in the sign of Cancer at summer solstice on behalf of earth and her evolutions.
4. The Freedom conference in the year that this dictation was given was entitled *The Coming Revolution in Higher Consciousness*. The ascended master Mighty Victory dictated during this conference.
5. John 11:1–44.
6. See Isa. 55:11.
7. Luke 19:13.
8. Matt. 24:27.

CHAPTER 14: **The Words of My Father**

1. After converting Paul (Acts 9:1–20), Jesus raised him up as his apostle. In *The Masters and Their Retreats* (pp. 133–34), the ascended master Hilarion, who was embodied as the apostle Paul, recalls his encounter with the Christ: "Jesus the Christ we called him, and we were called of him as you are called this day. I recall the memories of his coming to me, empowering me with his Word. Yet first he humbled me... that I might bow to my own Christ flame that he revealed to me, as he also gave to me the key of meditation upon that flame that I might walk in his footsteps.... Thus, I was turned around, converted by the Spirit of the Lord in the full manifestation of Jesus Christ upon me." *The Masters and Their Retreats* is available at https://Store.Summit Lighthouse.org.
2. During the sermon before the dictation, the messenger read from the Book of Ezekiel, chapters 1, 3, and 4.
3. Sanat Kumara gave to Ezekiel a vision (Ezek. 1:1–28) and commission (Ezek. 2:3). In *The Opening of the Seventh Seal*, Sanat Kumara describes Ezekiel's response to his call: "He gave his life for Israel. He set the example as the man of Aquarius.... He did not let me down...." (pp. 42–43) "The LORD chose to reveal himself to Ezekiel as the

Creator, ... as the one Jehovah, at once the impersonal sacred fire, at once the personal Presence walking and talking with him as friend, as teacher—as God himself. I was that God Presence unto Ezekiel. I gave to him the commission as Watchman of the Word...." (pp. 73–74) "The living soul Ezekiel, a daring and devout witness ... responded to me with the exercise of his free will. He accepted from me the Calling, the Commission, and the Covenant...." (p. 74) Sanat Kumara bids us to "call for the initiations which I gave to Ezekiel to be given unto you, step by step." (p. 76) See *The Opening of the Seventh Seal,* available at https://Store.SummitLighthouse.org.

4. The day of this dictation, May 24, 1979, is the day of the celebration of Jesus' ascension. According to Christian tradition it is a moveable date, most often celebrated in May, forty days after Easter.
5. Jesus may be referring to what was called "Ascension Hill" located at Camelot, the headquarters of The Summit Lighthouse from 1978 through 1986. "Ascension's hill" may also be referring to the "hill," the place and location of each one's ascension.
6. See Ezek. 1:5–28.
7. See Gen. 15:17.
8. The Freedom conference that was held at Camelot from June 30, 1979, through July 5, 1979, was entitled *The Coming Revolution in Higher Consciousness.* The "Upper Room training" refers to the Seminar of the World Teachers held in the Chapel of the Holy Grail at Camelot from July 9, 1979, through July 20, 1979. The messenger explained that this seminar was for those who are "called to be representatives of the World Teachers ... to convey to you the ability to teach, to give you the initiations necessary ... and ultimately to prepare you for the bestowal of the mantle."
9. The retreat of the God and Goddess Meru is known as the Temple of Illumination, located in the etheric plane over Lake Titicaca in the Andes Mountains on the Peru-Bolivia border. This retreat is the focus of the feminine ray of the Godhead to the earth. For further information, see *The Masters and Their Retreats,* pp. 478–80.
10. The messenger Elizabeth Clare Prophet was embodied as the representative of the Divine Mother on the lost continent of Lemuria, which extended to what are now the shores of California. The messenger's return to Lemuria/California coincided with the period of the mission at Camelot.
11. Jeanette MacDonald (1903–1965) and Nelson Eddy (1901–1967) were movie stars and singing partners in the 1930s and early 1940s, best known for their work together in eight classic operettas, such as *Rose Marie* (1936) and *Maytime* (1937). The ascended masters

have revealed that they are twin flames.
12. The ascended masters have taught that Los Angeles is the seat-of-the-soul chakra of America, focusing the violet flame for the nation.

CHAPTER 15: Willingness to Confront the Adversary

1. *The turning aside of my father and my mother by Serpent.* (Gen. 2:15–17; 3) In the Genesis account of Adam and Eve in the Garden of Eden, which was on Lemuria, God commanded, "Of the tree of the knowledge of good and evil, thou shalt not eat of it: for in the day that thou eatest thereof thou shalt surely die." But Adam and Eve believed the Serpent's lie, "Ye shall not surely die," and they partook of the fruit of the tree. For their disobedience, the LORD God exiled them from the Garden. Mark Prophet has said, "By the knowledge of relative good and evil, the consciousness of absolute Good that was once in man and woman in the Garden, able to directly apprehend the Father and the unity of the Father's expression, was cut off. It no longer lived in man." Driven away from the Garden of Eden, Adam and Eve were required to pass the same tests they had failed in the Garden but under much more difficult conditions. Elizabeth Prophet has said that God told Adam and Eve that they would have to wait for their redemption until the coming of his Son, indicating the long journey into night that succeeding generations would have to bear.
2. *Death at the hand of Cain.* (Gen. 4:1–8) After Adam and Eve left the Garden of Eden, Eve gave birth to Cain and then to Abel, who was an embodiment of Jesus. Abel, a righteous man, was a keeper of the sheep and his offering was accepted by the LORD. But when his brother Cain, a tiller of the ground, brought his offering, the LORD did not accept it. In anger Cain rose up and slew Abel.
3. *Jesus placed under Lord Maitreya . . .* relates to his position in the lineage of Gurus of the Great White Brotherhood called the hierarchy of the ruby ray. The chain of hierarchy in this lineage descends from the Ancient of Days (Sanat Kumara) to Gautama Buddha, to Lord Maitreya, to Jesus Christ and then to Padma Sambhava.
4. *I stood as David before Goliath.* (I Sam. 17:48–51) Prior to his final incarnation as the Nazarene master, the soul of Jesus was embodied as David (c. 1043–973 B.C.), one of the most loved and revered figures in Hebrew history. As a young shepherd boy, David single-handedly slew the Philistine giant Goliath. The messenger Elizabeth Clare Prophet has said that Goliath represented David's dweller-on-the-threshold. She said that David could not have defeated Goliath if he had not slain the dweller within himself. It was a spiritual initiation

that he had to pass in order to eventually rise in stature to become the king of Israel.
5. Rev. 17:8.
6. The Lamentations of Jeremiah is a book in the Old Testament in which the prophet Jeremiah weeps and mourns the condition of his people—their having been manipulated by the fallen ones, their cowardice, their nonreceptivity to God's teachings, and their suffering the karmic recompense for their iniquities and transgressions.
7. The Temple of the Resurrection, or the Resurrection Temple, is the retreat of Jesus and Mary over the city of Jerusalem in the Holy Land. For more on the Resurrection Temple, see *The Masters and Their Retreats,* pp. 456–58; available at https://Store.SummitLighthouse.org.
8. Rev. 22:11.
9. The shortening of the days for the elect of God. Matt. 24:22; Mark 13:20.
10. Luke 2:49.

CHAPTER 16: **Rekindling the Essential Identity of Every Living Soul**

1. Matt. 5:13; 6:23.
2. John 18:37.
3. Matt. 9:13.
4. Rev. 3:4, 5; 5; 6:9–11; 7:9–17; 17:14; 19:7–9; 21:9–27; 22:1–5.
5. John 10:1–30; 14:6.
6. Matt. 7:13, 14.
7. John 6:29.
8. John 14:15–18, 26; 15:26, 27; 16:7–15.
9. John 14:12.
10. Phil. 2:5.
11. Acts 10:42; I Pet. 4:1–6.
12. John 12:31, 32.
13. Matt. 11:7; 3:11, 12.
14. John 20:22.
15. Luke 24:49.
16. Gal. 5:1–6; James 2:8–13.
17. I John 4.
18. I Cor. 3:16, 17.
19. Matt. 26:17–29.
20. Rev. 7:3, 4; 14:1–5.
21. Ps. 23:3.
22. Isa. 11:1–10.

23. Each Easter Sunday, Jesus receives the children at the altar. Children, counted through age eighteen, pass by the messenger and receive the blessing of the Lord Christ. The baptisms of the new infants, coming from all over the world, are also received.
24. Rev. 12:1–6.

CHAPTER 17: "Almost Free!"

1. See Saint Germain, "A Victory Celebration: Almighty God Is the Winner!" in 1980 *Pearls of Wisdom,* vol. 23, no. 46, delivered November 5, 1980, one day after the landslide election of Ronald Reagan.
2. Mal. 4:2: "But unto you that fear my name [I AM THAT I AM Sanat Kumara] shall the Sun of righteousness [the Sun of the mighty I AM Presence] arise with healing in his wings [manifest in the Person of the Christ Self]; . . ." Thus beloved Jesus is proclaiming the present era as the hour of the fulfillment of the LORD's prophecy given through Malachi—that the children of God should know the LORD by the power of his name and should behold him "in their midst" as the blazing Sun of their own God Self revealed through the Christ.
3. Matt. 7:1.
4. John 7:24.
5. John 6:29.
6. Behind bars on Sirius. Satan was seized and bound by Archangel Michael in 1968. On February 1, 1982, Jesus said, "I announce to you that the Word has gone forth on Wednesday past, in the very triumph and the hour of the twenty-seventh, for the remanding to the Court of the Sacred Fire of the one you have known for so long as Satan." (1982 *Pearls of Wisdom,* vol. 25, no. 16) For more information see "The Final Judgment of Satan" in *The Word,* volume 5, chapter 5.
7. Rev. 21:2, 10–27.
8. Luke 24:49.
9. Matt. 27:51.
10. Acts 10:34.
11. Isa. 1:18.
12. Ps. 24:1; I Cor. 10:26, 28.
13. Matt. 26:36–46.
14. Mark 14:36; Gal. 4:6.
15. Luke 22:42.
16. Matt. 26:28; Heb. 9:22.
17. John 8:1–11.
18. John 6:53, 54.

19. Isa. 25:8; I Cor. 15:54.
20. John 6:35.

CHAPTER 18: **The Sacred Walk to the Immaculate Heart of Mary**

1. Rev. 12:1.
2. John 10:10.
3. Luke 1:38.
4. Rev. 12:17.
5. Refers to the Book of Revelation, recorded by John the Evangelist.
6. Isa. 40:31.
7. John 6:35.
8. Matt. 10:16.
9. Rev. 15, 16. See *Vials of the Seven Last Plagues: The Judgments of Almighty God Delivered by the Seven Archangels.*
10. Rev. 9:3–11.
11. Gen. 2:9; 3:22, 24; Rev. 2:7; 22:2, 14.
12. See Sanat Kumara, *The Opening of the Seventh Seal,* chapters 32, 33, and 34.
13. Rev. 20:1–3. See also chapter 17, this volume, note 6.
14. Eph. 6:12.
15. Matt. 24:22.
16. Those whose works must be tried have been tried. On November 22, 1980, Saint Germain said: "You have seen that fiery vortex descend in that city of sin, Las Vegas. You have seen it descend in Los Angeles, which is not yet a city free of sin. You may wonder how the judgment can descend and innocent life be taken. You must understand that salamanders are supremely obedient to the divine will. Their orders are cut by the Karmic Board. They bypass those who are under the protection of the guardian angels. And no life lost ever occurs by accident, but in supreme fairness and justice this transition becomes a point of maximum opportunity for that soul to rise from the ashes of greed into a higher evolution—if they so choose." See "The Watchman of the Night," 1980 *Pearls of Wisdom,* vol. 23, no. 48. Endnote 8 in that *Pearl* provided additional information: On November 21, 1980, the MGM Grand Hotel in Las Vegas, Nevada, burst into flames in the second worst hotel fire in U.S. history. Eighty-three persons died and 534 were injured. On November 16, Santa Ana winds gusting up to 90 m.p.h. whipped wildfires across more than 63,000 acres of brushland through the foothills and canyons of Los Angeles, Orange, Riverside, and San Diego Counties. In six separate

fires, 64 homes were destroyed. Property damage exceeded $25 million in Los Angeles County alone. On November 24, 90 m.p.h. winds drove a fire from the foothills into the city of San Bernardino, destroying at least 200 homes and 100 other structures. That same night, just two days following Saint Germain's dictation, a 2,600-acre brush fire in Malibu Canyon fanned by hurricane-force winds threatened to destroy Camelot. It was turned back on West Mulholland Highway just across the street from Camelot by a large number of firefighters, including the Camelot staff and the dynamic decrees of the community. All felt the intense presence of the Watchman of the Night, our dear Saint Germain. Praise the Lord! (I Cor. 3:13)
17. See the Book of Job.
18. On March 23, 1980, Cyclopea announced that "it is the ascended lady master Portia [Goddess of Justice, twin flame of Saint Germain] who shall be present at Summit University fall quarter 1980 for the purpose of the fulfillment of this dispensation whereby Saint Germain's causal body—by the feminine ray transmitted by Portia—shall be anchored in the world in a physical dimension that shall be the greatest opportunity that the world has ever known to become and to enter into the oneness of the God flame.... It is a final opportunity for those who are to come into the flame in this age to do so." Then on June 13, 1980, Portia said: "How I rejoice to descend out of octaves of light in the name of the God of Freedom. I come from the very heart of Sanat Kumara. As we took our vow to fulfill his glorious light of freedom, so we anticipated the hour when, through those who had gone before, we might be almost physical in the full intensity of the magnet of our heart's love."
19. Josh. 24:15.

CHAPTER 19:   **The Hour of the Sword Is Come**

1. Matt. 10:34.
2. Mark 11:15–18.
3. Rev. 6:8.
4. Rev. 9:1–11.
5. Jer. 2:8; 10:21; 12:10; 23:1, 2.
6. Pallas Athena announced the onset of the Coming Revolution in Higher Consciousness in her dictation at *Higher Consciousness: A Conference for Spiritual Freedom,* June 30, 1976. The messenger defines the Coming Revolution as "our involvement with the heavenly hosts and their cooperation with us, as prophesied in the Old and New Testaments at the end of the millennium when 'there shall

be a time of trouble, such as never was since there was a nation. . . . ' It is the hour of the coming of Archangel Michael, the protagonist who leads the armies of light against the rebellious ones. . . . It is time for every injustice to be challenged—not by the bloodbaths of prior revolutions, but by the acceleration of atoms and molecules of consciousness to the plane of the universal mind. One in that mind, one with the hosts of the LORD, we can say with Jesus Christ, 'All power is given unto me in heaven and in earth!'"

7. Gen. 6:3.
8. Matt. 13:45, 46.
9. During the Carter administration, the leaders of Western Europe began to chart a course increasingly independent of United States foreign policy. By the Venice Summit of June 1980, the U.S. seemed to have lost the position of dominance in the Western Alliance, with West Germany and France exerting greater leadership. (See "Carter's Impact on Europe," *U.S. News and World Report,* 7 July 1980, p. 16; "Fencing with the Soviets," *Newsweek,* 7 July 1980, p. 16.) One of the major areas of disagreement between U.S. and NATO leaders cropped up over the U.S. plan for economic sanctions against Iran. President Carter called for an embargo on April 7, 1980. Heads of state in NATO countries, particularly France and West Germany, were reticent to apply sanctions. The Carter administration threat to blockade Iran or to take direct military action persuaded the European Common Market nations to declare on April 22, 1980, that they would impose sanctions if no progress was made in the hostage negotiations by May 17, 1980. Then on May 22, 1980, 45 days after President Carter had made the public request for our allies to join the U.S. in imposing sanctions against Iran, Western European nations imposed a watered-down version of sanctions which, by one estimate, affected only 8 percent of Europe's $1.1 billion monthly trade with Iran. West Germany and France are major trading partners of Iran and had much to lose by the embargo. They were unwilling to jeopardize their own well-being and agreed to sanctions only under duress and with considerable misgivings. See Norman Kempster and Don Irwin, "Carter Severs Ties with Iran, Adds New Sanctions," *Los Angeles Times,* 8 April 1980, p. 1; Oswald Johnston, "U.S. Urges Allies to Back Iran Sanctions," *Los Angeles Times,* 9 April 1980, p. 1; "France," *Intelligence Digest,* 23 April 1980, p. [2]; Scott Sullivan, "The Shaky Alliance," *Newsweek,* 12 May 1980, p. 48; David Fouquet, "EC Scowls As It Starts Iran Embargo," *Christian Science Monitor,* 23 May 1980, p. 10; and James A. Phillips, "Iran, the United States and the Hostages: After 300 Days," Heritage Foundation *Backgrounder,* 29 August 1980.

10. Jer. 23:5, 6; 33:15, 16.
11. Jer. 23:1–4; John 10:11–13.
12. Matt. 8:11, 12; 13:47–50; 22:11–14; 24:48–51; 25:29, 30; Luke 13:24–28.
13. *Nephilim* [Hebrew *Nephilim* "those who fell" or "those who were cast down," from the Semitic root *naphal* "to fall"]: a biblical race of giants or demigods (Gen. 6:4). According to scholar Zecharia Sitchin, ancient Sumerian tablets depict the Nephilim as an extraterrestrial superrace who "fell" to earth in spacecraft 450,000 years ago. The ascended masters reveal that the Nephilim are the fallen angels cast out of heaven into the earth (Rev. 12:7–10, 12). They are of the lineage and descent of "the Watchers" revealed in the Book of Enoch.
14. Matt. 13:24–30, 36–43.
15. Rev. 19:14, 19–21.
16. On December 23, 1980, Patrick Wall, a Canadian environmentalist, made a daring underwater raid to free about 650 dolphins earmarked for slaughter by Japanese fishermen. Wall, wearing a wet suit, rode a rubber boat into the Futo harbor (Izu Peninsula, about sixty miles southwest of Tokyo), dived into the sea, and untied the net, allowing the dolphins to escape. "I did it," Wall said, "because I felt sorry for the dolphins destined for the killing as Christmas drew near."
17. John 14:2.
18. Matt. 28:18.
19. Rev. 12:1–8.
20. Each of the seven archangels is referred to as "Lord."
21. Rev. 19:11–16.
22. Pss. 35:19; 69:4; John 15:25.
23. John 14:18.
24. Isa. 11:10, 12.
25. Isa. 7:14; 9:6; Matt. 1:23.
26. The Dark Cycle of the return of mankind's karma began on April 23, 1969. It is a period when mankind's misqualified energy (i.e., their returning negative karma), held in abeyance for centuries under the great mercy of the Law, is released according to the cycles of the initiations of the solar hierarchies for balance in this period of transition into the Aquarian age. April 23, 1980, commenced the twelfth year of the Dark Cycle (initiation under the hierarchy of Sagittarius and their God consciousness of victory). On April 23, 1981, the initiations of the karmic return continued to mount under the hierarchy of Capricorn. The Dark Cycle concluded on April 22, 2002. For more information, see 1990 *Pearls of Wisdom*, vol. 33, no. 6, pp. 77–86.

27. Matt. 25:1–13.
28. Luke 22:53.
29. Isa. 6:9, 10; Matt. 13:13–15; II Thess. 2:10–12; Rom. 3:8.
30. Luke 24:13–16.

THE WORD

Mystical Revelations of Jesus Christ through His Two Witnesses

Volume 8 (1993-1998)   372 pp • ISBN 978-1-60988-370-6

Volume 7 (1989-1992)   304 pp • ISBN 978-1-60988-385-0

Volume 6 (1985-1988)   364 pp • ISBN 978-1-60988-403-1

Volume 5 (1981-1984)   402 pp • ISBN 978-1-60988-424-6

Jesus Christ is the avatar of the ages—the same yesterday, today, and forever. We knew him when he walked the streets of Atlantis and Lemuria. We also knew him in eras of darkness, when he sought to lead men to the light.

His message did not begin with the Bible, nor did it end with the Book of Revelation. He has never stopped speaking to his own.

Two thousand years ago, he foretold a time of tribulation—the end of an age. That time has come. It is the era when the mystery of God should be finished, when the Two Witnesses should prophesy "a thousand two hundred and threescore days."

And so Jesus once more delivers his Word to a world in transition. As always, the message is one of judgment to the fallen angels, admonishment to those who would walk in the light, hope for all who are striving on the path, and the vision of a golden age to come.

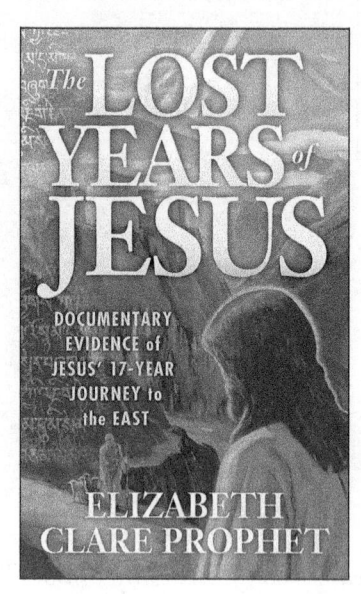

480 pp • ISBN 978-0-916766-87-0

THE LOST YEARS OF JESUS
Documentary Evidence of Jesus' 17-Year Journey to the East

"Reads like a detective thriller! It picks you up and never lets go of you."
—**Jess Stearn**, bestselling author of *Edgar Cayce: The Sleeping Prophet*

Ancient texts reveal that Jesus spent 17 years in the Orient. They say that from age 13 to age 29, Jesus traveled to India, Nepal, Ladakh and Tibet as both student and teacher. For the first time, Elizabeth Clare Prophet brings together the testimony of four eyewitnesses—and three variant translations—of these remarkable documents.

She tells the intriguing story of how Russian journalist Nicolas Notovitch discovered the manuscripts in 1887 in a monastery in Ladakh. Critics "proved" they did not exist—then three distinguished scholars and educators rediscovered them in the twentieth century.

Now you can read for yourself what Jesus said and did prior to his Palestinian mission. It's one of the most revolutionary messages of our time.

"Well-written and provocative.
The research was not only thorough and accurate but very, very careful."
—**Robert S. Ravicz, PhD**, Professor of Anthropology, California State University, Northridge

THE LOST TEACHINGS OF JESUS SERIES

THE LOST TEACHINGS OF JESUS 1

Missing Texts • Karma and Reincarnation

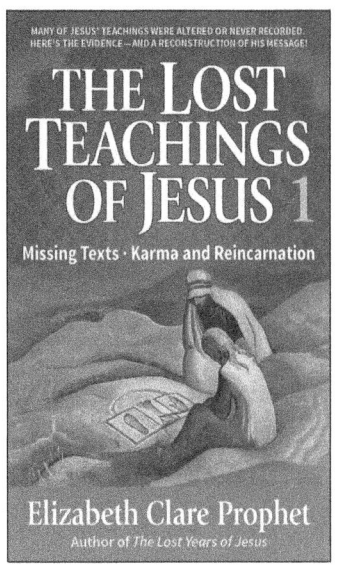

Mark L. Prophet and Elizabeth Clare Prophet prove that many of Jesus' original teachings are missing. They show that the New Testament records only a fragment of what Jesus taught—and that what was written down was tampered with by numerous editors or suppressed by "guardians of the faith."

Now, in their landmark series The Lost Teachings of Jesus, the Prophets fill in the gaps with a bold reconstruction of the essence of Jesus' message. They unfold the lost teachings Jesus gave in public to the multitudes and in secret to his closest disciples. And they answer questions that have puzzled readers of the Bible for centuries.

358 pp • ISBN 978-0-916766-90-0

THE LOST TEACHINGS OF JESUS 2

Mysteries of the Higher Self

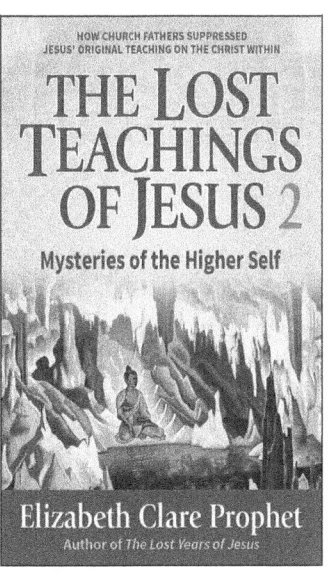

How Church Fathers suppressed Jesus' original teaching on the Christ within.

This volume reveals how early churchmen distorted Jesus' true teachings and robbed you of what he wanted you to know about the power of your own inner Christ. It recaptures the heart of Jesus' message—that you, like Jesus, can reconnect with your Divine Source to realize your full potential.

352 pp • ISBN 978-0-916766-91-7

PRAYER AND MEDITATION

A combination of Christian mysticism and Eastern meditation that teaches the art of unceasing communion with God and the way of higher meditation to open the heart. Eighteen Chinese-style prints of great spiritual masters.

302 pp • ISBN 978-0-916766-19-1

CORONA CLASS LESSONS

For Those Who Would Teach Men the Way

Reveals the many treasures to be found on the spiritual path, with rare insights on love, habit, mercy, brotherhood, charity, the soul, vision, mission and faith. Unveils new interpretations of the Bible.

408 pp • ISBN 978-0-916766-65-8

ELIZABETH CLARE PROPHET is a world-renowned author, spiritual teacher, and pioneer in practical spirituality. Her groundbreaking books have been published in more than thirty languages and over three million copies have been sold worldwide.

Among her best-selling titles are *The Human Aura, The Science of the Spoken Word, Your Seven Energy Centers, The Lost Years of Jesus, The Art of Practical Spirituality,* and her successful Pocket Guides to Practical Spirituality series.

The Summit Lighthouse®
63 Summit Way
Gardiner, Montana 59030 USA
1-800-245-5445 / 406-848-9500

Se habla español.

info@SummitUniversityPress.com
SummitLighthouse.org

Printed in July 2023
by Rotomail Italia S.p.A., Vignate (MI) - Italy